EXAMINING SPORTS DEVELOPMENT

Sports development takes place in continually evolving – and expanding – territory. If new policies are to be implemented effectively, it is vital to understand how development policy translates into the real world. Until now no single text has examined how sports development policies are implemented and experienced 'at the coal face' of community and performance sport.

As well as critical analysis of models and concepts in sports development, *Examining Sports Development* presents original case studies from practising sports development professionals working in a variety of areas, including:

- national and regional policy
- school sport
- talent identification and development
- sports club development
- coach development
- sport and social inclusion
- sport and crime prevention
- sport and health promotion.

Sports development is evolving as a profession, especially in matters of education and training. This book encourages critical reflection, pointing the way to accountable policy making and a long-term future for sports development professionals. It is essential reading for all students and practitioners working in sports development.

Mike Collins was a Senior Lecturer in Recreation Management at Loughborough University for over ten years before 'retiring' to part-time work in Sports Development and Faith Communities at the University of Gloucestershire. Prior to holding this position he founded and then directed the Institute of Sport and Recreation Planning and Management at the same university for five years.

EXAMINING SPORTS DEVELOPMENT

EDITED BY MIKE COLLINS

Routledge
Taylor & Francis Group

LONDON AND NEW YORK

First published 2010
by Routledge
2 Park Square, Milton Park, Abingdon, Oxon, OX14 4RN

Simultaneously published in the USA and Canada
by Routledge
270 Madison Avenue, New York, NY 10016

Routledge is an imprint of the Taylor & Francis Group, an informa business

Transferred to Digital Printing 2010

Typeset in Zapf Humanist and Eras
by Keystroke, Tettenhall, Wolverhampton
Printed and bound in Great Britain
by CPI Antony Rowe, Chippenham, Wiltshire

British Library Cataloguing in Publication Data
A catalogue record for this book is available from the British Library

Library of Congress Cataloging-in-Publication Data
Examining sports development / edited by Michael F. Collins.
p. cm.
Includes bibliographical references and index.
1. Sports–Great Britain. 2. Sports administration–Great Britain.
3. Sports–Social aspects–Great Britain. 4. Sports and state–Great Britain.
I. Collins, Michael F. (Michael Frank)
GV605.E93 2010
796.0941–dc22
2009023688

ISBN 0–415–33989–8 (hbk)
ISBN 0–415–33990–1 (pbk)
ISBN 0–203–46198–3 (ebk)

ISBN 978–0–415–33989–6 (hbk)
ISBN 978–0–415–33990–2 (pbk)
ISBN 978–0–203–46198–3 (ebk)

To Sue and Hannah

Long-suffering in my busy 'retirement'

CONTENTS

FIGURES

TABLES

XVI

tables

CONTRIBUTORS

Len Almond is the Foundation Director and Senior Adviser of the British Heart Foundation National Centre for Physical Activity and Health, and the former Director of Physical Education at Loughborough University from 1991 until 1997. He has co-authored and edited many books and research papers on physical activity, health and physical education and is a member of many strategy and cross-partnership groups. He is also an active member of the National Coalition for Active Aging in England.

Barbara Bell is Senior Lecturer in Sport Development in the Department of Exercise and Sport Science at Manchester Metropolitan University, delivering and developing sport development courses to undergraduates and post-graduates. Previously her experience included ten years in community sport with various local authorities, and over fifteen years in Higher Education, with main academic interests in sport development and management, sport policy and the promotion of sport participation, particularly where this is used also to address social objectives. Her Ph.D. analysed policy in youth sport and coaching, focusing on the work and legacies of Champion Coaching in the NW. Her previous research included work on youth sport, evaluating the impacts of sport events on sport development, social sport marketing and social capital contributions of sport programmes. Her first book, *Sport Studies,* was published by Learning Matters (Exeter) in 2009.

Niki Bolton is Principal Lecturer at the Cardiff School of Sport, University of Wales Institute, Cardiff (UWIC). She led the UWIC team evaluating the Welsh Assembly Government's Free Swimming Initiative. Her research interests lie in sports development and management, public policy, strategy and evaluation. She is currently researching young people's attitudes towards extra-curricular sport and physical activity for the Sports Council for Wales, referred to as the 5X60 initiative. Formerly employed in local government and the Sports Council for Wales, she has extensive experience of preparing and implementing organisational strategy and policy. She has served as a member on the Sport Council for Wales and was until April 2007 a Board Member of ISPAL.

Tony Charlton is Senior Lecturer in Sports Development at Edge Hill University, where he is Associate Head of Department with responsibility for designing and implementing degrees in sports studies and sports development. His research interests include partnership development and networking in sport, the role of sport in regeneration and major events, and capacity building at grassroots to increase and sustain sport participation (his case study of Lancashire Sport is based on his Ph.D.). Tony is heavily involved in community sports development through working with groups and agencies at different levels of the delivery process, with a main focus of ensuring a lasting legacy from the forthcoming Olympic Games in London.

Mike Collins is Visiting Professor at the University of Gloucestershire, where he is heading new courses and research on sport and faith communities. Prior to that he was a Visiting Research Fellow and Senior Lecturer at Loughborough University, specialising in sport and planning, sports development and sport and social policy, and authoring *Sport and Social Exclusion* (Routledge, 2003). He trained as a geographer and town/transport planner, and was Head of Research, Planning and Strategy at the Sports Council from its founding in 1972 to 1989, managing 500 research projects in over a dozen disciplines and two strategies in 1982 and 1987.

Steve Conway is Sports Development Manager with Leicestershire and Rutland Sport (County Sports Partnership) where his expertise is around PE and School Sport. Steve has presented at various national conferences and has previously been a Youth Sport Trust national trainer. He trained as a PE teacher and has been involved in PE and school sport for over twenty-five years. He is married with three children and is a lifelong Hull City FC supporter.

Nikki Enoch founded VAGA Associates consultants in 2003 and has directed and delivered 150 assignments for a wide range of clients. With the CCPR and five Sports Councils, she piloted the Equality Standard for Sport with 38 UK NGBs. She joined Sport England in Nottingham in 1988, responsible for Beyond the Barriers, the East Midlands Sport and Recreation Strategy for 1992–7, and led campaigning to successfully make Sport England a statutory consultee on planning matters affecting sport. Later she became Head of Active Sports, delivering opportunities in eleven sports through 45 embryonic County Partnerships, and helping to establish the Millennium Youth Games, the Club Mark accreditation standard (with 21 NGBs), and the Child Protection in Sport Unit. On behalf of Sport England, she received two Cabinet Office Modernising Government Awards for partnership working in the public sector.

Stuart Lindeman is Strategic Director for Education for Partnerships for Schools (the Government organisation managing the Building Schools for the Future programme) with the additional responsibility for PE & School Sport and the Arts. He is a board member for Leicester, Leicestershire and Rutland County Sports Partnership. Earlier, he was Assistant Director of Education for Leicestershire for school/college support, establishing the Connexions Service for the City and County, and responsible for outdoor education. Earlier still he was an LEA/OFSTED Inspector/Adviser, Director of TVEI Related In-Service Education and Training, Head of Dartington Tech, and a secondary/primary school teacher and senior manager. He is also a trained teacher, professional counsellor and groupworker.

Fiona McCormack is Senior Lecturer in Sport, leisure and tourism at Buckinghamshire New University. After her M.Sc., she became training manager for an international resort consultancy working throughout Europe. Previously Fiona had been a sailing instructor and yacht skipper specialising in working with young people on sailing adventures and other outdoor recreation programmes. Her Ph.D. research at Loughborough was based on a study of sport and active leisure interventions with young offenders, and is reflected in her teaching and in a new project study of youth development in sailing. Having developed undergraduate and postgraduate programmes in outdoor learning, she has an interest in pedagogy in HE, especially the growing demands for vocational skills for sports and outdoor education. In her leisure time, she enjoys sailing and volunteering as a youth coach in a local club.

Andy Pitchford is Deputy Head of the Department of Sport and Exercise at the University of Gloucestershire. He teaches on undergraduate and postgraduate courses in sports development and has research interests that embrace the sociology of childhood, grassroots football and community sports development, including several years working with a team on projects for the Football Association, co-authoring *Child Welfare in Football* (Routledge, 2006). Andy previously worked as a Sports Development Officer for the London Borough of Bromley, and has published numerous papers on this emergent profession in his time in Higher Education.

David Sparkes is Chief Executive of the Amateur Swimming Association. While running his engineering business, he worked as a successful voluntary coach to county, district and national swimmers and was a member of the ASA Coach Certificate Committee, and the Education Committee which he chaired for five years. He was appointed CEO in 1994 and has overseen many developments in lifesaving, and recreational and competitive swimming in Britain and internationally.

Ian Thomson was Director of Physical Recreation at the University of Stirling from 1969 to 1989. He introduced sports scholarships and developed an extensive programme of community access to University sports facilities, as well as helping to establish National Centres for tennis and swimming on campus. He served as an Honorary Professor from 1999 to 2009. His research interests and publications have been mainly concerned with policies for elite sport and national policies for sport in other countries in Europe. Most recently he led a 3-year study of Stirling Council's 'Integrated Sports Strategy' (October 2008) which followed 140 children for three years from late primary into secondary education.

Rod Thorpe trained and taught as a PE teacher and then returned to Loughborough College to train teachers in 1968. During his thirty-five years at the College and University, alongside his academic work, Rod coached rugby and tennis (for ten and twenty-seven years respectively). Rod directed the Sport Development Centre until retiring in 2004, and was awarded an Honorary Ph.D. for his work in coaching children and developing Loughborough as a world-class training venue. He was central to developing 'sports leadership' programmes in the UK. He co-authored *Rethinking Games Teaching* (Loughborough University, 1982) and after working with the Australian Coaching Council adapted it to coaching as *Games Sense*. He was a Director on the Board of sports coach UK and now likewise of the Youth Sports Trust. Rod has been invited to present at PE conferences worldwide, and he received the International Olympic Committee's Biennial Award for Services to Sport, the Munrow Award for services to sport in Higher Education, and was inducted into sports coach UK's 'Coaching Hall of Fame'.

Caron Walpole has, since mid-2008, been working part-time as a sports consultant to spend more time at home with her young family. Her first post was as manager of a North London programme which gave unemployed people opportunities for training and work experience as sports coaches and leaders. Thereafter, Caron moved to Leicestershire where she worked for the next seven years as a Sports Development Officer for local authorities, including North West Leicestershire, Rutland District and Leicester City Councils. She then worked for five years as a Sport England Senior Regional Development Manager, based in Nottingham, before taking up the post of Sport Action Zone Manager for Braunstone Community Association in 2000. Another five years later she joined Leicester, Leicestershire and Rutland Sport (County Partnership) as its Community Sport Manager.

contributors

PREFACE AND ACKNOWLEDGEMENTS

This book was conceived over a cup of coffee in a break in the Manchester Commonwealth Games conference in Manchester with Simon Whitmore, editor for Routledge's sports list. It was agreed that despite the proliferation of courses teaching sports development (see Chapter 14), there was little in the way of case study material for students or working professionals. There has been some more recently in the renewal.net database, and in some Sport England documents and scattered journal/magazine articles, but only a few extend beyond description and quasi-journalism. The purpose of the text was to provide a range of material from across Britain, covering both community and performance sport.

Most contributors produced their material on time. Then I was taken up by early retirement and a bout of minor illness, and the second editor responsible for the performance sport element withdrew for personal reasons. This required some rebalancing of case studies to cover GB for community sports, and new authors came in.

Simon meantime had worked for another publisher and returned to Routledge, and on his return our judgement was that the book was still needed. I am grateful for his patience and that of the contributors during the delay. In those case studies where further developments have occurred, updating postscripts have been provided by me and the authors. All errors are mine and not theirs.

I would like to acknowledge the encouragement of my Gloucester colleagues, Andy Pitchford and Jon Cryer, Kate Mori, Phil Shirfield and Andrew Parker, and those hardworking and inventive SDOs whom I meet in my various guises.

Shepshed, April 2008

ABBREVIATIONS

AS (P)   Active Sports (Partnership) *now CSN (Community Sports Network)*
CC   Champion Coaching
CLOA   Chief Leisure Officers Association
CSD   Community Sports Development
CEO   Chief Executive Officer
CSP   County Sports Partnership
DCMS   Department for Culture Media and Sport
DCSF   Department for Children, Schools and Families
DES   Department for Education and Skills
DETR   Department of Environment, Transport and the Regions
DoH   Department of Health
EIS   English Institute of Sport
FSI   Free Swimming Initiative
HEI   Higher Education Institution
ILAM   Institute of Leisure and Amenity Management, *now ISPAL (Institute of Sport, Parks and Leisure)*
ISRM   Institute for Sport and Recreation Management
LA   local authority
LEA   Local Education Authority
NASD   National Association of Sports Development
NCF   National Coaching Foundation
NGB   National Governing Body
NHS   National Health Service
PCT   Primary Care Trust
PESSCL   *Physical Education, School Sport and Club Links*, now *PESSYP (Physical Education and Sport Strategy for Young People)*
scUK   sports coach UK
SC   Sports Council
SD (O) (U) Sports Development (Officer) (Unit)

SSc	Specialist Sports College
SSCo	School Sports Coordinator
SSP	School Sports Partnership
TAES	*Towards an Excellent Service*
UKS	UK Sport

PART A

EXAMINING SPORTS DEVELOPMENT

CHAPTER 1

INTRODUCTION

Mike Collins

DEFINITIONS

This book was commissioned specifically to provide case studies of two sorts of project: those still in development, focusing on the partnership/stakeholder arrangements put in place to drive and manage them, and established projects, focusing on outputs and outcomes of a period of operation.

Books usually begin with definitions. Houlihan and White (2002: 1–2) commented that this was more difficult for sports development (SD) than some other policy areas because it:

1. was a sub-area of sports policy;
2. had been subject to several changes of objectives;
3. was (then but no longer) at the margins of HMG's field of vision;
4. is in a policy field crowded with other more powerful interests (education, health, foreign policy, social services).

SD officers (SDOs) started as promoters of youth participation in the youth service and promoters of performance in the national governing bodies of sport (NGBs). In one of the guises now familiar, in local authorities (LAs), SD had been operating for a decade before the Sports Council offered this definition below (which is rather wordy in its attempt to be comprehensive):

> Sports development is a process whereby interest and desire to take part may be created in those who are currently indifferent to the message of sport; or by which those not now taking part, but well disposed, may be provided with appropriate opportunities to do so; or by which those currently taking part may be enabled to do so with meaningful

frequency and greater satisfaction, thus enabling participants at all levels to achieve their full potential.

(Sports Council, NW, 1991: 3)

This was in a document to help people making policy or practice in areas of disadvantage. Two years later, in the first 'manual' for teaching and training, Eady (1993: 1) first an SDO in Lancashire and then a consultant, wrote of the role of an SDO as normally 'to operate in an interventionist and proactive manner improving/increasing sporting opportunities for people'. Two more years later, in reporting on a survey of SD work and roles, I wrote of SD (Collins 1995: 21) as,

> a process whereby effective opportunities, processes, systems and structures are set up to enable and encourage people in all or any particular groups and areas to take part in sport and recreation or to improve their performance to whatsoever level they desire.

Most who have quoted this have ignored the sentences in which this was set, namely '[an] appropriate definition now relates to SDOs' work as analysts and "fixers" of organisational weaknesses and strengths for promoting sport. While in an ideal world SDOs would do themselves out of a job, current changes in policies and systems suggest that they will be needed for a good while yet.' Fourteen years later, I think this is still true. At much the same time, the Sports Council (1993: 1) produced a succinct definition that SD is,

> about ensuring the pathways and structures are in place to enable people to learn basic movement skills, participate in sports of their choice, develop their competence and performance, and reach levels of excellence.

This is a more process-oriented definition, than a policy one, but I will stick by my guns, as explained in the Conclusions (Chapter 15).

OUTLINE

When looking for case studies I first wanted to look at different areas of Britain, so there are two located in the NW, one each in the west and east midlands, one in Wales and one in Scotland. The group most focused on is youth and six chapters look at young people in school and community. Chapter 2 gives a very personal view on how sports development has evolved over the past three decades – not a detailed history nor a complete social and leisure policy context, for others have laboured to produce these. But I was privileged to work at the policy centre in the Sports Council, as it then was, from its inception to 1989.

Organisations take their shape from either their vision or their function, and the first group of studies examines how this has happened. In Chapter 3 Nikki Enoch tells a first-hand story about how Active Sports evolved from 1998 to the time when County Sports Partnerships were set up as an intermediary – the bridge between national policy and action and their local equivalents. In Chapter 4 Stuart Lindeman and Steve Conway tell, again from first hand, how the community education set up in Leicestershire grasped the opportunity of sports development to benefit children in and out of school. Leicestershire was one of the few exceptions in England where the far-sightedness of Chief Education Officer Fairbairn had set up high schools and colleges with sports and arts facilities for evening and weekend use by the public, before the 'dual-use' policy was introduced elsewhere, usually led by local authority leisure departments rather than education.

Chapter 5 is another study by a participant-observer, Tony Charlton, critically viewing the development of a County Sports Partnership – Lancashire, one of the largest and most complex in design, with many partners, and for those reasons prey to human failings and tensions in its development. Chapter 6 tells the story of a new facet of SD, in Higher Education, where Rod Thorpe, with Mike Collins, describes the growth of sports functions which he headed in the class leader, Loughborough University, now emulated nationwide.

Constitutional devolution brings the possibilities of difference and diversion, and in Chapter 7 Ian Thomson retails the first nine years of Scottish sports policy, a story of an over-ambitious strategy, relatively minor new investments streams, a closer relationship with health-promoting physical activity than in England but no leap forward in school sport like that south of the border. It remains to be seen what catalytic effect on policy the awarding of the 2014 Commonwealth Games to Glasgow brings.

The second group of case studies attempt to map out some of the outputs and initial outcomes of SD schemes. Some policy makers and reviewers of this book may say, 'Oh, these are old hat'. Politicians in Britain's two-party see-saw system always seek and expect quick results (i.e. before the next election) and painless ones, often cheaply, and many senior managers, willingly or otherwise, have gone along with that. They ignore the considerable frictional costs of policy and organisational change; they believe the obvious rightness of their rhetoric will overcome any doubt about or opposition to their ideas. They ignore the communication problems in three- and four-level sports organisations, they forget the fact that non-statutory public services and autonomous voluntary ones are to a lesser or greater degree only loosely linked and not susceptible to orders or grant bribery when push comes to shove. Above all, they think naively that managers, customers and organisations will change in a matter of months as a result of them talking a lot and waving their hands about. Major change is slow and incremental and not without personal stress, pain and loss as well as gain. So it is not surprising that the small-scale research that is usually commissioned – with still fairly basic methods and short time spans – does not always capture major change.

In Chapter 8, Barbara Bell seeks to tease out – from records and going back after some years to adolescents, teachers and coaches – the legacy of a decade of Champion Coaching for youth sport in NW England. (This was a legacy that the Sports Council was not interested in tracing because it was on to the next wave of policy development.) She does find a legacy, if rather fragmentary, in participation and in coach development. Sport England and Minister for Sport, Richard Caborn were determined to 'modernise' NGBs and make them 'fit for purpose', respectively. It was a case of 'do or be done to', and in Chapter 9 ASA Chief Executive David Sparkes and Mike Collins recount the challenges faced in getting the Amateur Swimming Association's voluntary clubs to examine their vision for their club, tighten the focus and plan for change through self-improvement. This process was seen as a few years' work, but will take two decades to complete; at the same time there are the challenges of modernising or replacing pools, of overcoming social inequalities and of using the government's free swimming initiative as a springboard to further development, and not a cost.

In Chapter 10, Caron Walpole gives an insider's view on the evolution of Braunstone in Leicester, England's smallest Sport Action Zone, where bottom-up working with citizens yielded a rich return, with sport spearheading the regeneration of the estate and recovery of citizen confidence in their city council. Likewise, in Chapter 11, Fiona McCormack describes the effective mentoring and sports leadership of the Streetsport team in the open spaces of deprived housing estates in Stoke-on-Trent, doing what several years later the government spent £25m on doing in its Positive Futures schemes, and learning the same lessons, but this time involving continuous monitoring and annual evaluation, producing models and marketing and research tools.

In Chapter 12, Len Almond brings thirty years of experience in health-related PA to bear on the sport–PA relationship, though the UK is not as fertile or well-prepared soil for such programmes to flourish as Finland, which the government would have us emulate. In Chapter 13, Nicola Bolton relates the findings of her monitoring of the Wales Free Swimming Initiative, a product of the semi-autonomous Welsh Assembly that England has decided to copy, and fore-shadowing some of the issues that English local authorities will face in 2009/10.

These eleven case studies demonstrate the range of tasks, roles and relationships SD Officers now undertake. In Chapter 14, Andy Pitchford and Mike Collins compare the profiles of the SDOs that the former found with the latter's survey a decade earlier. The workforce has grown and aged, and doing more work in community development in response to New Labour's urging to combat the cross-cutting issues – 'sport for good', as Fred Coalter (2007a) would term it. How will this workforce adapt to another policy swing, back to 'sport for sport's sake', but in a much higher profile setting and complex of agencies than in the 1950s and 1960s when this stance last operated? They also examine the content of the new HEI courses in sports development, and the tentative moves towards a single chartered institute for sports management. In Chapter 15, Mike Collins summarises the chapters' findings and tries to draw some threads from them, notably the many and varied ideas of partnerships that they demonstrate.

ASPECTS THAT THE BOOK DOES NOT COVER

This book focuses on community sports development, and there are four aspects of SD not covered – two relating to community SD, one to performance sport and one to sport-in-development.

Sports clubs

Sports clubs are obviously a major part of the provision system and a major agency of SD. But there is a disproportionately small literature about their structure, management and how they operate. Even though Britain has the largest number of small, mainly single-sport clubs (150,000) in Europe, there is not even a decent up-to-date survey of numbers, sizes and trends, despite the fact that Sport England expects them to recruit 300,000 new regular participants in 2008–2011. Two main reasons can be attributed:

1. Despite their 6.5 million members and their federal body, the Central Council for Physical Recreation (CCPR), sports clubs are not accorded political clout. Compare the German Sports Federation with its signed-up and subscribing 21 million members, which is consulted on every piece of Federal legislation.

2. Partly because of that, for nearly twenty years, Germany has undertaken quadrennial clubs surveys, most recently with a sample of 13,000 (Breuer and Wicker, 2008), which give details of plant, financial and human resources, their aspirations, and the challenges faced. These revealed a minority of very large multi-sports clubs (6 per cent with 1,000 or more people) who cover a third of all club members, and undertake much of the new activity and programmes on behalf of the state for sport for all and target groups (Lankenau and Dagli, 1987; Anders, 1991). In Britain, some partial glimpses appeared in surveys on volunteering (e.g. Taylor et al., 2003), but there has never been a survey comparable with the German ones. The CCPR's 2007 survey was a small, totally unrepresentative snowball sample. Such clubs barely exist in Britain, making widespread take-up more difficult under the new strategy. A Sport England officer said that she hoped that the Whole Sport Plans submitted for grant aid under its 2008–2011 strategy (as yet mostly unpublished), would contain such detail, but even if they do, this only covers a third of the sports on offer. It is a major gap in knowledge.

There is a wider point. Sports clubs, like arts groups, are a form of mutual help organisation, producing and consuming (mainly) their own products and performances (Bishop and Hoggett, 1986). They are not like the much larger, overwhelmingly altruistic welfare sector, about which there is a vast international literature and body of research. Yet across Europe, sport alone represents 26 per cent of all volunteering, so Sport England and others, like Putnam (2000), believe that this movement must generate substantial social capital. But as Collins (2007) and Coalter (2007a) point out, the nature of the social capital, and how it is generated and sustained, have not been spelt out. This mutual-aid nature is likely to bolster the bonding links (of similar people) and may set limits to the bridging links (with 'other' types of people) so valued by policy makers. Autonomous, they can choose to play a constructive or defensive role in helping public policy (e.g. Garrett, 2003; Harris et al., 2009).

Sports development and the impact of mega-events

There is now a voluminous literature of mega-events, especially for sport, like the Olympics, the Commonwealth Games, the World Cup and world championships. Much is now being written about their facilities and environmental legacies, but little is known about whether they produce long-term benefits for sports participation or the sports system. Weed et al. (2009) disingenuously suggest therefore that unidentified benefits may have occurred, but there is no

8

practical evidence of post-Games increases in participation beyond fads (like parks tennis after every Wimbledon, golf frenzy after UK and Europe won the Ryder Cup, and so on) – as confirmed by Brown and Murray (2001), Coalter (2004, 2007b, 2008a: 141–50) and Murphy and Bauman (2007). Nor is there evidence of a stronger club network for the future. Volunteering to help continues to grow with each succeeding Olympics, but there is no evidence that the (mainly young) people feed into the regular competitive sports.

In *Game Plan* (DCMS, 2002: 66) the government was guarded about the benefits of major events, saying they were 'more about celebration than economic returns', but gave enthusiastic support for the London bid, and after a successful campaign, has now found the overwhelming bulk of the rising costs of reclaiming the East London site and building the venues. In its 2008–2011 strategy, Sport England avers, without convincing evidence, that 'the Olympics provide a focal point for developing a world-leading community sport system'. Meantime, UK Sport is pursuing vigorously a programme of hosting major events.

Sports development for performance and elite sport

While the other issues are not covered for lack of material, the same cannot be said of developing elite sport. Other texts have started to deal with this, and Houlihan and White (2002) suggested that it had developed its own policy network/advocacy coalition. Sebastian Coe, while Deputy Chair of the Sports Council, constantly complained about the inadequate level of support for elite athletes, especially that they did not get 'broken time' payments to help them with the costs of intensive training. In 1995 the first White Paper for twenty years, *Sport: Raising the Game* (DNH), had elite sport as its dual priority with youth sport. Within two years, the Lottery brought the funds that would allow support on an unprecedented scale – for facilities, for individual athletes and for NGBs to appoint performance directors and coaches and develop/commission related sports science and medicine services, with a network of regional institutes (copying Australia) and costing some £100m (Theodoraki, 1999). This led to major developments in coaching – which is closely related to but distinct from SD (Lyle, 2008).

In 1989, Kamphorst and Roberts foresaw the delegation of the task of promoting mass participation to regional and local governments and the increasing interest of federal/central governments in elite sport. Green and Houlihan (2005) spelt this out in comparisons between Australia, Canada and the UK, and more recently Houlihan and Green (2008) compared nine other countries – from China to Norway and New Zealand. At the same time, university colleagues from Belgium, Canada, The Netherlands, Italy and Norway formed a consortium with UK Sport (De Bosscher et al., 2008) to gather evidence on the nine pillars leading to sporting success, namely:

1. adequate financial support;
2. integrated approach to developing policy;
3. participation in PE and sport;
4. talent identification and development;
5. athletic and post-career support;
6. specialist training facilities;
7. coaching provision and coach development;
8. international competition opportunities;
9. scientific research.

Quite simply, despite large sums, this support is much cheaper, easier to measure (success = medals), more visible for the nation, the media and the politicians and far surer of achievement than the much larger sums needed for mass participation, which is a conundrum for all the developed nations, who see little growth after two decades of investment (e.g. Stewart et al., 2004).

Sport-in-development

For many years, several other European countries operated programmes of technical support and sports development expertise in Africa, Latin America and Asia, while the Foreign Office and Overseas Development departments told the Sports Council it was only a domestic department. The United Nations developed an interest after two conferences in Magglingen, through its Sport for Development and Peace International Working Group (2006), as described by Beacom and Levermore (2008) and Coalter (2007a: 68–91). The latter outlines how in such underdeveloped state mechanisms, sport as a powerful attraction for youth rapidly becomes a tool of wider social development – fighting the ravages of HIV/Aids, encouraging the empowerment of girls in mainly oppressive, patriarchal societies, and encouraging citizenship, including environmental clean-ups. From the 1990s, UK Sport (2009) has offered a range of programmes which now includes:

- International Inspiration – a London 2012 legacy programme now operating in five countries, including curricular work with 250,000 rural primary schools in India and sports leaders in NE Brazil;
- International Sports Development programmes which have operated in eighteen South and East African countries.

UK Sport's staff complement is now 112, including 17 in International Events, 37 in Performance and 23 in Drug-free Sport (who will presumably transfer to the new independent agency).

For UK Sport, Coalter (2006) worked with local sports interests in India and East Africa to produce a monitoring and evaluation manual, using realistic evaluation techniques of scientific realism and logic models described on pp. 142–3. The crowded policy spaces and numbers of specialised workers limit how far this can go in Britain, but some forms of community development come close, the nearest in our case studies being that of Braunstone Sport Action Zone (Chapter 10).

So this book attempts to give insights into what is now a significant function of local government. And it still is overwhelmingly a direct function – only 4.4 per cent delegating it to contractors and 3.5 per cent to trust or other agents. It also expends a net £115m a year (£2.26 per head) (CIPFA, 2009).

REFERENCES

Anders, G. (1991) Structures and functions of sports clubs in Germany: between service organisation and social community. Paper to RECMAN '91 conference, 28 February, Birmingham.

Beacom, A. and Levermore, R. (2008) 'International policy and sport-in-development'. In Girginov, V. (ed.) *Management of Sports Development*, Oxford: Butterworth-Heinemann.

Bishop, J. and Hoggett, P. (1986) *Organising Around Enthusiasms: Patterns of Mutual Aid in Leisure*, London: Comedia.

Breuer, C. and Wicker, P. (2008) *Sports Development Report 2005/6: The Situation of Non-profit Sports Clubs in Germany*, Cologne: Bundesinstitut für Sport.

Brown, A. and Murray, J. (2001) *Literature Review: The Impact of Major Sports Events*, Manchester: Manchester Metropolitan University, Centre for Popular Culture.

Chartered Institute of Public Finance and Accountancy (2009) *Culture, Sport and Recreation Statistics* [including charges], London: CIPFA.

Coalter, F (2004) Stuck in the blocks? A sustainable sporting legacy? In A. Vigor and M. Mean (eds) *After the Gold Rush? The London Olympics*, London: Institute for Public Policy Research/Demos.

Coalter, F. (2006) *Sport-in-Development: A Monitoring and Information Manual*, Edinburgh: SportScotland.

Coalter, F. (2007a) *A Wider Social Role for Sport: Who's Keeping the Score?*, London: Routledge.

Coalter, F. (2007b) London Olympics 2012: The catalyst that inspires people to lead more active lives, *Journal of the Royal Society for the Promotion of Health* 127(3): 109–10.

Collins, M. (1995) *Sports Development Regionally and Locally,* Loughborough: Loughborough University for Sports Council and Institute of Leisure and Amenity Management.

Collins, M. (2007) Leisure Studies and the social capital discourse. In M. Collins, K. Holmes and A. Slater (eds) *Sport, Leisure, Culture and Social Capital: Discourse and Practice* (Leisure Studies Association publication 100), Eastbourne: University of Brighton.

De Bosscher, V., Bingham, J., Shibli, S. and de Knop, P. (2008) *The Global Sporting Arms Race: An International Comparative Study on Policy Factors Leading to International Sporting Success (SPLISS),* Oxford: Meyer & Meyer Sport.

Department for Culture Media and Sport (2002) *Game Plan: A Strategy for Delivering the Government's Sport and Recreation Objectives,* London: DCMS.

Department for National Heritage (1995) *Sport: Raising the Game,* London: DNH.

Eady, J. (1993) *Practical Sports Development,* Harlow: Longman.

Garrett, R. (2003) The response of voluntary sports clubs to Sport England's lottery funding: cases of compliance, change and resistance. In G. Nichols (ed.) *Volunteers in Sport,* (Leisure Studies Association publication 80), Eastbourne: University of Brighton.

Green, M. and Houlihan, B. (2005) *Elite Sport Development: Policy Learning and Political Priorities,* London: Routledge.

Harris, S., Mori, K. and Collins, M.F. (2009) Great expectations: voluntary sports clubs and their role in delivering national policy for English sport, *Voluntas* 20(4).

Houlihan, B. and Green, M. (2008) *Comparative Elite Sport Development: Systems, Structures and Public Policy.* Oxford: Butterworth-Heinemann.

Houlihan, B. and White, A. (2002) *The Politics of Sports Development.* London: Routledge.

Kamphorst, T. and Roberts, K. (eds) (1989) *Trends in Sports: An International Perspective,* Culemborg, Netherlands: Giordano Bruno.

Lankenau, K. and Dagli, J. (1987) *Sports Clubs: Sport for All and Organisational Structures,* Cologne: Federal Institute of Sport (mimeo).

Lyle, J. (2008) Sports development and sports coaching. In K. Hylton, and P. Bramham (eds) *Sports Development: Policy, Process and Practice,* London: Routledge.

12

McDonald, D. and Tungatt, M. (1991) *National Demonstration Projects: Major Lessons and Issues for Sports Development,* London: Sports Council.

Murphy, N.M. and Bauman, A. (2007) Mass sporting and physical activity events: are they 'bread and circuses' or public health interventions to increase population levels of physical activity?, *Journal of Physical Activity and Health* 4(2): 193–202.

Putnam, R. (2000) *Bowling Alone: The Collapse and Revival of American Community,* New York: Simon & Schuster.

Sports Council, NW (1991) *Sportnews Factfile Two: Sports Development,* Manchester: Sports Council.

Sports Council (1993) *Black and Ethnic Minorities and Sport: Policy and Objectives,* London: Sports Council.

Sport England (2008) *Grow, Sustain, Excel: Strategy 2008–11,* London: Sport England.

Sport for Development and Peace International Working Group (2006) *Sport for Development and Peace: From Practice to Policy,* Toronto: UNDP.

Stewart, B., Nicholson, M., Smith, A. and Westerbeek, H. (2004) *Australian Sport – Better by Design: The Evolution of Australian Sport Policy,* London: Routledge.

Taylor, P. *et al.* (2003) *Sports Volunteering in England,* London: Sport England.

Theodoraki, E. (1999) The making of the UK Sports Institute, *Managing Leisure* 4(4): 187–200.

UK Sport (2009) *Annual Review 2008, Part 1,* London: UK Sport.

Weed. M. *et al.* (2009) *A Systematic Review of the Evidence Base for Developing a Physical Activity and Health Legacy from the London 2012 Olympic and Paralympic Games,* Canterbury: Canterbury Christchurch University.

CHAPTER 2

THE DEVELOPMENT OF SPORTS DEVELOPMENT

Mike Collins

INTRODUCTION

In this chapter I give a first-hand account of the development of sports development and sports policy from an insider position of Head of Research Planning and Strategy at the Sports Council (later Sport England) from 1972 to 1989, and thereafter from an involved commentator/analyst stance at the Universities of Loughborough and Gloucestershire, and as a member of the two professional bodies, the Institute of Leisure and Amenity Management (ILAM – now ISPAL – the Institute of Sport, Parks and Leisure) and the Institute of Sport and Recreation Management (ISRM). I will make reference to, but not repeat, the various analyses of leisure policy development (Bergsgaard *et al.*, 2007; Collins, 2002, 2008; Henry, 2001; Houlihan, 1991, 1997, 2002; Houlihan and White, 2002; Green and Houlihan, 2005; Coalter, 2007; Hylton and Bramham, 2008). Table 2.2 (p. 23) summarises milestone documents and events in each phase.

The first phase of sports policy was concerned to provide enough facilities to increase participation, mainly among youth (Wolfenden 1960, Sports Council, 1971). As Houlihan and White said, sports development as defined in Chapter 1 had its antecedents in youth work and school sport, but in fact it started farther back in national governing body programmes in the late 1940s and 1950s. But in the community it was closely linked with people employed as youth workers, PE teachers and sports coaches and team managers. The original model for sports development was Action Sport, whose origin is an interesting anecdote, not yet told.

The Sports Council had been concerned about the nexus of social deprivation in inner cities (much more graphically outlined in *Bringing Britain Together* thirty years later (SEU, 1997)). It had a standing Advisory Group of academics and practitioners chaired by Professor Gordon Cherry, mostly from outside sport, and produced *Sport and Recreation in the Inner Cities* (Collins, 1977) which foresaw

14

social tensions but not specifically the1981 riots in Brixton that led to the Scarman report (1982), so it was sensitised to a range of issues. This resulted in a policy paper arguing for small area initiatives (not then called Sport Action Zones!) and targeted polices including ones for youth, three years ahead of the Minister for Sport's inner city review group (DOE, 1989) which focused more narrowly on youth and schools.

A STRATEGY OF TARGETING AND THE EVOLUTION OF SPORTS DEVELOPMENT, 1982–1991

In 1981 Denis Howell was Labour Minister for Sport for his second spell (he often said that he was minister for sport, whoever was in power! But he cared passionately about it). He was also Minister for Water Supply (or, after a very dry summer dubbed by the press 'Minister for Drought'). At that time, growing demand for industrial and agricultural water supplies had led to building new dams, but a cold, wet winter meant that pouring concrete was difficult and expenditure delayed. He came to the Sports Council HQ offices, and said to the Director and the author, the only other senior staff on site, 'I know what you want to do with your budget [then about £20.9m] and what you would do if you had ten per cent more, and it's basically more of the same. I have £1 million a year for three years, and I would like to see it spent on something new for youth sport. You have ten days to produce a credible idea.'

Such an offer could not be ignored, politically and practically, and after consulting with the Head of Sports Development, the nine Regional Directors and some senior Council members, 'Action Sport' was born – a programme to put young, credible sports leaders on the streets, to use existing purpose-built and borrowed facilities to engage youth, especially disaffected and unaffiliated youth in inner cities, particularly boys and from black and ethnic minorities. The money was not enough to spread countrywide, so it was focused on the West Midlands (six projects) and London (nine projects), and local authority partners were offered up to 100 per cent contribution to get off the ground quickly, unlike the minority contribution in other Sports Council programmes. The London programme had an objective also to involve girls and over 55s.

In policy terms, within months it was an unqualified success, and long before the evaluation commissioned from the Policy Studies Institute was completed (Rigg, 1986), it had been taken up by other local authorities across the country, and soon there were over 300 SDOs, with the aim of getting 50 per cent Manpower Services Commission (MSC) funding to attract suitable young unemployed people, though that was curtailed before reaching a target of 900

15

SDOs (*Sports Council Annual Report 1987*: 7). This MSC phase was called 'Operation Sport' in Wales and had a particular focus on unemployed youth; it reached 400 employees, of whom a high proportion obtained jobs as SDOs (Rigg, 1989: 86). The speed of this development helps to explain why policy documentation was somewhat sparse. The 1981 riots spurred the expansion of this method of working but did not spark them, so the accounts by Houlihan and White (2002: 35–9), Henry (2001) and Hylton and Bramham (2008: 48) are not completely accurate.

By 1989/90 the Sports Council was grant-aiding 560 SDOs, divided as shown below.

'SPORT FOR SPORT'S SAKE' SDOs
- **Target group SDOs**
  (119 grant-aided by 1989)

  Children
  Youth
  Women
  Disabled people
  Ethnic minorities

- **Sport-specific SDOs**
  (208 grant-aided by 1989)
  Including football and the community

- **Small area SDOs**
  (233 grant-aided by 1989)
  Serving several sports/groups in particular estates/village clusters

- **Schools SDOs**
  Including community use

- **Strategic SDOs**

'SPORT FOR GOOD' CDOs
- **Sport and PA/health SDOs**

The author was responsible for producing the Council's first strategy, *Sport in the Community: The Next Ten Years* (Sports Council, 1982). This was a response to HMG's requirement for such documents from government agencies – as in business practice – to publicly nail down objectives, to aid measuring achievement, and to underpin spending plans. It was an opportunity to produce a broad-based strategy (the earlier 1972/3 documents being overwhelmingly facility plans). *Sport in the Community* had elements covering elite sport and new facility provision, but focused, as its title suggested, on community sport. The projected finance was insufficient to fund all that needed doing, so it took a targeted approach, seeking to develop sport at two points of strategic and structural change in people's lifecycles – school leaving and people in the retirement phase at ages 55–64. (Men in particular were beginning to retire early because of redundancy in the sunset industries and by choice for some with index-linked pensions.) Others targeted were lower participant groups – women and girls, disabled people, ethnic minorities and concentrated areas of deprivation.

The Review of this strategy (Sports Council, 1987: 1, 24) foresaw an increasingly polarised society, presaging government policy on this issue by ten years:

> In the foreseeable future there will be two markets for sport:
> - The first is generally affluent, in work, healthy, well educated, and will increase its expenditure on both leisure and other goods [offering] considerable opportunities for providers of sport and recreation.
> - The second . . . is generally poor, has poor health, may be unemployed, often lives in inner cities or rural areas with a poor economic base, and contains many ethnic minority groups. The benefits of increased leisure and Sport for All have largely passed it by. [It] offers not an opportunity but a challenge and . . . the need for a strong public sector will be vital.

This turned out to be true, and the strength of the public sector was variable and poorly supported by government from 1990 onwards. Remans (1993: 18) identified this as a pattern common throughout Europe.

Within this framework, the National Demonstration Projects (NDPs) were launched to extend the proven Action Sport methods to other groups, but with two other specific elements:

- to make use of existing facilities in communities – schools, church and village halls, youth and community centres;
- to involve new partners to broaden the networks and skills base and connect with other agendas and open up other local resources – health centres, working men's clubs, pubs, Women's Institutes.

So, fifteen five-year projects emerged between 1984 and 1990, five providing new forms of outreach and partnership, six experimenting in new fields for SD and so with new partners, and four developing SD in schools and with extra-curricular programmes, as set out in Table 2.1 (London Sport ,1990; McDonald and Tungatt, 1991).

17

Table 2.1 Sports Council National Demonstration Projects

Project	Partners and aims
NEW OUTREACH	
1984 Activities promoter for women	Norwich City – develop Action Sport model for women
1984 Women and sport (WI)	Women's Institutes in Cambridgeshire – develop new and existing women's programmes in voluntary groups
1984 Associated Sport and Recreation (ASR)	Cleveland County Council and Working Men's clubs – open up clubs to women and the community
1984 Community sport and recreation (COMSPORT)	Northants county and district councils – adapt AS model to rural areas
1984 Tolly's sportline	Tollemache & Cobbold brewery and pubs in Suffolk – use pubs as a base to develop sport
EXPERIMENTS	
1984 Health and Recreation Team (HART)	Regional Health Authority – to develop sport and exercise promotion via Liverpool 8 inner city health centres
1985 Staff Health and Fitness Training Scheme (SHIFTS)	Notts Health Promotion Unit, then Notts County Council – corporate health and fitness in NHS and local businesses
1985 Solent Sports Counselling (SOLENT)	Hants Probation Service – sport to help young people at risk of offending
1986 Every Body Active (EBA)	Local authorities, clubs, school in NE England – overcoming constraints in sport for disabled people
1989 Scunthorpe Ethnic Minorities	Scunthorpe Council and clubs, schools – overcome barriers in sport for Asian and European minority citizens
1988 Langbaugh Motorsports	Local authorities, clubs – develop motorsports in the community
EDUCATION-BASED	
1984 Active Lifestyles (ALS)	Coventry Education Authority – to develop curricular and community sport & PE
1986 From school to community teacher training	Gloucester College of HE – to train teachers in reaching beyond the school
1990 Primary teacher training	Dudley LEA – in-service training and support
1990 Local Management of schools for sport (Sport's Cool)	3 schools in NW – community SD in light of new local management framework

Source McDonald and Tungatt, 1991.

The NDPs demonstrated the vital role of partnerships, including not only the crucial need to make them compatible with partners' aims and organisational culture (then expressed as 'ways of working'), but also their limitations, especially in the commercial and voluntary sectors (McDonald and Tungatt 1991: 42–3). Only two NDPs could be said to have failed. The attempt to open up pubs for boules and small-space indoor sports foundered on trying to work with brewery management rather than individual landlords, who would have had more incentive and local knowledge. And the Cambridgeshire WI project was initially very successful, with one full-time and one half-time Development Officer, but when offered an equivalent workforce for each county, the WI with its tiny HQ paid team took fright at becoming an employer of ten times as many staff – a real loss of potential momentum for women's SD – and potentially a great partnership still, since one in three local branches had (and has) some sport or PA in their programme. The Solent project was curtailed after two years' local management when probation budgets were cut and staff reorganised, despite being praised by the Home Office as an exemplary scheme (Collins with Kay, 2003: 173–93). One feature of the NDPs bemoaned by the Sports Council was a hint of the future – a tendency for 'drifting from initial objectives, with non-sporting objectives being allocated a higher priority' (Sports Council 1991 Annual Report: 31).

Action Sport and the NDPs set a model whose influence can still be seen for the role and functioning of SDOs locally, working with 'target groups' and in small areas (see Pitchford and Collins' account in Chapter 14). One issue was that two out of five SDOs worked alone (Collins, 1995) as generalists, combining area, target group and sport-specific work, often in small, frequently rural authorities – doing non-conventional, often discretionary outreach work mostly away from base, often with non-specialist line managers, and often lonely, not having a knowledgeable, sympathetic colleague (Whitely International, 1993). This led to regional groups forming, and eventually to the National Association of Sports Development. The difficulties were exemplified by a lone SDO being appointed to a Norfolk district where there was no leisure department, and she was managed by a Deputy Chief Executive. No prior assessment of resources and links had been made and this took her six months. She was expected to work over the large area, with several sports and target groups. Needless to say, despite a huge devotion of time and labour often leading sessions herself, as a lone person she could make only limited inroads, and after thirty months a new Committee chair decided that too little had been achieved, halved the finance and replaced her with a half-time Arts Development Officer. By 2005 the proportion of lone SDOs had halved (see Chapter 14).

The basic grade of SDO was a sports leader, sometimes paid, sometimes voluntary; the Central Council for Physical Recreation (CCPR) ran a Community

Sports Leaders award. Thorpe (1988) argued for a better codification of skills and better coordinated and resourced training; this slowly evolved, and the CCPR developed a higher award (Hansen Leadership Award), and a Basic Expedition Training Award for people running outdoor sports and expeditions. An evaluation of a sample of completers in 1989–91 showed a gender balance, a proportionate representation of ethnic minorities, a young age profile (70 per cent under 24), and a quarter intending to go on to further sport and recreation study, a third having done the award for personal development reasons (Lawson, 1990).

Alongside this, two other forms of SD work were developing. First, extending community use of schools beyond the level stimulated by 1960s regulations led to posts focused on opening them up and establishing district/county partnership management arrangements. Secondly, early interest in local projects to promote health through PA began, leading to the pattern of SD roles shown above, p. 14.

The Sports Council's model was very much top-down, service-specific (Houlihan and White, 2002). In parallel with this model, however, another had existed outside sport since before the Second World War but it was boosted by the needs of new communities of relocated citizens in New and Expanded towns, and began to take in sports work: Community Development (CD) is predicated on getting to know local communities and being accepted by them, and adopting and implementing local agendas with local interests and people. This is bottom-up work, often contended politically or socially, often in tension or opposition to local authority or commercial interests, and consequently often slow (AMA, 1989; McDonald and Tungatt, 1993; Taylor et al., 2000). Indeed, the CD Foundation will not get involved in any project that does not have seven years' secure funding, believing that not five (and certainly not the three years that is most common still) is long enough to ensure firmly based developments and enduring legacy frameworks. But it operates across a broad base of welfare, housing, employment, environmental and community needs, and some Directors of Sport and Leisure in larger metropolitan authorities (and districts with large populations that later became unitary authorities) with their own education and social services, thought it a more appropriate mode of operation. This was especially true as sport became drawn into seeking wider social outcomes, initially in the 1980s social cohesion for disaffected youth and some urban regeneration, and then under New Labour the full range of cross-cutting issues.

Hylton and Totten (2008: 65) wrote that an uncritical functionalist view of SD would ague that:

> SD polices gaps in provision and participation. It distributes social justice in the face of market trends. It circumvents barriers to participation. It

spreads the benefits of sport. It presides over competing plural interests. It advocates on behalf of marginalized groups. It applies the glue to bind diverse strands into an integrated whole.

Elsewhere, Hylton and Bramham (2008: 52) comment 'what we rarely see in the public domain is a challenge to these optimistic claims of smooth, systemic pathways to sporting success'. They go on to argue that Community SD responds better to concerns about equity and participation.

Pressure from the Thatcher government for public bodies to be more business-like extended to health and local authorities, and ideas of developing client units and contracted deliverers were developed. Perhaps because sport and leisure had a customer orientation, it had adopted some of the rhetoric and techniques of marketing, taught on many of the new graduate courses (Collins and Glyptis, 1992). So, sport was included along with grounds maintenance and catering for Compulsory Competitive Tendering (CCT). Coghlan, formerly a Deputy Director General of the Sports Council made a contemporary comment that sport was,

> subjected more and more to the market place, to the notion of 'value-for-money', to the concept if you want it you must pay for it, and if you cannot pay the market rate you cannot have it. This may well be sound in the purchase of a car, a washing machine or an expensive holiday, but is it so if Sport for All is a national policy? Such a philosophy takes no account of the 'social wage', the value society places on something intended to be of value to all.
>
> (Coghlan, 1990: 262)

This approach had been buttressed by a review by HMG's financial watchdog, the Audit Commission, which in *Sport for Whom?* (1989) argued that the still relatively narrow base of participation justified users paying more and taxpayers paying less for local sport and recreation services. Coghlan was gratified that Sports Council chairman Peter Yarranton wrote that 'the main concern of most people is that access to sport should be readily available and affordable' (*Annual Report 1989/90*: 5). But, despite the lack of sports management companies in the market, CCT was imposed. Local authorities had to draw up specifications and tenders, and choose between in-house operators and commercial companies, many formed by former municipal officers. Less than one in ten contracts went to contractors, who nevertheless formed their own association (Leisure Management Contractors Association) and most local authorities retained sports development on the client side. But the minority who contracted out their SD function had to think harder about objectives, targets and performance indicators. But most threats and least protection were given to 'services most likely to be deserving of public subsidy – sports development [where] between 41 and 49 per cent [of authorities] claim that the threat . . . takes the form of reducing services' (Taylor and Page, 1994: 22; see also Nichols and Taylor, 1995).

But measurement was more about throughput than social effectiveness (Coalter, 1994). CCT won economic efficiencies but the emphasis was on 'the bottom line' and, from this time on, prices for public sports services increased above inflation, which must have limited access for poor people, whose needs had already been recognised by the Sports Council with growing income inequalities (Sports Council, 1987: 1, 24). Nor did it encourage increases in service quality, sought under 'Best Value' by New Labour after they came into power in 1997. The government's own judgement on CCT was that it had 'provided a poor deal for employees, employers and local people' (DETR 1999: 6).

At the end of this phase, local authorities were also being encouraged to develop sport and recreation strategies (SSc, 1990), with emphasis on sport aiding wider social policies. This required examination of the needs of various population groups which SD officers were well-placed to do; larger authorities had developed teams with middle-level leaders, and the Sports Council wanted to encourage all authorities to have this coverage, so it started to fund Strategic SDOs, especially in LAs which had made no appointments, to the annoyance of some which had developed this function themselves, with no grant-aid. Reviewing trends, Lentell (1993) argued that the difficulty of achieving and measuring the social aims, and the growth of extrinsic purposes – what Coalter (1998) called 'sport for welfare' – suggested that England was waving 'goodbye to community recreation'.

Also at this time, sport was moved for a short period from the new Department for National Heritage to the Department for Education and Science which 'exhibited an attitude which combined neglect, disdain and incomprehension' (Houlihan and White, 2002: 63), and the Sports Council became more isolated from the DoE which oversaw most local government policy. The irony of this Department finding a new impetus for school sport and PE in a couple of years, as soon as sport had moved back to the Department for Culture Media and Sport will not be lost on sport historians.

Table 2.2 Milestones in sports development policy

Documents and decisions	Effects
1. FACILITIES BASE DEVELOPMENT 1960s–1982	
1964 A Chance to Share White Paper	Community use of schools (DES, 1964)
1971 Sport in the 70s	Community and specialist facilities (SC, 1971; Collins 1973)
1972, 75 Regional Councils for Sport, and then, Sport & Recreation	Regional advisory mechanism linking Sports Council LAs, LEAs, countryside interests
1975 Sport & Recreation White Paper	Identified social role for sport (DOE, 1975)
1977 Sport & Recreation in the Inner city	Foresaw social polarisation and problems (Collins, 1977)
1981 Action Sport	Concept of sports leadership (SC, 1986)
2. STRATEGY OF TARGETING AND EVOLUTION OF SPORTS DEVELOPMENT 1982–1991	
1982, 1987 Sport in the Community	Targeting groups, improved administration, sports medicine (SC 1982, 87)
1983 National Coaching Foundation	To support/professionalise coaching
1984–1990 National Demonstration Projects	Rolling out SD concepts with new partners, settings
1989 Sport for Whom?	Market testing of local sports services (AC, 1989) leading to Compulsory Competitive Tendering
1991/2 English Sports Council formed	Separation of powers for UK and domestic matters
3. SHIFTING PROVISION TO SCHOOLS, PERFORMANCE AND EXCELLENCE 1991–1997	
1992 Allied Dunbar National Fitness Survey	Sports Council's first serious engagement with health/PA (SC/DoH et al., 1992)
1993 National Sports Medicine Institute formed	Policies for youth, women, disabled, ethnic minorities (SC, 1993a–c, 1994)
1993 Sports equity replaces targeting	Ensure 2 hours a week quality sport and PE; extend school–clubs links; develop HE/FE role; talent development and Academy of Sport
1995 Sport: Raising the Game White Paper	To provide support for PE teachers and coaches
1994 Youth Sport Trust set up	Ambitious targets for participation, coaching and medals (ESC, 1997)
1997 England: The Sporting Nation	Review and development of individual volunteering (Gratton et al., 1997; Taylor et al., 2003; ESC, 1997)
1997 Valuing Volunteers	

Table 2.2 Continued

Documents and decisions	Effects
4. SOCIAL EXCLUSION AND MORE MEDALS 1997–2008	
1999 *Policy Action Group 10 Report: Sport and Arts*	Social exclusion identified as sport policy issue (Collins *et al.*, 1999; DCMS, 1999)
2000 *A Sporting Future for All*	Programmes for school facilities, new 5% contribution from TV income for grassroots sport
2002 *Game Plan*	Major new Active People survey 2006 to aid participation; twenty priority sports identified via Whole Sport Plans and Long-term Athlete Development model adopted; cautious strategy on mega-events; sector skill training; Best Value Performance Indicators (DCMS, 2002a)
2002 Coaching Task Force plan	Increase training and professionalisation (DCMS, 2002b; SCUK 2006)
2003 *Physical Education, School Sport and Club Links* (PESSCL)	400 specialist Sports Colleges and Partnerships, 3,200 School Sport Coordinators, Step into Sport youth volunteering in 200 SSPs
2004 *Framework for Sport in England*	*Towards an Excellent Service* quality accreditation; multi-sport hub clubs; workforce development
2005 *Review of National Sport Effort* (Carter report)	UK cabinet committee; single system for sport with County Sports Partnerships as link; £30m social marketing; Everyday Sport campaign (UK Sport 1999, 2005)
2005 Strategy for hosting mega-events, London wins bid for Olympics 2012	
2006 *Power of Sport*	Cantle identifies role of sport in social cohesion (ICC, 2006) after riots in northern cities
5. MEDALS AND SPORT FOR SPORT'S SAKE 2008 –?	
2008 *Playing to Win: A New Era for Sport*	Creating a 'world-leading SD system'; free swimming for <16 and 60+; sport for sport's sake for SC and NGBs; other agencies responsible for PA (DCMS, 2008)
2008 Strategy 2008–2011	Seek 1.25 million new participants from NGBs, HE/FE, commerce 3rd sector – of £205m, 58% to NGBs – but still seeking benefits to cohesion, employment, safer communities and fulfilled lives (SE, 2008a–f)

SHIFTING PRIORITIES TO SCHOOLS, PERFORMANCE AND EXCELLENCE, 1992–1997

The separation of UK elite sport and English functions was not a clean one; the English Council had national centres, and established more, and set up the National Sports Medicine Centre in London and the National Coaching Foundation in Leeds. Then in 1995 the Major government produced *Sport: Raising the Game*, the first White Paper on sport for twenty years (DNH, 1995). This was what Kingdon (1984) termed a 'focusing event' for government policy, pointing to school and youth sport (seeking two hours a week of 'quality sport', encouraging coaching and volunteering and school–community links and pursuing excellence via the English Institute of Sport, starting to focus on sport and scholarships in universities). The Regional Councils for Sport and Recreation which had linked national policy with the main delivery agency then – local authorities – were replaced with smaller, weaker 'Forums' in the guise of being more business-like. HMG's main triumph of the period, however, was to introduce the National Lottery, which engaged more of the population (especially women) in socially acceptable, nay sanctioned, betting than its proponents foresaw. It yielded money which could support NGBs and individual elite athletes as never before, leading to a rash of new national facilities countrywide (but with major clusters at Loughborough, as recorded in Chapter 6, and in Sheffield) and enabling the hiring of top-quality coaches, harnessing sports science and providing a means of medium-term secure planning, which was to yield a harvest of medals in future Olympics. It also enabled large numbers of grants to be given for local projects, but neither *Raising the Game* nor *The Sporting Nation* gave any major mention to local authorities. In 1997, the ESC produced its strategy, with a host of (over) ambitious targets for increasing participation (Collins, 1997). Even under Labour, the advent of the Lottery brought in a bidding culture rather than a planning culture, rewarding those who could make the best bids (often communities and clubs with professional advisers/members with legal, financial and professional skills), rather than those who had the greatest need (Oatley, 2000).

SOCIAL INCLUSION – 'SPORT FOR GOOD' – AND MORE MEDALS, 1997–2008

Earlier policies were rapidly overtaken in the landslide of a Labour election victory, and the introduction of policies aimed at reducing social inequality (SEU, 1997 – with poverty having climbed from 7 per cent of the population to 24 per cent between 1979 and 1994, under the Tories) which was exacerbated by other social factor (gender, ethnicity, disability, age and lack of transport (Collins *et al.*, 1999; Collins with Kay, 2003). New Labour was determined to have joined-up strategies to combat concentrations of social exclusion, in which sport was to play a part (Policy Action Team 10, DCMS 1999). ESC was now branded as Sport England and embarked on an agenda of *More People, More Places, More Medals* (ESC, 1998), under which 110 Specialist Sports Colleges (SSCs) would be identified with good club links capable of extension, and 600 secondary School Sport Coordinators (SSCOs) to link with 3,000 feeder primary schools.

The emphasis became on cross-cutting, 'wicked' issues with very broad intentions and outcomes, to:

■ support life-long learning, including developing new sports-related job skills;
■ improve health through fitness and meaningful activity and social contacts;
■ help make safer communities with greater cohesion across cultures and classes;
■ aid urban and rural development, with job generation as one consequence;
■ reduce social exclusion, especially in the most concentrated areas of deprivation.

In 1999, sports minister Kate Hooey extended this work in a DCMS (2000) strategy, *A Sporting Future for All*, mostly rehashing previous announcements (Collins, 2000), but proposing Performance Plans for NGBs, and multi-sport 'hub' clubs to promote participation locally, a vain hope in a traditional system of small, parochial single-sport clubs – quite unlike Germany where such clubs were a major agent of public policy (Anders, 1991). A new survey showed 5.8 million sports volunteers, supporting 106,000 clubs in England and contributing the equivalent help of 720,000 full-time workers, valued at £14bn (Taylor *et al.*, 2003), and emphasising the crucial nature of this part of the third sector to SD. Oakley and Green (2001) spoke of this period as one of 'selective reinvestment'.

Then the DCMS (2002a) produced *Game Plan*, significantly subtitled *A Strategy for Delivering the Government's Sport and Physical Activity objectives*, which:

■ set up a Sport and PA Board, but produced no programme as vigorously promoted or coordinated as in Scotland (see Chapter 7);
■ demanded better evidence on facilities and participation, setting up the online 'Active Places' database, and instituting the largest-ever participation survey, 'Active People', with 364,000 telephone interviews;
■ reinforced the importance of evaluation and penalties for failure (e.g. swimming was penalised £300,000 for poor results at the Sydney Olympics);

- supported the Long-Term Talent Identification model for elite athletes (see pp. 61–2, 66, 210) and identified twenty priority sports for funding;
- demanded of Sport England simpler funding streams, and saw SE and UKS roles as distributors of public funds more than technical advisers – their earlier roles;
- under the Audit Commission's regime of Best Value (2000) sought a set of performance indicators for local authorities, though when put out for consultation most were rejected by district councils as too costly and difficult to construct, leaving the sector open to the accusation that 'what cannot be measured, doesn't matter' (Collins, 2005).

Subsequently, and somewhat ironically, Sport England co-operated with the IDeA (2006) to provide a performance management framework for local authority sport (*Towards an Excellent Service – TAES*) under the new regime of Comprehensive Performance Assessment.

By this time, Sport England's Royal Charter no longer conveyed the 'arms-length' principle of the 1970s, and it was effectively an agency of government. Minister for Sport, Richard Caborn, made it clear he wanted a new start in leadership, and Derek Casey, CEO of Sport England for six years, left two years early with a considerable pension enhancement and an understanding that he would not work in England in any official role (Bourne, 2000: 1). He became chair of World Leisure, and later of the Glasgow bidding committee for the 2014 Commonwealth Games, resigning as soon as it was successful. Lord Carter, who has advised the government on getting out of messes regarding major facilities in the Lea Valley and the rebuilding of Wembley stadium, became chair.

Sue Campbell was then adviser to ministers in both DCMS and DfES, and in 2003 the latter produced a multi-strand strategy called *Physical Education, School Sport and Club Links (PESSCL)*, into which £1.5bn would be put over the next seven years. Its target of 75 per cent of schools offering the two hours of quality PE/PA a week in and outside the curriculum was comfortably exceeded, but questions have been raised about how to ensure the quality of the out-of-school element in particular.

This was incorporated in Sport England's (2004) *Framework for Sport in England* which promoted *PESSCL*'s targets, supported LTAD and hub clubs, and extended *TAES* to County Sports Partnerships, and to NGBs. The NGBs showed little interest (though they were directed to pursue Equality Standards (Sport England, 2004) throughout their organisations), because several of the cross-cutting issues and the form of *TAES* struck them as inappropriate. (*TAES* was soon extended to cover parks and open spaces and cultural services generally.) The *Framework* also:

- Committed Sport England to work with DfES on Extended Schools (an elaboration of the out-of-hours community-use policy that SC/SE had pursued since 1965), and sought evidence to underpin policy via the Value of Sport monitor which summarised and assessed the best research worldwide on the cross-cutting issues. Wallace *et al.*'s (2009) evaluation of Extended Schools use suggested that sport still led community use, with lunchtime and after-school clubs for 39 per cent of boys and 30 per cent of girls in the 1,901 schools surveyed. But 'pupils least likely to be using activities and childcare are those from deprived backgrounds, those where parents do not work or only one parent works, those attending special schools and those where parents are dissatisfied with the school' (2009: 7). Social gradients ruled again.
- Launched a Lottery-linked programme of projects called Active England to implement the recommendations from PAT 10 five years earlier.
- Started research on participants' motivation and barriers.
- Announced a social marketing campaign called 'Everyday Sport' which allegedly had a national budget of £30m matched by sponsors, large enough for real awareness impact, but which seemed to run into the sand after pilots in northern England.

The monitoring of Active England (Hall Aitken/Bearhunt, 2009) covered £94.8m of investment with another £132m levered in, in 241 capital and revenue projects of various sizes, whose managers were inducted into the importance of monitoring and reporting (though sadly, not until after most had started work). Some were large health/PA or sports centres, as in Burnley and Woodhouse Park in Manchester. Over the three years, this provided participation for 1.4 million people, of whom 12 per cent had been inactive in the previous year (16 per cent in local authority projects, but only 5 per cent in projects at sports clubs – see the end of this chapter and Chapter 15), and a throughput of 7 million visits. 636,000 were young participants (4 per cent at risk), 665,000 people were from deprived communities, and 101,000 had disabilities. 803,000 benefited from coaching. Two-thirds were promoted by public providers, a fifth by voluntary organisations and one in eight by sports clubs. Some 200 jobs and 11,000 qualifications were generated. Most projects intended to continue, but only three-quarters had measures in place to do so.

The consultants devised a measure of output per £10,000 of input – see Table 2.3. Some differences could be explained by:

- outdoor projects making use of existing land and water resources (e.g. Coastal and extreme water sports, for youth in North Cornwall) or mobiles (stadiums in Great Yarmouth, gyms in Eureka using futuristic animated figures);

Table 2.3 Monitoring Active England: output per £10,000 of input

Average	Centre-based	Out-door	Out-reach	Youth	Women	BME	Disabled	Disadv.
165 Participants	42	135	161	54	121	22	18	90
1,055 Visits/ throughput	359	246	821	550	937	240	225	194
2.1 Coaches	0.9	1.2	2.1	1.3	n/a	n/a	n/a	1.7
5.4 Active members	12.2	4.7	10.8	12.6	n/a	n/a	n/a	n/a
1.8 Volunteers	0.7	0.6	2.9	1.3	1.4	n/a	2.5	0.8

Source Hall Aitken/Bearhunt, 2009, Technical Appendix.

- some projects having smaller demand pools (e.g. BME projects) or requiring high staff/volunteer ratios (at risk, disabled; the Bolton Lads & Girls Club had 360 volunteers to support its 4 staff and 83 sessional workers).

It was not clear why participants and throughput were lower for youth and for women's projects.

Three out of five projects were with hard-to-reach/deprived and under-represented groups. The evaluation demonstrated that this work involved:

- assessing needs and aspirations and not assuming them, and matching supply to demand;
- considering psychological and motivational barriers;
- packaging activities to appear less like sport and more like fun;
- doing whatever it takes to make them accessible;
- using outreach and communicating well;
- using great, even iconic design wherever possible; and crucially
- choosing good staff and leaders who are 'boundary-busters'; 'People make projects'.

None of this is new to those involved in SD and CD for the last thirty years (see the same comments re the SAZ and ACDF reports on pp. 207–9). Indeed the consultants say that Sport England and its regions were inclined to play safe with traditional projects rather than innovative ones. They remarked on high staff turnover at some projects and the problem of staff leaving some months before the end of the three years, an established issue; as early as 1993 Collins commented 'Sports Development based solely on rapid turnover is a travesty of the term' (see also Collins with Kay, 2003: 219). Also it is not possible to estimate how much of this work would have proceeded with Active England, using other grant sources.

Sport England's new chair, Lord Carter, undertook a wide-ranging review of English structures, resources and policies, collecting perhaps the best back-up evidence since *Sport in the Community* in 1982. Perhaps with optimism beyond realism, he sought a single system for SD from Whitehall to village green, in which the CSPs were the essential link between local and national policy (see Chapters 3 and 5). But the rest of the recommendations made little impact. Neither did a rival 'Independent Sports Review' (2005) by former sports ministers Kate Hooey and Colin Moynihan (soon to take the chair of the CCPR) which had none of the sweep and vision of Lord Wolfenden's1960 report.

Six other issues raised their heads at this time:

1. *Coaching.* Coaching for both community and elite sport developed professionally through a Coaching Task Force review (DCMS, 2002b) which proposed forming 3,000 Community Sports Coaches (CSCs), a network of Coach Development Officers, and a nationally accredited certificate. This led to sports coach UK's (2006) plan. Of 1.1 million coaches in the UK in 2008, 76 per cent were volunteers, 3 per cent full-time paid, and the remainder paid part-time (SCUK 2009). Only two in five had an NGB qualification (MORI, 2004), but this had climbed to half by 2007 (Townend and North, 2007). A National Coaching Certificate with five levels was developed. In its new framework, SCUK (2006) saw differentiation of children's, participation, performance, high-performance and talent-development coaches, as part of a 'professionally regulated vocation'. Sport England had a programme to encourage CSCs, with £1.8m to fund 3,800 bursaries for courses via partners SkillsActive and the National Skills Academy, training for 1800 coach educators/tutors, and training resources. Active People 2008 showed that 7.5 million people undertook coaching tuition in 2007/8. SCUK (2009) looked to getting another 93,000 coaches by 2016.
2. *Helping elite sport.* The Talented Athlete Scholarship Scheme (TASS) was launched via Higher Education to help18–25 year-olds in thirty-two mainstream and fifteen disability sports to prepare for competition, and in 2005 smaller bursaries were offered to talented younger children.
3. *Health threats.* Concerned by rapidly growing overweight and obesity in adults and children, and consequential health threats, the Chief Medical

Officer (2004) produced a review arguing for five sessions of 30 minutes moderate exercise a week, but this did not pull national sports and health ministers closer; in 2008 both were contributing separately to programmes via the CSPs (Chapter 12).

4. *Using schools.* Extended use of schools should be helped by a major 'Building Schools for the Future' programme. But much management is still left to schools, many of which do not employ trained recreation managers or employ the same stringent quality and performance standards expected of local authorities and their trusts or contractors. A similar programme in Scotland produced 300 new schools by 2008 (Coalter and Genesis, 2008).
5. *PESSCL* strategy. In 2008 the strategy rolled on and was extended into Further Education Colleges, intensifying coaching support (Table 2.4). With Big Lottery money, £2.2bn will have been spent 2003–2011 on school sport. If/when it finishes it will leave a large hole in CSP programmes.
6. *Urban unrest.* Inner city cross-cultural unrest flared again in northern cities, and Cantle identified the potential for sport to aid social cohesion (ICC, 2006).

Green (2006: 234) said that by this time Sport for All had been long declining as a prominent and guiding policy ethos; perhaps its flexible boundaries, constantly shifting priorities and lack of specificity (McIntosh and Charlton, 1985: 99–101; Houlihan and White, 2002: 25) did not help. The Audit Commission (2006: 28) could write of local sport and recreation services 'only 15 per cent of the councils . . . had included outcome-focused targets, such as participation by target groups or customer satisfaction', concluding (p. 58) 'if councils fail to adopt clear comprehensive approaches to strategy decisions, they will fail to meet participation targets and community needs'. The challenge for them and Sport England is clear: Sport England is at last looking at customer satisfaction, but Chapter 14 will debate how coherent the current approach is.

So in this period the programmes for both school/youth and elite sport clarified, and extended and developed their own small policy/advocacy networks, even though Houlihan (2000) could rightly describe the former as a 'crowded policy space with many agencies and politicians and managers seeking a share of the action and success', which both undoubtedly achieved. Despite what Richard Caborn called 'sport for good', for extrinsic social benefits, by comparison community sport had no more clarity, resources or coherence than hitherto; a problem shared with other nations (Collins, 2008).

Houlihan and White (2002: 22) had written 'what is conspicuous by its absence is any sustained attempt to defend the promotion of sport for its intrinsic benefits'. A new Secretary of State and Minister for Sport at DCMS were soon to change that.

Table 2.4 Physical Education, School Sport and Club Links and Physical Education and Sport Strategy for Young People programmes, 2003–2008

DfEE 2003 elements	Developments and PESSYP 2008
■ From 62% in 2003, PSA targets of 75% of children having 2 hours high-quality PE and sport a week by 2006, 85% by 2008; £1.5bn 2003–2008	Exceeded – 90% by 2007–08); but only 71% and 66% in Years 10 and 11 (Quick et al., 2008); a five hour target is being set (DCSF, 2008) with £755m for 2008–2011
■ 400 Specialist Sport Colleges (SScs) by 2005	DfEE say exam results improved; still struggle between PA, competitive and lifelong recreation; help raise the floor rather than raising the ceiling (Houlihan and Wong, 2005); SScs obtain above-average GCSE scores for 5 subjects graded A*–C (YST, 2000)
■ 450 School Sport Partnerships (SSPs)	Do develop networks, help teacher development , and focus on neglected primary PE (Loughborough Partnership, 2005); £30m for coaches in SSPs 2008–2011
■ 3,200 School Sport coordinators (SSCOs) by 2006, linked to 18,000 primary teachers	Appoint FE college coordinators (FESCOs) linked to SSPs
■ Increase proportion entering clubs	Club links increase from 5 to 7.6 per school 2003–2007, and volunteers from 12% to 16%
■ Gifted and talented development programmes, including talent camps	Those registered as gifted and talented rise from 3% to 7%
■ Step into Sport to encourage youth volunteering in 200 SSPs	SScs developing interest in sports leadership £45m for Playing with Success schemes with professional clubs to increase numeracy/literacy Create at least 1 multi-sport club for disabled children in each SSP

Sources: DES, 2003; DCSF, 2008.

MEDALS AND 'SPORT FOR SPORT'S SAKE', 2008–

Towards the final writing of this book, the see-saw of British sport policy tipped again. Derek Mapp, former chair of the East Midlands Development Agency had been appointed chair of Sport England and was trying to grapple with a new strategy for increasing moderate-intensity sports participation linked to PA, taking responsibility for encouraging take-up of three of the five half-hour activity sessions required ('Engaging the Nation' speech to the CCPR conference, 9 May 2007). Newly appointed at DCMS, Secretary of State James Purnell, with a background in broadcasting rather than sport, took exception to Mapp's criticisms of money being diverted to supporting London 2012, and asked him to resign.

Mapp commented, 'I am bound to say I think it's unfair. I was mandated to produce an agenda which I was delivering on, but now that has been changed and I have been dumped on' (D. Bond, *Daily Telegraph*, 30 November 2007). He also said, 'Purnell is an arrogant young man who doesn't reflect what I thought this Government was trying to do' (A. Hubbard, *The Independent*, 2 December 2007). Purnell was soon moved to Work and Pensions, but the review of policy continued.

DCMS rhetoric (2008) continued to speak of a 'world-class sports development system', and a switch to promoting 'sport for sport's sake' mainly through the NGBs; though whether the NGBs had lobbied behind the scenes, saying, 'give us the money and we'll do this job' is not known. The strategy for 2008–2011 was soon published (Sport England, 2008a). Despite health and fitness having the strongest evidence for sport's extrinsic benefits (Coalter, 2007), health promoting activity was to be undertaken by health agencies, though County Sports Partnerships were to hold the two types of work together in return for a tiny £10m (see Chapters 5 and 12). NGBs were to get £120m (58 per cent of the total) and be expected to generate 500,000 new participants and 200,000 taking part with increased intensity; but HE/FE were expected to produce another 300,000 from among their students, commercial providers 150,000 and other voluntary bodies another 100,000 (see Table 2.5).

Sport England's CEO, Jennie Price, said that having half the total numbers to come from just eight sports could be seen as a confidence factor or a risk. She also warned that NGB funding will be stopped if action is not taken when gaps or slow progress is indicated, and clawed back if money or assets are not used for the approved purposes. Sport England will undertake a satisfaction survey of 300 regular participants, 300 club members and 300 people from the sport's talent pool, asking about ten domains – facilities and playing environment, coaching, people and staff, three aspects of playing (ease of participating, diversion and release), exertion and fitness, performance, social aspects and value for money – what Julian Misell called 'the DNA of sport'. He was from Ipsos MORI, the same company who undertook the Active People surveys (at 'Building Partnerships that Deliver' conference, London, 11 March 2009).

The strategy was supported by the Conservative and LibDem shadow ministers, and by the Local Government Association, perhaps surprisingly since local

Table 2.5 'World-leading community sport'

Grow (15% of investment)	Sustain (60 % of investment)	Excel (25% of investment)
1 million adults taking part in more sport by 2012–13	More people satisfied with the aspects of sport important to them	Talent support systems appropriate to each sport to enable identified performers to move to elite programmes
Helping more young people access five hours of sport a week	25% fewer 16–18 year olds dropping out of selected sports	

Source Sport England, 2008a.

authorities were given no more money directly or through general funding. The NGBs must be delighted. British Cycling was the outstanding success of the Beijing Olympics and the archetype of what Sport England and UK Sport would like to see. At the same event, its CEO, Ian Drake, outlined British cycling's solid growth in the last decade, but also its meteoric rise in international success, with a very clear elite mission, top-quality coaching and innovative world-class sports science, and its aspirations in its Whole Sport Plan (Table 2.6). Chapter 10 outlines British Swimming's plans.

The NGBs in English sport command only some 6 million members, not all playing (though Active People now suggests some 10 million involved, who may not all be (or have to be) members). Without exception, the NGBs argue that they need more volunteers to cope with the growing roles the government expects them to play; they struggle with working out the expressed aims of equality, of increasing involvement of more women, ethnic minorities, disabled people and other hard-to-reach groups. This clearly shows politicians continuing to value elite performance over community sport after nearly two decades, in common with most developed sports economies (De Bosscher et al., 2008; Houlihan and Green, 2008). Politicians' rhetoric reinforces the mythopoetic (myth-making) qualities of sport as character-building and foundational to society (Coalter, 2007).

David Pickup (1996: 172) saw the need for a close focus of policy and agency for elite sport, but thought that plurality was a virtue for 'modest levels of participation'. But English sports ministers have little budget, power or even authority and have not encouraged their civil servants or Sport England in recent years to have great technical know-how (compared to the 1970s and 1980s), being more strategic distributors of funds, and perhaps that is why they struggle to cope with the plural system (Roche, 1993; Henry, 2001; Oakley and Green, 2001). Tessa Jowell said in her preface to *Game Plan* (DCMS, 2002a: 11):

34

Table 2.6 British Cycling changes, 1996–2002 and Whole Sport Plan outcomes, 2009–2013

	1996	2008	Desired outcomes 2009–2013
Members (000)	13	25	100
Licences (000)	8	13	5% p.a. growth in competitors, 125,000 cycling for sport; 5% increase in satisfaction
Olympic/Paralympic medals	0	25	Growth, and success in Tour de France
World ranking	17th	1st	Retain 1st
Income	£1m	£10m	
Staff	16	153	21,000 youth club members 'Significant increase in cycling for recreation, physical activity, utility'

Source Ian Drake, CEO British Cycling, 'Whole Sport Plan 2009–2013: NGB process', paper to Sport England conference 'Building Partnerships that Deliver' London, 11 March 2009.

Sport defines us as a nation. It teaches us about life. We learn self-discipline and teamwork from it. We learn how to win with grace and lose with dignity. It gets us fit. It keeps us healthy and then those of us who carry [this blueprint] out must take our responsibilities seriously. But we should always remember that sport should be fun.

That was as near as she got to a statement of belief in the intrinsic value of sport. (She had made an explicit statement about the intrinsic value of culture, and promised but never delivered one on sport.) So, in the next policy phase it seems likely that school and elite sport will continue to thrive, and mass sport will struggle with local authorities, low in priority and funding. I will examine the proposed strategy in the light of the 2006 and 2008 Active People data at the end of my conclusions (Chapter 15). Now we turn to the case studies of developing SD.

REFERENCES

Anders, G. (1991) Structures and functions of sports clubs in Germany: between service organisation and social community, paper to RECMAN '91 conference, 28 February, Birmingham.

Association of Metropolitan Authorities (1989) *Community Development: The Local Authority Role*, London: AMA.

Audit Commission (1989) *Sport for Whom?* London: Audit Commission.

Audit Commission (2000) *A Step in the Right Direction? Lessons from Best Value Performance Plans,* London: Audit Commission.

Audit Commission (2006) *Public Sport and Recreation Services: Making them Fit for the Future,* London: Audit Commission.

Bergsgaard, N.A. et al. (2007) *Sport Policy: A Comparative Analysis of Stability and Change,* Oxford: Butterworth Heinemann.

Bourne, J. (2000) *Report of Auditor and Comptroller General to Parliament on the Departure of Mr Derek Casey, Former CEO of Sport England,* London: National Audit Office.

Carter, P. (Lord) (2005) *Review of National Sport Effort and Resources,* London: DCMS.

Chief Medical Officer (2004) *At Least Five a Week: Evidence on the Impact of Physical Activity and its Relationship to Health,* London: Department of Health.

Coalter, F. (1994) *Compulsory Competitive Tendering and Sports Development Planning in Scotland,* Research Report 41, Edinburgh: Scottish Sports Council.

Coalter, F. (1998) Leisure studies, leisure policy and social citizenship: The failure of welfare or the limits of welfare, *Leisure Studies,* 17: 21–36.

Coalter, F. (2007) *A Wider Role for Sport: Who's Keeping the Score?* London: Routledge.

Coalter, F. and Genesis Consulting (2008) *Use of School Sports and Cultural Facilities,* Research Digest 100, Edinburgh: sportscotland.

Coghlan, J. (1990) *Sport and British Politics since 1960,* London: Falmer Press.

Collins, M. F. (ed.) (1973) *Provision for Sport, vol. II: Specialist Facilities,* London: Sports Council.

Collins, M .F. (1977) *Sport and Recreation in the Inner City: Report of a Sports Council Seminar in Manchester,* November, London: Sports Council.

Collins, M.F. (1993) Sports development: the lessons learned and future challenges, in *Sport for All: in Pursuit of Equality,* Bedford: Eastern Council for Sport and Recreation.

Collins, M. (1995) *Sports Development Locally and Regionally,* London: Sports Council/ILAM.

Collins, M.F. (1997) Sporting nation, *Leisure Management,* (17)12, sports management section: 16–18.

Collins, M.F. (2000) Sporting future (Review of DCMS strategy), *Sports Management,* July 6–8.

Collins, M.F. (2002) England: Sport for All as a multifaceted product of domestic and international influences, in L. Da Costa and A. Miragaya (eds) *Worldwide Experiences and Trends in Sport for All,* Oxford: Meyer & Meyer Sport.

Collins, M.F. (2005) Where next with CPA?, *Recreation,* 64(12): 14.

Collins, M. (2008) Public policies on sports development: Can mass and elite sport hold together?, in V. Girginov (ed.) *Management of Sports Development,* Oxford: Butterworth-Heinemann.

Collins, M.F. and Glyptis, S.A. (1992) Marketing public leisure services in the UK, *Library Management*, 13(4): 33–42.

Collins, M.F. with Kay, T. (2003) *Sport and Social Exclusion* London: Routledge.

Collins, M.F., Henry, I., Houlihan, B. and Kennett, C. (1999) *Research Review: Sport and Social Exclusion,* London: Department of Media Culture and Sport.

De Bosscher, V. et al. (2008) *The Global Sporting Arms Race: An International Comparative Study on Sports Policy Factors Leading to International Sporting Success (SPLISS)*, Oxford: Meyer & Meyer Sport.

Department for Children, Schools and Families (2008) *PESSYP: Creating a World-Class System for PE and Sport,* London: DCSF.

Department for Culture Media and Sport (1999) *Report on Sport and Arts, to Policy Action Team 10 Social Exclusion Unit*, London: DCMS.

Department for Culture Media and Sport (2000) *A Sporting Future for All*, London: DCMS.

Department for Culture Media and Sport (2002a) *Game Plan: A Strategy for Delivering the Government's Sport and Physical Activity Objectives,* London: DCMS.

Department for Culture Media and Sport (2002b) *The Coaching Task Force: Final Report,* London: DCMS.

Department for Culture Media and Sport (2008) *Playing to Win: A New Era for Sport,* London: DCMS.

Department for Education and Skills (2003) *Learning Through PE and Sport: A Guide to the Physical Education, School Sport and Club Links Strategy,* London: DES.

Department for National Heritage (1995) *Sport: Raising the Game,* London: DNH.

Department of Environment (1975) *Sport and Recreation,* White Paper, London: HMSO.

Department of Environment (1989) *Sport and Active Recreation Provision in the Inner Cities: Report of the Minister for Sport's Review Group 1988/9,* London: HMSO.

Department of Environment, Transport and the Regions (1999) *Modernising Local Government: Improving Local Services through Best Value,* London: HMSO.

English Sports Council (1997) *England: The Sporting Nation,* London: Sports Council.

English Sports Council (1998) *More People, More Places, More Medals,* London: Sports Council.

Gratton, C. et al. (1997) *Valuing Volunteers in UK Sport*, London: Sports Council.

Green, M. (2006) From *Sport for All* to not about *Sport* at all? Interrogating sport policy interventions in the UK, *European Sport Management Quarterly*, 6(3): 217–38.

Green, M. (2007) Olympic glory or grassroots development? Sports policy priorities in Australia, Canada and the United Kingdom 1960–2006, *International Journal of History of Sport*, 24(7): 921–53.

Green, M. and Houlihan, B. (2005) *Elite Sport Development: Policy Learning and Political Priorities,* London: Routledge.

Hall Aitken/Bearhunt (2009) *Active England, Sport and Physical Activity: Final Report,* London: Sport England/Big Lottery Fund.

Henry, I. (2001 2nd edn) *The Politics of Leisure Policy,* Basingstoke: Palgrave.

Houlihan, B. (1991) *The Government and Politics of Sport,* London: Routledge.

Houlihan, B. (1997) *Sport, Policy and Politics,* London: Routledge.

Houlihan, B. (2000) Sporting excellence, schools and sports development: the politics of crowded policy spaces, *European PE Review*, 6: 73–92.

Houlihan, B. and Green, M. (2008) *Comparative Elite Sport Development: Systems, Structures and Public Policy,* Oxford: Butterworth-Heinemann.

Houlihan, B. and White, A. (2002) *The Politics of Sports Development,* London: Routledge.

Houlihan, B. and Wong, C. (2005) *Report on 2004 Survey of Specialist Sports Colleges,* Loughborough: Institute of Youth Sport, Loughborough University.

Hylton, K. and Bramham, P. (2008) Models of sport development, in V. Girginov (ed.) *Management of Sports Development,* Oxford: Butterworth-Heinemann.

Hylton, K. and Totten, M. (2008, 2nd edn) Community sports development, in K. Hylton and P. Bramham (eds) *Sports Development, Policy Process and Practice,* London: Routledge.

Improvement and Development Agency (2006) *Towards an Excellent Service: A Performance Management Framework for Sport and Recreation Services in Local Government,* London: IDeA.

Independent Sports Review (2005) *Raising the Bar,* London: ISR.

Institute for Community Cohesion (2006) *The Power of Sport,* Coventry: Coventry University for Sport England.

Kingdon, J.W. (1984) *Agendas, Alternatives and Public Policy,* Boston, MA: Little, Brown.

Lawson, P. (1990) Evaluation report of the Community Sports Leaders Award, *British Journal of PE*, 25(3): 29–31.

Lentell, R. (1993) Sports development: goodbye to community recreation?, in C. Brackenridge (ed.) *Body Matters: Lifestyles and Images,* Leisure Studies Association Publication 47, Eastbourne: Brighton University.

London Sport (1990) *Sports Development: Hitting the Target,* London: London Council for Sport and Recreation.

Loughborough Partnership (2005) *School Sports Partnership Annual Monitoring and Evaluation Report*, Loughborough: University Institute of Youth Sport.

McDonald, D. and Tungatt, M. (1991) *National Demonstration Projects: Major Lessons and Issues for Sports Development*, London: Sports Council.

McDonald, D. and Tungatt, M (1993) *Sport and Community Development*, London: The Community Development Foundation.

McIntosh, P. and Charlton, V. (1985) *The Impact of Sport for All Policies 1966–1984 and a Way Forward*, London: Sports Council.

MORI (2004) *Sports Coaching in the UK*, Leeds: sports coach UK.

Nichols, G. and Taylor, P. (1995) The impact on local authority leisure of CCT, financial cuts and changing attitudes, *Local Government Studies*, 21(4): 607–22.

Oakley, B. and Green, M. (2001) Still playing the game at arm's length? The selective re-investment in British sport, 1995–2000, *Managing Leisure*, 6: 74–94.

Oatley, N. (2000) New Labour's approach to age-old problems, *Land Economy*, 15: 286–97.

Pickup, D. (1996) *Not Another Messiah: An Account of the Sports Council 1998–1993*, Edinburgh: Pentland Press.

Quick, S. *et al.* (2008) *School Sport Survey 2007–08*, London: DCSF Research Report RW063.

Remans, A. (1993) *Sport for All: From Theory to Practice, KKU Seminar Report*, Strasbourg: Council of Europe, Committee for the Development of Sport.

Rigg, M. (1986) *Action Sport: Community Sports Leadership in the Inner Cities*, London: Policy Studies Institute for the Sports Council.

Rigg, M. (1989) *Operation Sport: Leadership in Wales*, Cardiff: Sports Council for Wales.

Roche, M. (1993) Sport and community: rhetoric and reality in the development of British sport policy, in J. Binfield and J. Stevenson (eds) *Sport, Culture and Politics*, Sheffield: Sheffield Academic Press.

Lord Scarman (1982) *Brixton Disorders 10–12 April 1981*, Harmondsworth: Pelican Books.

Scottish Sports Council (1990) *Sports Development Groups and Plans*, Report OP1, Edinburgh: SSc.

Social Exclusion Unit (1997) *Bringing Britain Together*, London: SEU/Cabinet Office.

sports coach UK (2006) *UK Action Plan for Coaching*, Leeds: sports coach UK.

sports coach UK (2009) *The Coaching Workforce 2009–16*, Leeds: sports coach UK.

Sports Council (1971) *Sport in the Seventies: Making Good the Deficiencies*, London: Sports Council.

Sports Council (1982) *Sport in the Community: The Next Ten Years*, London: Sports Council.

Sports Council (1987) *Sport in the Community: Into the Nineties*, London: Sports Council.

Sports Council (1990) *Recman 90 Seminar Report: Sports Development*, London: Sports Council.

Sports Council (1993a) *Sport in the Nineties: New Horizons*, London: Sports Council.

Sports Council (1993b) *Young People and Sport: Policies and Frameworks for Action*, London: Sports Council.

Sports Council (1993c) *Women and Sport: Policy and Frameworks for Action*, London: Sports Council.

Sports Council (1993d) *People with Disabilities and Sport: Policy and Current/Planned Actions*, London: Sports Council.

Sports Council (1994) *Black and Ethnic Minorities in Sport: Policy and Objectives*, London: Sports Council.

Sports Council/Department of Health et al. (1992) *Allied Dunbar National Fitness Survey, Main report*, London: Sports Council.

Sport England (2002) *The Equality Standard*, London: Sport England.

Sport England (2004) *Framework for Sport in England: Making England an Active and Successful Sporting Nation: A Vision for 2020*, London: Sport England.

Sport England (2008a) *Grow, Sustain, Excel: Strategy 2008–11*, London: Sport England.

Sport England (2008b) *Shaping Places through Sport: Executive Summary: Developing Strong, Sustainable and Cohesive Communities through Sport*, London: Sport England.

Sport England (2008c) *Shaping Places through Sport: Transforming Lives – Improving Life Chances and Focusing the Energies of Children and Young People through Sport*, London: Sport England.

Sport England (2008d) *Shaping Places through Sport: Increased Prosperity – Increasing Skill, Employment and Economic Prosperity through Sport*, London: Sport England.

Sport England (2008e) *Shaping Places through Sport: Creating Safer Communities – Reducing Anti-Social Behaviour and the Fear of Crime though Sport*, London: Sport England.

Sport England (2008f) *Shaping Places through Sport: Building Communities – Developing Strong, Sustainable Communities though Sport*, London: Sport England.

Taylor, P. and Page, K. (1994) *The Financing of Local Authority Sport and Recreation: A Service under Threat?* Melton Mowbray: Institute of Sport and Recreation Management.

Taylor, M., Barr, A. and West, A. (2000, 2nd edn) *Signposts to Community Development*, London: Community Development Foundation.

Taylor, P. *et al.* (2003) *Sports Volunteering in England*, London: Sport England.

Thorpe, R. (1988) *Sports Leadership*, unpublished report for the Sports Council, mimeo Loughborough: Loughborough University.

Townend, R. and North, J. (2007) *Sports Coaching in the UK II*, Leeds: sports coach UK.

UK Sport (1999) *Major events: The Economics of Measuring Success*, London: UK Sport.

UK Sport (2005, 2nd edn) *Major Events: The Guide*, London: UK Sport.

Wallace, E. *et al.* (2009) *Extended Schools Survey of Schools, Parents and Pupils*, London: Ipsos/MORI for DCSF.

Whiteley International (1993) *Sports Development in Wales: People in Action*, Study 14, Cardiff: Sports Council for Wales.

Wolfenden, J. (Sir, later Lord) (1960) *Sport and the Community*, London: Central Council for Physical Recreation.

Youth Sport Trust (2000) *Know the Score: Collection of Evidence to Support the Impact of the Sports College Network*, Loughborough: YST.

PART B

CASE STUDIES OF ORGANISING FOR SPORTS DEVELOPMENT

CHAPTER 3

TOWARDS A CONTEMPORARY NATIONAL STRUCTURE FOR YOUTH SPORT IN ENGLAND

Nikki Enoch

INTRODUCTION

'Changing forever the way we provide sport for young people so they can be the best they can be' was the mission that Sport England's Active Sports (AS) Team set itself in 1998. The Active Sports Programme (ASP) and its funding was the carrot to bring different provider agencies together and initiate a way of partnership working never before achieved across England, through creating a County Sports Partnership (CSP) network. Considerable achievements have been made, with forty-five CSPs.

CSPs are at a critical stage in their evolution. Moving beyond Active Sports to a much wider agenda, they were presented as and accepted by HMG as an essential part of the sub-regional structure for sport in England. This new role brings with it opportunities and threats, including a danger of regression if CSPs try to move their focus too wide, too fast and without the investment and support needed to ensure effective evolution. CSPs were set up to help create a single development pathway for young people in different sports. This is their core business. Whilst they could do much more, it should never be at the expense of the young people they were designed to serve.

This case study sets out to:

1. share understanding of the research and principles that underpinned the AS approach;
2. offer insight into the business planning process and challenges AS faced;
3. highlight the strengths, weaknesses, and current challenges that remain in developing the CSP network for young people.

The case study covers, successively: the key issues affecting youth sport in England in the late 1990s; the aspirations of the ASP and lessons learned during 2000–2004; and the evolving role of CSPs within the emerging framework for youth sport.

YOUTH SPORT AT THE MILLENNIUM

This section describes what youth sport was like in the late 1990s and highlights seven major influences that impacted on AS's work.

1. The sports development continuum

The concept of the sports development continuum describes a logical progression from learning the basic skills at foundation level to performing as an elite performer at the excellence level (Tungatt and MacDonald, 1991). The concept had been around for a decade (see Figure 3.1). It was logical, easy to explain and widely accepted, but it was also open to interpretation and selective use. This is illustrated in the Regional Strategies produced by the Regional Councils for Sport and Recreation in the mid-1990s (e.g. *Beyond the Barriers*, East Midlands Council for Sport and Recreation, 1994). All made reference to the continuum model as an underpinning concept to explain the process of sports development, but none used it as a 'driver' to influence the holistic

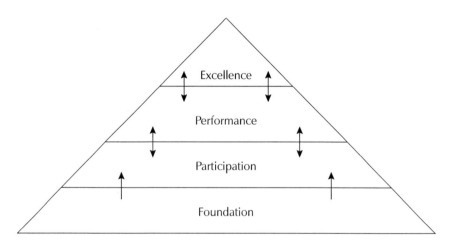

Figure 3.1 The sports development continuum model

46

nikki enoch

development of sport. As such it was rarely translated meaningfully into the business plans of policy makers.

2. Early specialisation in sport

Early specialisation in sport – identifying talent at an early age and subjecting young people to intensive performance programmes in a single sport – became the norm for National Governing bodies (NGBs) during the 1990s (Rowley, 1992a, 1992b). The original 'pyramid' of the Sports Development continuum was being distorted into a narrow vertical 'pipe' by colleagues working in the field of excellence (who were influenced by the need to win more international medals and by funding limitations that restricted investment programmes to a relatively few individuals). The philosophies underpinning grassroots development and performance programmes were becoming opposed. This was a major issue in need of reconciliation.

3. TOPs

By the end of 1990s the Youth Sports Trust's TOPs programmes, that initially targeted training of teachers, and subsequently expanded to cover school–community links and children with disabilities, were reaching very large numbers of schools and young people (YST, 1998, 1999), who would soon need access to the organised sports system to pursue their interest and skills. TOPs was 'a child-centred approach', being both fun and enjoyable whilst developing skills and physical literacy.

4. A sports development network

As Chapter 2 described, after the NGBs, local authorities (LAs) were the first to employ sports development officers (SDOs), followed by local education authorities (LEAs) when the national policy emphasis was increasingly on young people. In the late 1990s the biggest gap was of sports-specific officers operating locally with clubs, coaches and volunteers. Clubs and volunteers are often described as the 'bedrock', 'backbone' or 'grassroots' of English sport, but were rapidly becoming the weakest link, as a combination of changing lifestyles, ageing population and increasing responsibilities of duty-of-care and child protection were stretching to their limits the small-sized clubs that predominate (Collins and Randolph, 1994).

5. Changing local government structures

Unitary authorities for major urban areas were introduced (outside the metro-politan counties) in 1996, weakening county council remits and their Council Tax income bases, and potentially damaging opportunities for strategic countywide sports development. In reality, no NGB has the capacity to work with all 388 district and unitary authorities. Similarly, most local authorities do not have the capacity to work with all thirty or so 'core' NGBs. A strategic network of a manageable number of appropriate 'catchment' areas was needed to build a bridge between grassroots and national high-level performance programmes.

6. Modernising governance

The requirements to achieve Best Value and then comprehensive performance in local government, and the recommendations of the PAT 10 report (DCMS, 1999) challenged the justification of public intervention and investment, pro-moting community engagement and requiring integrated thinking and partner-ship working. Inspection systems were looking for decision-making based on evidence and underpinned by good quality organisational practices; soon struc-tural change was being required also of NGBs by UK Sport and Sport England.

7. The 'Big Picture'

Sport's 'Big Picture' was introduced by Sport England with the aim of 'building the most comprehensive sports development system in the world' (Sport England, 1998a–c) through the Active Schools, Active Communities, Active Sports and World Class Start, Potential and Performance programmes. For the first time ever, sports development was at the heart of sports policy, and substantial Lottery funding was available for revenue funding of local schemes, individual athletes and NGBs, on a solicited basis (Figure 3.2).

In summary, these were exciting times, offering both major opportunities and challenges. In theory, the ASP and CSPs were the central link within that 'Big Picture'. In reality, there was:

- no widely accepted practical framework for developing youth sport across the sports development continuum, or indeed in any single major sport;
- no mechanism or structure for bringing the different provider agencies together;

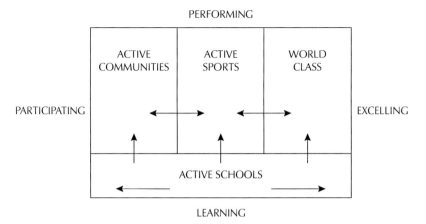

PERFORMING

| ACTIVE COMMUNITIES | ACTIVE SPORTS | WORLD CLASS |

PARTICIPATING ←→ ←→ EXCELLING

ACTIVE SCHOOLS

LEARNING

Figure 3.2 English sport's 'Big Picture', introduced by Sport England, 1998c

- highly charged views on who should lead this work and receive the new Lottery funding: NGBs, LEAs or LAs?;
- resistance to the concept of CSPs from several parties (notably the newly established unitary authorities in large cities) that wished to flex their political and financial muscles;
- no natural 'champion' for the 'middle ground' of sport's 'Big Picture', such as those for other programmes (LEAs, the YST, the DfES for Active Schools, local authorities for Active Communities, and the NGBs for World Class), as contended by Houlihan and White (2002);
- a culture in sports development practice that was not tuned into quality standards and business processes.

ACTIVE SPORTS

The ASP got off to a false start. In fact, it emerged out of the World Class Start programme for people seeking to follow the elite sport pathway. In 1997 Sport England published its first policy paper on World Class Start and established a national team to implement it, led by the author. It was heralded as a 'strategic' grassroots leadership and coaching programme, with a seamless link into the World Class Potential programme (for young people on the fringe of national squads). The team's first task was to undertake market research to identify where on the sports development continuum it would be most effective, to test support for the concept of CSPs, and to identify how best to invest the £10m annual budget allocated from the Lottery Sports Fund.

49

Market research with thirteen NGBs (Sport England, 1998d) identified a need for it to be positioned at the top of the continuum, involving a relatively small number of participants, about 1,000 in each sport – on average 22 in each CSP area. The same market research with twelve potential CSPs identified support for strategic alliances between LAs, county GBs and education services to provide a co-ordinated system for young people to develop their interests and skills in sports, and to support the development of clubs, coaches, officials and volunteers. To achieve these outcomes, the programme would need to be positioned significantly lower on the continuum and to involve significantly larger numbers of people than envisaged by the NGBs. The findings from both parts of the market research were understandable and justifiable, but incompatible.

A key issue was at whom should this £10m a year programme be targeted: a larger number of young people enjoying sport and wanting to improve, or a much smaller number identified as talented, so they could reach the top? The easy, short-term option would have been to 'fudge' the issue, and proceed as originally intended. In the longer term, this tension would have remained and damaged the programme. High-level political debate caused delays and frustrations, especially for the 150 people and organisations involved in the market research, who in turn would network with many others. Eventually, it was decided to increase the overall resources and proceed with two programmes – 'World Class Start' and 'Active Sports'.

World Class Start would fit directly beneath World Class Potential, and be led by NGBs as part of an integrated World Class Programme, targeted at a relatively small number of youngsters. Active Sports would build up from the grassroots and link into the NGB county and performance programmes, targeted at substantially more young people, who already liked sport and wanted to improve.

This bold decision took courage, and caused embarrassment and short-term pain, but was absolutely right in the circumstances. It presented major challenges and lessons for those staff in Sport England charged with developing yet another new programme at a time of 'initiative overload', and when its credibility was low.

The lessons learned from this false start are listed in Table 3.1.

Four research projects influenced the design of the ASP:

1. A public opinion survey (Sport England, 1998e) in which nine out of ten respondents agreed that Lottery grants should be available to improve coaching opportunities for young people, and to fund developing young people with talent.

Table 3.1 Early lessons built into the Active Sports programme

Lesson	Learning
Focus	Ensure clarity of purpose is understood and agreed by decision makers and stakeholders.
Political support	Check out – don't make assumptions.
Market research	Vitally important to undertake, involving partners and delivery agents, but *prior to* the design and development stage and definitely without a 'brand name'.
Timeframe	Resist pressure to make short cuts, and be realistic.
Communication and promotion	Think through the strategy and act only when ready.
Reactions	Develop a defendable rationale that can be explained to and accepted by the majority; antagonists will make their views known.

2. The *Development of Sporting Talent* study (ESC, 1997) which confirmed that most talented performers were selected from a very narrow base of the population, those in professional, managerial (A, B) socio-economic groups. Indeed, a major conclusion was that 'a selected few have a first-class ticket to the podium and the majority have no ticket at all'. It revealed a varying level of understanding of talent selection processes by NGBs, and a resistance from them to sharing expertise. It highlighted that, whilst most performers were satisfied with their coaches, many felt they had been lucky to find one of good quality.

3. A *Young People and Ethics* study (Sport England, 1998f) which identified what young sports competitors most valued – enjoyment, improving personal performance and playing in a sporting manner (without cheating). So it was crucial that these values were embedded into the ASP.

4. A *World Class Start Interim Report* (Sport England, 1998d) which confirmed support for a programme of this nature to be sports-led with sport-specific frameworks, devised nationally, but delivered through strategic countywide partnerships.

Purpose, aim and objectives

The purpose of the ASP was summarised by Trevor Brooking, then Chair of Sport England:

For the first time the whole country will be covered by a network of Sports Partnerships whose main purpose is to make it easier for young people who enjoy sport, and want to be more involved, to improve and achieve their best. Through this network we will help such young people to become more committed to sport and more fully involved in our clubs and performance programmes. From Penrith to Penzance we must guarantee the same high quality opportunities for any young person who wants to progress in sport.

(Sport England, 2000: Foreword)

The three fundamental principles of access to all, top-down policy and bottom-up delivery, and effective local alliances of education, community and sports bodies were enshrined in operations.

The Programme's aim was to:

Help young people with the ability and the desire to improve their sporting skills through a coordinated programme across England that will provide access to organised sport.

The Programme's objectives were to:

1. identify and support innovative approaches and action for ensuring the benefits are *equally accessible* to all young people with the ability and desire to progress in sport, including: women; disabled people; black, Asian and other ethnic minorities; and those living in designated priority/ disadvantaged areas;
2. coordinate and improve *coaching and competitive opportunities* for young people, including the new Millennium Youth Games;
3. create and support local *assessment and development squads* in specific sports;
4. develop and support high opportunities for juniors in *clubs;*
5. increase both the number and quality of *coaches* working with young people at different levels;
6. increase both the number and quality of *officials* working with young people at different levels;
7. increase both the number and quality of *volunteer helpers* working with and on behalf of young people;
8. provide a range of *specialist services* for young people, parents, coaches, officials and volunteers as set out in the national guidance documents to support the development of Active Sports at national and local levels.

nikki enoch

Delivering the objectives involved a very simple strategy:

- NGBs and other national agencies to design national frameworks for local delivery;
- CSPs to coordinate and manage local delivery through appointing forty-five Active Sports Managers and teams;
- funding allocated on a population-linked basis, and released on approval of action plans, so that there would be no 'dash for cash', but time and resources available for quality planning.

Initial five-year targets were agreed as set out in Table 3.2.

Table 3.2 The scale of the Active Sports programme

Published targets	By 2003*	
	Number	%
Sports Partnerships formed with Active Sports Managers	45	100
Sports Partnerships with Lottery awards	45	100
Sports Partnerships 'active' with programmes for young people	45	100
Participants	300,000	7**
Profile of participants in Stage 1	(Max)	
Girls and young people	150,000	50
Black, Asian and other ethnic minorities	30,000	10
Disabled people	6,000	2
In Priority areas (original designated areas)	120,000	40
Coaches	20,000	n/a
Profile of coaches		
Girls and young people	5,000	25
Black, Asian and other ethnic minorities	1,000	5
Disabled	400	2
In Priority areas (original designated areas)	6,000	30
Volunteers	30,000	n/a
Sports clubs supported	2,000	n/a
Equity policies and action plans	45	100
Child protection policies and plan	45	100

Source Sport England, 2000.
Notes * Assuming the programme would be fully operational by the end of 2003 in all County Sports Partnerships; ** Of total population of 10–16 year olds.

53

The original programme budget averaged £10m a year and £73m in total. It was a big business, and needed to be planned as such. In the market research phase, the European Business Excellence Model (EFQM, 1998) was suggested by a potential CSP as a good framework for designing and delivering the business plan. In the absence of anything customised for the sports industry, and with *Quest for Sports Development* (Sport England et al., 2000) still being designed (and in any case being underpinned by the widely applied EFQM), it seemed a good suggestion. Table 3.3 provides a summary of the six major components of the business plan.

Some aspects of the plan worked better or faster than others (e.g. the spirit of teamworking with AS managers (ASMs) and NGB lead officers). Some elements needed fundamental rethinking (e.g. the design of the initial audit and the application process). Overall, as a framework for building and improving this particular sports SD business, it worked well and produced evidence of achievements in line with stated objectives.

Active Sports hit all of its major planning milestones in establishing the CSPs, as follows:

- 45 established, with ASMs in post, achieved by April 2001;
- 45 with Lottery awards, achieved by April 2002;
- 45 with Child Protection Policies, achieved by April 2002;
- 45 with Equity Policies and Action Plans, achieved by April 2002;
- 45 with activities for young people in at least three sports, achieved by Autumn 2002.

Details are documented in the *Mid Term report* (Sport England, 2002). Most CSPs opted for introducing three or four sports in their first year and building up to all nine sports by year three (rugby league was the tenth sport in its 'heartland' areas of northern England). By March 2003 CSPs had 383 Sport Action Groups planning or implementing local programmes, which equated to 92 per cent of the total roll-out. 292 of these Action Groups (70 per cent of the total roll-out) had received Lottery awards for delivering activities, as shown in Figure 3.3.

By December 2004 the scale of the activity had grown, as shown by data registered on the AS database, though (as Table 3.4 shows) relatively few had reported Year 4 data. These statistics (unpublished) highlight the significant numbers of participants, coaches and clubs involved in the ASP over its four-year life. Whilst there was some element of double counting those involved for more than one year, the overall totals were impressive and exceeded the targets set, with 435,000 young people, 28,800 coaches and 5,900 clubs participating.

Table 3.3 Summary of Active Sports programme's business plan

Approach	Tactics	Rationale and learning
Leadership	Recognise and support those in leadership positions who are able to help and influence: ▪ Active Sports Managers (ASMs) and Chairs ▪ NGB lead officers and Chief Executives ▪ Sport England members, senior management and lead officers nationally and in regions ▪ National equity lead officers ▪ DCMS and government advisers ▪ Sports Partnership Sounding Board (a national advisory group) ▪ National presence at County Youth Games and Active Sports launches.	Success depends on the quality of leaders to inspire, create and 'do the right things'. Significant effort on managers, lead officers and Sport England senior management and members that had desired effect. Less effort was invested in CEOs, Chairs, Sport England unit heads and government departments, who continued to challenge the role of CSPs.
Policy and strategy	Provide high-quality pre-application support, so as to achieve 100% success in Lottery applications, and encourage CSPs to make the most of their allocated resources, by: ▪ Setting clear purposes, aims and objectives that applied to all aspects of policy and programme development ▪ Being development-led, and not application-led ▪ Agreeing policy based on shared funding ▪ Selecting sports that could make a major contribution ▪ Designing NGB and partnership services frameworks ▪ Establishing CSPs and appointing ASMs in three phases ▪ Designing and improving funding processes ▪ Managing the roll-out of sports over five years ▪ Encouraging innovation within Partnership services.	Policy and strategy designed to achieve intended objectives and outcomes, and help translate theory into practical actions. This aspect of the business plan was rated in the top 3% of all submissions for the 2002 TNT Modernising Government Award. Difficult decisions cannot be avoided, e.g. allocating funds and selecting sports, and there will always be perceived 'winners' and 'losers'. Defendable rationale, consistency of message and adherence to approach helped to reinforce the policy.

Table 3.3 Continued

Approach	Tactics	Rationale and learning
People	Create a team spirit and working approach with everyone getting the support they need to fulfil their roles, inspiring commitment, winning hearts and minds, and providing two-way channels of communication, through: ■ An ASM welcome package, induction and project-planning training ■ An NGB lead officer network ■ A Sport England lead officer network ■ ASM regional and supra-regional networks ■ AS seminars and workshops ■ AS specialist advisers ■ Weekly email ■ Leadership development ■ Recognising achievements.	Ultimately it's people who make things work. Making everyone involved feel part of the team and recognising their contribution in the collective game plan was a culture we tried to nurture, which gained us a reputation for listening and caring. Although enormous effort was put into communicating, it was never enough. Early training focused on programme matters. Much more was achieved when this shifted to personal and skill development, highlighting how little attention and understanding sport invests in this area.
Partnerships and resources	Maintain strong relationships with all stakeholders through a network structure linked into the national team, and market test need for resources: ■ AS and Youth Games funding and development guides ■ Partnership roles and responsibilities framework ■ AS one-stop website ■ Player registration package ■ Coach Management Information System ■ Web design and sponsorship packages	Coordinating effort to provide a single system for young people to access, and impetus behind CSPs. Originally more were sceptics than believers, many adopted a neutral position to see what happened. Convincing people in key political positions by using evidence from the more established Partnerships swung the debate. The challenge in 2005 was managing the transition beyond Active Sports, and the increasing pressures and expectations on CSPs.

	<ul><li>Clubmark standards, resources and accreditation</li><li>Child-protection standards, guidelines and workshops</li><li>Partnership database.</li></ul>	Use effective and efficient processes systematically to make life much easier and less frustrating for all.
Processes	Market test processes prior to introduction, and review after the first wave of users, publishing improvement proposals:<ul><li>Framework design and approval process</li><li>ASM pre-application support service</li><li>Lottery application process</li><li>ASM post-award support service</li><li>Monitoring and review of performance-based self-assessment</li><li>Stakeholder development groups for new products.</li></ul>	Giving more attention to processes and challenging existing 'rules' were two of the biggest lessons learned – the hard way.
Results	Collect and disseminate evidence of impact and achievement by:<ul><li>Key performance indicators linked to objectives and targets</li><li>Annual customer and stakeholder surveys</li><li>Interpret evidence from annual Partnership Reviews</li><li>Longitudinal impact study by external consultants.</li></ul>	Articulating success and then measuring it is a basic business requirement and needs high priority. The issue that emerged is how much should be done nationally, regionally and locally, and whether information systems can be synchronised without excessive bureaucracy.

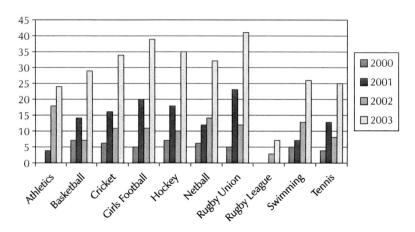

Figure 3.3 Number of Sport Action groups with a Lottery award

Table 3.4 Active Sports national statistics, April 2003

Headline Performance Indicators	Year 1 44 CSPs	Year 2 42 CSPs	Year 3 32 CSPs	Year 4** 11 CSPs	Total*
No. of participants across all stages and Youth Games	94,773	166,779	153,074	20,535	435,181
No. of coaches	6,219	12,484	9,209	857	28,769
No. of clubs	1,289	2,234	2,101	249	5,873

Source Sport England AS Database, December 2004.
Notes * Figures are cumulative and will double count those involved in ASP for more than one year; ** Very few CSPs have completed the fourth year of operation in ASP or inputted their achievements.

Dorset Sport, Greater Sport (Greater Manchester Sports Partnership) and Merseyside Sport were the first three CSPs to have registered their Year Three statistics, provided in Table 3.5.

The data for Greater Sport in Table 3.6 demonstrates a dramatic rise in the number of youngsters involved in AS in Year Three. Both Dorset and Merseyside experienced significant growth in Year Four, with the number of participants increasing in Dorset from 2,500 to 7,100, and in Merseyside from 5,400 to 9,400. (Equivalent figures for Greater Sport were not available at the time of writing.)

Table 3.5 Overall key statistics for Year 3 in three CSPs (September 2002–August 2003)

Headline Performance Indicators	Dorset (Pop: 644,000)		Greater Manchester (Pop: 2,497,000)		Merseyside (Pop: 1,402,000)	
	Target	Actual	Target	Actual	Target	Actual
Total number of participants across all stages and PYG	4,385	2,482	n/a	19,238 (8%)	5,876	5,375 (4.1%)
% of young people moving from AS Stage 1 to Stage 2	49	60	n/a	69	31	29
% of young people female (all stages and PYG)	51	56	55	67	58	54
% of young people with a disability (all stages and PYG)	6.7	4.7	5.0	8.0	7.8	9.0
% of young people from BEMs in AS Stage 1	7.4	4.9	12.0	10.0	2.1	4.5
% of young people from Priority Areas in AS Stage 1	2.9	3.2	41	44	44.6	50.6
Total number of coaches involved in ASP	235	168	n/a	121	387	336
Number of clubs (CSP actively working with) that are working towards NGB accreditation/ Clubmark	65	67	n/a	234	70	65

Notes Stage 1: coaching centres and courses; Stage 2: participation in clubs; Stage 3: selection events for partnership development squads; Stage 4: partnership development squads.

Data for Merseyside showed particular progress in involving youth who were disabled, from black and ethnic minorities and from priority areas, and coaches who were women (Figure 3.4).

It is widely accepted that, of the young people involved in CSP programmes, only a fraction was registered and profiled, since such data takes substantial effort to obtain, but the emerging statistics demonstrated the considerable scale and breadth of the ASP. The trends demonstrated by Greater Sport (Manchester) and Merseyside suggest that the equity targets were not only being achieved at

Table 3.6 Young people involved in the Greater Sport Partnership (Greater Manchester)

Stages	Year 1	Year 2	Year 3
Total number of participants across all stages and PYG	5,127	7,073	19,238
Total number in Stage 1	3,380	4,555	10,433
Priority areas	1,498	1,008	4,632
Females	2,399	2,766	7,030
Black and ethnic minorities	170	386	1,043
With disability	172	295	835
Total number in Stage 3	299	660	1,980
Priority areas	n/a	91	566
Females	212	410	1,526
Black and ethnic minorities	5	24	103
Total number in Stage 4	177	359	1,324
Priority areas	n/a	41	365
Females	90	271	1,094
Black and ethnic minorities	0	18	49

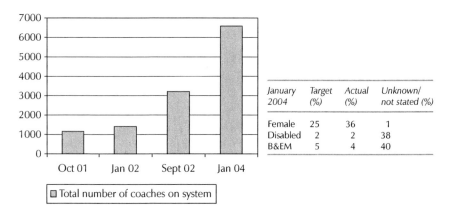

January 2004	Target (%)	Actual (%)	Unknown/ not stated (%)
Female	25	36	1
Disabled	2	2	38
B&EM	5	4	40

☐ Total number of coaches on system

Figure 3.4 Total number of coaches on Coach Management Information System

Stage 1, but were maintained in the Stage 4 development squads. Should these trends be replicated across the country and maintained over time, a change in the structure of English sport will be evident, with safer and more equitable systems in mainstream sport.

In early 2004 more than 6,500 AS coaches were registered on the national Coach Management Information System. Figure 3.4 shows their number and profile, and that recruitment was hitting its target for disabled and female

nikki enoch

coaches, but not for those from black, Asian and other ethnic minorities. Such statistics provide a small part of the overall picture, because it is the positive relationships developed with NGBs, clubs, volunteers and coaches that is the real strength of how the work impacted, supported and encouraged innovation at the grassroots. Consequently, most NGBs involved, and especially their development teams, grew to value and appreciate the role of CSPs. Many saw a continuing role for them as they developed their One Stop and Whole Sport Plans.

The profile, successes and future of the ASP were suppressed after the modernisation of Sport England in 2003 and the decision to rationalise its many funding programmes into two main streams (community and national). Instead, ASP's legacy was communicated to people who had invested considerable effort in setting it up and were still actively involved in delivering it, along two discrete but interdependent dimensions:

- community – the evolution of the CSPs' role to be wider than that of ASP;
- national – incorporating sub-regional delivery of elements of most NGB plans.

THE EVOLVING ROLE OF COUNTY SPORTS PARTNERSHIPS

Even in 2000, sports minister Kate Hoey questioned the value of CSPs relative to one of her Department's babies – School Sport Partnerships (SSPs), but by 2002 the DCMS concurred on their importance (DCMS, 2002). A framework for the structure of English sport was emerging (as illustrated in Figure 3.5), championed by Sue Campbell, then Ministerial Adviser on Sport and interim Chair of UK Sport (e.g. Campbell, 2003). This put CSPs at the centre of the web.

The framework applied the principles of the Long Term Athlete Development model (Balyi, 1999) backed by Sport England. This is a slightly more sophisticated version of the traditional sports development continuum, with the key difference being its stages from 'fundamentals' to 'training to win' (from bottom to top of the right-hand side of Figure 3.5), and growing evidence of its application. It gained the support of HMG and of many people developing sport at both grassroots and world-class levels. It provides some basis for aligning many different agendas, but there are critics who say it is just a hyped up model of training periodisation, generalised originally from Alpine skiing, based on no good, peer-reviewed research. Chris Earle, Director of Sports Development at Loughborough University (see Chapter 6) describes it as not a high-performance model, but an athlete-retention one (www.sportsdevelopment.org). Also there

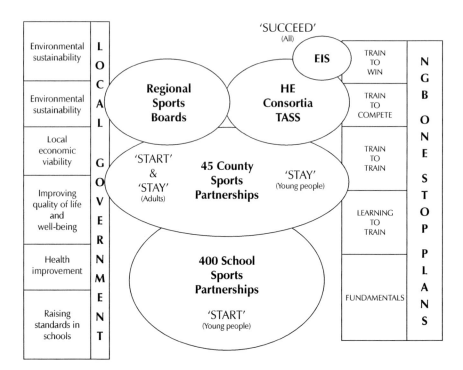

Figure 3.5 The emerging framework for English sport (Campbell, 2003)

has been some realisation that it takes ten years to get the right structures in place (DCMS, 2002; Sport England, 2004a).

A fundamental role of a CSP is to bring together three sectors in a way that adds value to their individual efforts for developing sport across their geographic area, namely:

- *education*, including schools, LEAs, Further and Higher institutions;
- *community*, including health, inclusion, cohesion and other cross-cutting themes;
- *sports*, including voluntary, public and commercial enterprises.

CSPs have a dual purpose:

- a *sports focus* – building and improving a coordinated sports system for people in their areas to enter, participate and progress;
- a *partnership focus* – building a high-performing partnership of agencies across the three sectors to help them increase their collective influence, work better together, and attract investment to benefit sport.

Whilst both are essential, there is an argument that the sports focus should come first to give the CSP a tangible basis for demonstrating its role and impact and for attracting investment from a wider range of partners. This is exemplified by the scale of activity taking place in Greater Sport (and Lancashire Sport among others, see Charlton, Chapter 5) giving a profile and level of credibility that has attracted interest from community agencies.

Through the Regional Sports Boards, Sport England confirmed its commitment to invest in CSPs and help to get them fit for purpose in their new roles by April 2006, using IDeA's *Towards an Excellent Service (TAES)* tool. The CSP model that Sport England (2004b) proposed is illustrated in Figure 3.6.

Good partnership relationships need a clear shared understanding of their purpose and added value, and the unique roles and contributions of the different members/stakeholders. Even when these are agreed, they need constantly to be revisited and reinforced through action. Charlton's exploration of the development of Lancashire Sport (Chapter 5) makes this clear. CSPs had to review

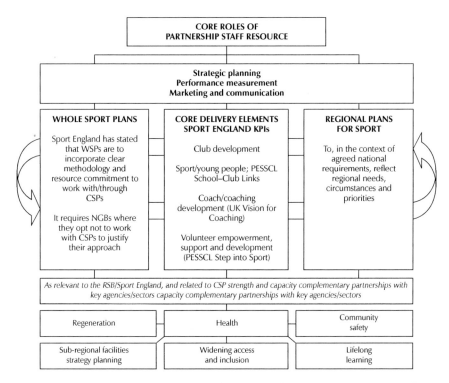

Figure 3.6 Sport England's model of the role of County Sports Partnerships (Sport England, 2004b)

their vision and core purpose in 2004 and are now doing so again in the light of Sport England's 2008 strategy, with effects on their governance, staffing and organisational design, strategic frameworks, operating models and decision making.

There is recent evidence suggesting that CSPs have begun to move towards integrated operations with the SSPs, as exemplified by the South Yorkshire Sport Improvement Plan (Sport England and YST, 2004c). Likewise, Lancashire Sport (see Chapter 5), Merseyside Sport (2003), Somerset Sport (2004) and Sport across Staffordshire (2004) have all been developing joint strategies with their colleagues in education. These trends suggest tangible progress towards creating a single system for young people.

Relationships with the community sector and the cross-cutting themes like health, crime, economic growth and regeneration are less well developed and more complex, in that they need to work both at county and local levels. In those CSPs that have agreed the basis of local sports/PA alliances (variously referred to as sporting hubs, community sports networks or forums), these form an important component of their structure (as in Derbyshire, Durham and Northumbria, Lancashire, Leicestershire, Merseyside and Oxfordshire. Examples of good working practices of this concept are few, and would benefit from national research rather than informal exchange.

Transforming CSPs into their new roles requires strong strategic leadership and effective change management processes. The leadership abilities and perfor-mance capabilities of the people responsible for making them work (principally the Chairs, Executive Board members and the Director/Chief Executive/ Partnership Manager), will be critical in determining the extent of perceived and measured success. There are significant lessons to be learned from the nine CSPs that employed Partnership Managers in addition to AS Managers; many of these postholders have found themselves in the front line of cultural change, in the middle of interests, holding everything together, staying motivated, whilst absorbing the demands from numerous partners, and trying to interpret a confused and uncertain external environment. While some received regional and national support, it is doubtful whether this has been enough. At the time of writing five of them had moved on to roles outside CSPs. It is important to discover why and to learn from their experiences: did they jump because of the pressures, or move to capitalise on their steep learning curves, for better rewards, or for more satisfying roles? High staff turnover (including Director posts, as in Lancashire Sport) also has been a feature of the Neighbourhood Renewal Unit's flagship New Deal for Community Partnership, being cited as a factor for poor performance (NRU, 2004). Figure 3.7 illustrates the typical pressures experi-enced by Directors at the centre of multi-agency partnerships.

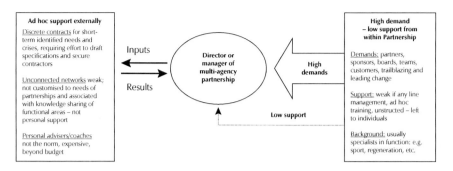

Figure 3.7 Pressures and support experienced by Partnership directors

This evidence suggests a need for proper investment in leadership development and in creating a supportive environment for Directors and Executive Board members to operate and thrive. Leadership programmes held in the North and South West regions were perceived to be invaluable by those involved. Despite this evidence, this new national structure has not been afforded a nationally coordinated leadership development and support programme.

CONCLUSIONS: FUTURE CHALLENGES

This final section deals with seven key questions regarding the proposed structure for the development of sport in England:

1. Are the components right?
2. Are the conditions right?
3. How do the interdependencies work?
4. Are the leaders capable of leading?
5. Are we involving the young people?
6. How is success defined and measured?
7. Is there the time and resources for it to work?

Components

Key components now included, accepted and being translated into action are:

▪ a common development framework based on a child- or young person-centred approach, applying the principles of the Long-Term Athlete

Development model (Balyi, 1999). Whether this will meet all its claims should come to the crucial test in the years leading to London 2012;

- a single coordinated system centred around CSPs;
- a strong rationale for significantly investing in PE, sport and physical recreation;
- new nationally agreed and published equality and child-protection standards for sport.

These components have become much clearer and much stronger recently. Clubs remain a vital resource for providing and developing opportunities for young people. They could be the backbone of English sport or its weakest link (Collins, 2003). This is a complex issue inadequately dealt with, in the author's opinion.

Conditions

Traditionally, sports providers operated independently and provided a fragmented service to young people, hence the need for the CSPs to play a co-ordinating role. This task is impossible if the key agencies themselves do not recognise this need, accept that CSPs have this role, and actively support them in fulfilling it. For the past five years this issue has been the crux of the debate, has caused frustration, and slowed progress. There are signs that a threshold has been reached, and major players (e.g. PCTs) have made their commitment clear, and in doing so have swung the majority.

Interdependencies

Given their role to put in place a 'single system' for sport that feeds into the performance structures of NGBs, CSPs depend on many other sports agencies. Sport England's recent strategy of investing in individual agencies through an outcome-led approach, where success is judged on results, ignores the importance of managing the relationships between agencies that depend on each other. At a practical level, CSPs do not have the capacity to negotiate with all NGBs and national, regional and local sports agencies, nor is it cost-effective or efficient for them to do so. So making the right choices is critical, and aligning the aspirations and proactively managing the interfaces of the major players is required for the framework to cohere.

Leadership

Leaders are people who innovate, develop, inspire, motivate, have a vision and a long-term view, ask what and why, originate, challenge the status quo and do the right things. Collins (2001) proposed five levels of effective leadership (see below). After examining sustainable business successes, he concluded 'good-to-great transformations don't happen without Level 5 leaders at the helm. They just don't!'. Level 5 leaders combine humility and will. If something goes right they look out of the 'window' to see who they can praise. Conversely, if something goes wrong they look in the 'mirror' to see how they themselves can improve.

Collins's five levels of effective leadership are:

Level 5 – Executive
Builds enduring greatness through a paradoxical combination of personal humility and professional will.

Level 4 – Effective leader
Catalyses commitment to and vigorous pursuit of a clear and compelling vision; stimulates the group to high performance standards.

Level 3 – Competent manager
Organises people and resources towards the effective and efficient pursuit of predetermined objectives.

Level 2 – Contributing team member
Contributes to the achievement of group objectives; works effectively with others in a group setting.

Level 1 – Highly capable individual
Makes productive contributions through talent, knowledge, skills, and good work habits.

Compared to other industries in the public and private sectors, investment in developing leaders and leadership qualities in sport is woeful. Employers would not support a specialist MBA started at Loughborough University in the 1990s. The National Skills Academy aspires to running master classes for experienced senior managers. But in contrast, former Secretary of State Chris Smith promoted top level training for young arts and culture managers identified as future leaders, with sponsorship from the Clore Foundation.

The transformation of CSPs to be a dynamic, innovative and effective part of England's sporting infrastructure requires strong leaders, without whom success

67

will be limited. Clearly this area needs attention; the sports industry in state and commerce failed to support a new MBA in sports management at Loughborough, all candidates having to support themselves financially, and often having to use their own leave to attend.

Young people

Meaningful consultation with intended target markets is a prerequisite for successful service and product delivery. Town planning and regeneration agencies were slow to learn this (Fitzpatrick *et al.*, 2000), but have now done so. The emergence of young people's forums and efforts to engage the youth themselves in decisions affecting their future is becoming more prevalent in local and national government, as illustrated by the Connexions Service. Sport has some mechanisms to do this, such as leisure cards, the use of whole-year school surveys and the potential for individualised website programmes (such as *sportsearch*), but there is limited evidence of progress.

Defining success

The Long-Term Athlete Development model begins to partly define and explain what success looks like in performance sport. For the population at large, there is a growing acceptance of the need for five 30-minute sessions of moderate exercise every week to bring about substantial health benefits, both getting the best start in life and keeping fit throughout it (CMO, 2004), but in most countries there are politically set targets for participation but no researched basis for success. How such outcomes are translated meaningfully into the different parts of the framework and are measured (Coalter, 2007) is in the next round of challenges.

Time and resources

Changing once and for all how we provide sport for young people is not a quick fix, but a long-term mission. The changes now proposed are moving some theory and practice in the same direction and providing better understanding of how various structures, partnerships and plans fit together. The relative resources invested in NGBs (especially in their performance programmes) and in School Sports Partnerships are significantly higher than that proposed for CSPs and community sport. It is important that the CSPs do not become another weak link in the sports development chain alongside clubs, when they are being accorded such an important role. A relatively modest increase in investment to CSPs could help to bring about the transformation of English sport.

Final reflections

The author believes Britain now has the right building blocks to create a single system or pathway for young people to access, learn and progress in sport. Sport's biggest challenge is getting everyone to fulfil their own roles and to harness joint effort by working better together.

After leading the ASP for six years, my view on coping with major challenges is simple: if you still believe in the cause, keep going; hold to your principles, as they have got you where you are; and when obstacles appear, a good leader will know what to do and will find other opportunities to achieve results.

Looking forwards, never hitherto has English sport had such an infrastructure and resources to work with. Collectively, sport's decision makers should ensure they use them to build a solid structure around a young person-centred approach, and an entitlement to PE and PA for all. They should engage young people in its design and delivery, as happens in other services. They should also lever in further investment from major sectors like health and crime, and work hard to ensure that the different alliances and partnerships can demonstrate the benefits of their efforts for sustained success and growth.

REFERENCES

Balyi, I. (1999) Long-term planning of athlete development, multiple periodization, modelling and normative data, *UK Coaching Magazine*, 4: 7–9.

Campbell, S. (2003) Sports infrastructure, paper to the Sport Summit, London, 10 July.

Chief Medical Officer (2004) *At Least Five Times a Week,* London: Department of Health.

Coalter, F. (2007) *Sport: A Wider Role. Who's Keeping the Score?* London: Routledge.

Collins, J.C. (2001) *Good to Great: Why Some Companies Make It and Others Don't,* London: Random House.

Collins, M.F. (2003) *Sport and Social Exclusion,* London: Routledge.

Collins, M.F and Randolph, L.R. (1994) *Voluntary Sports: Fostering or Starving the Grass Roots?* Nottingham: East Midlands Council for Sport and Recreation.

Department for Culture Media and Sport (1999) *Policy Action Team 10: Sport and the Arts,* London: DCMS.

Department for Culture Media and Sport (2002) *Game Plan: Implementing the Government's Objectives for Sport,* London: DCMS.

East Midlands Council for Sport and Recreation (1994) *Beyond the Barriers: A Strategy for Sport and Recreation in the East Midlands 1994–1998,* Nottingham: EMCSR.

English Sports Council (1997) *Development of Sporting Talent Study,* London: ESC.

European Foundation for Quality Management (1998) *EFQM Excellence Model,* London: Quality Foundation.

Fitzpatrick, S., Hastings, A. and Kintrea, K. (2000) Youth involvement in urban regeneration: Hard lessons, future directions, *Policy and Politics*, 28(4): 493–509.

Hoey, K. (2000) Unpublished letter from Kate Hoey to Derek Casey, CEO Sport England, 14 July.

Houlihan, B and White, A. (2002) *The Politics of Sports Development,* London: Routledge.

Merseyside Sports Partnership (2003) *T.e.a.m. Works in Merseyside 2003–2008,* Liverpool: MSPartnership.

Neighbourhood Renewal Unit (2004) *Transformation and Sustainability: Future Support, Managing and Monitoring of the New Deal for Communities Programme,* London: Office of the Deputy Prime Minister.

Rowley, S. (1992a) *Training of Young Athletes: TOYA and Lifestyle,* London: Sports Council.

Rowley, S. (1992b) *Training of Young Athletes: Identification of Talent,* London: Sports Council.

Somerset Sport (2004) *Somerset Activity and Sports Draft Strategy*, unpublished, Taunton: Somerset Sport.

Sport across Staffordshire (2003) *Towards a New Era: Draft Strategy for PE, Sports and Physical Activity in Staffordshire 2003–2007,* Stafford: SAS.

Sport England (1997) *World Class Start,* unpublished policy paper ESC (97) 6.78.

Sport England (1998a) *Corporate Plan 1998–2002,* London: Sport England.

Sport England (1998b) *New Programme Development: Active Schools, Active Communities and Active Sports*, unpublished policy paper ESC (98) 10.4.

Sport England (1998c) *Active Sports Programme*, unpublished policy paper ESC (98) 10.5.

Sport England (1998d) *World Class Start Interim Report,* London: Sport England.

Sport England (1998e) (Lottery Panel) *Public Opinion Survey,* London: Sport England.

Sport England (1998f) *Young People and Ethics,* London: Sport England.

Sport England (2000) *The Active Sports Guide,* London: Sport England.

Sport England et al. (2000) *Quest for Sports Development: Managers' Guidance Pack,* London: Sport England.

Sport England (2002) *Active Sports Mid-Term Report*, London: Sport England.

Sport England (2004a) *A framework for English Sport,* London: Sport England.

Sport England (2004b) *Sport England Policy for County Sports Partnerships,* London: Sport England.

Sport England/Youth Sport Trust (2004c) *Making the Connections* London: Sport England.

Tungatt, M. and MacDonald, D. (1991) *National Demonstration Projects – Major Lessons and Issues for Sports Development,* London: Sports Council.

Youth Sports Trust (1998, 1999) *Annual Report,* Loughborough: YST.

CHAPTER 4

SPORT THROUGH EDUCATION

A county strategy

Stuart Lindeman and Steve Conway

INTRODUCTION

'Sport through Education' and 'Education through Sport' are equally valid titles for a strategy aimed at developing the whole young person. We chose the former, but the principle stands. As Chapters 3 and 8 show, PE and sport within education have never had such a high profile. The involvement of children and young people in a variety of activities provides them with an opportunity for self-discipline, healthy living, and personal and social development. More importantly, there is now growing evidence through QCA research and anecdotal evidence from Specialist Sports Colleges that undertaking physical activity can have a direct impact on behaviour, attendance, and on raising academic standards in our schools and colleges (Penney et al., 2002).

However, the challenge of any partnership is how to gain political support to bring together the right people to plan strategically and offer a range of exciting activities that enable progression for young learners.

This chapter is about such a partnership that preceded the current round of County Sports Partnerships described by Enoch and Charlton in their chapters. Doubtless, other similar ventures have developed across England, and we have learned from colleagues elsewhere. We reflect on the lessons to be learned, in the following sections:

- the background to the Leicestershire, Leicester and Rutland *Sport Through Education* strategy (STE), and its achievements and legacy;
- an analysis of the themes of planning, partnership and progression that emerge;
- the development of high quality PE and sport;
- key issues for readers to consider.

BACKGROUND

Leicestershire has strong sporting traditions through its Community College system. The policy basis for Leicestershire's school-based approach to Community Education was first set down in a 1948 memorandum by Director of Education (1949–1961), Stewart Mason. This stressed that there should be no 'diarchy of responsibility' between college and community management and that officialdom should be 'throttled down to the minimum', so a vice-principal was the community manager, and school secretaries doubled as receptionists. The Leicestershire Plan for Community Colleges was subsequently extended to incorporate primary schools in Andrew Fairbairn's (Director 1961–1985) *Memorandum on Primary School Community Centres* in 1972 (Fairbairn, 1979). The strategy was an exciting and innovative response to the educational needs of the community. Key characteristics included:

- an intention to integrate school/community learning;
- local autonomy;
- LEA financial support to any community which could raise half the cost of building a community room;
- LEA support for schools offering a community-related curriculum.

They were modelled on Henry Morris's concept of Village Colleges in Cambridgeshire (Jennings, n.d.). Adults used the buildings as an education and community centre in the evenings and weekends – for crafts and arts, sports, theatre and music. In Leicestershire they had cafés, and sometimes licensed bars too. Later youth wings were added. The strategic significance for the county was that education provided the widest range of indoor and outdoor sports provision – by 1999 there were 28 primary schools, and 26 secondary schools operating on this concept.

Unlike joint provision and use schemes in many counties, however, there was no agreed split of capital and maintenance funding with district councils. The district sports halls, pools and allied provision that appeared from the 1970s onwards were a function of local, independent political responses and were supplementary to that of the County. But it did mean that after 25–30 years of heavy use, the County alone was faced with the large bills for updating or replacing old facilities. And this was at a time when education authorities had been facing an unprecedented combination of factors – shrunken school rolls and surplus accommodation, reduced finance, and political scepticism about managing schools (decentralised under Mrs Thatcher) and their curriculum (now specified as a National framework). Also, the many new measures to improve professionalism of sports management in municipal centres (customer care and quality systems, performance indicators and benchmarking clubs) had bypassed the county systems, although introduced in many joint provision arrangements (Sport England).

The *Sport Through Education* strategy was conceived at a multi-agency workshop in January 1996, where colleagues from schools/colleges, district councils, governing bodies, the voluntary sector, the Youth and Community service, Loughborough University and sports associations all subscribed to the following aims:

- to develop a positive and enjoyable introduction to sport for young people;
- to develop an LEA framework providing strong sporting pathways across and beyond school;
- to ensure equality of opportunity;
- to encourage healthy lifestyles;
- to work with all potential partners.

The earliest outcomes were, first, an agreement that the purpose of the strategy should be to encourage all partners to work together to develop sport for young people and communities, and secondly to make the most effective use of educational resources as part of a wider 'Leicestershire, Leicester and Rutland Sport and Recreation Strategy'.

Four key areas of work were developed:

1. coordination and communication – to involve all partners;
2. curriculum – to ensure the Physical Education curriculum is balanced, has breadth and is relevant;
3. community sports links – to develop progressive programmes linking schools with local community groups, sports groups and other voluntary organisations;
4. facilities and resources – to provide good quality advisory support and training to increase community use of sports facilities on education sites.

These key aims were refined into a set of action plans and the strategy was launched in October 1997 (LCC, 1997). At a key conference in 1999, Trevor Brooking (then Chair of Sport England) ran a session for elected members to explore the value of PE and school sport for them, that proved a critical point in its development, and significantly allowed it to survive the local government reorganisation in April 1997. At a time when Leicester City councillors were

74

setting up their own unitary authority and Rutland was achieving county status, the political commitment in all three LEAs remained strong. This has been the case ever since, and it is even more apparent now how the work of the strategy can help elected members meet their own corporate 'cross-cutting' targets concerning health, regeneration, crime and disorder, and community safety and cohesion.

All partners, including Sport England, funded the strategy jointly, and as Sport England's funding diminished over 1997–2001, it was placed in the councils' base budgets. A strong project team was put in place. Probably more importantly, it has been firmly based within the countywide sports development structure to ensure integration with leisure departments, sports forums, district councils and the Active Sports programme and, latterly, the County Sports Partnership (CSP).

PLANNING, PARTNERSHIP AND PROGRESSION

Planning

Effective planning was an integral element of the partnership working. It encompassed the issues of leadership and of political power. Leadership of the planning process has probably been *the* key ingredient of the strategy's success. It can be described in three distinct stages:

1. *Prior to 1997.* There was a need to cement old relationships and establish new ones. Adequate briefing was essential, particularly for elected members who expected to jointly fund the outcomes. The agenda for the joint planning exercise had to be agreed with all partners.
2. *During the planning.* Cross-agency and multi-disciplinary groups considered the questions: Where are we now? Where do we want to go? How do we get there? How will we know when we have arrived? This process was, of course, not rocket science, but was one underused for partnership working in sports development. It called for good facilitative skills and a commitment from everyone to listen, contribute, reflect and above all put individual agency considerations aside. 'No power games' and 'no defensiveness' were but two of the ground rules agreed.
3. *During implementation.* The importance of agreed outcomes was articulated in clear, SMART action plans. Funding had to be secured and many reports written for formal committees. A communication plan was devised. Monitoring and evaluation systems were put in place.

An early realisation was that the only certainty was change, and everyone had to be ready to accept it.

A *Sport Through Education* Steering Group (chaired by the first author) was established with sub-groups reflecting the key areas of work – curriculum development, community sports links and facility use, and development/ resources.

The concept of leadership is well documented. However, the leadership we refer to depends not only on individual charisma or some special set of interpersonal skills, but also refers to developing shared leadership – the growth of a collective will to make something work through a shared understanding of a task, and not individual conception or action. The strategy has enhanced the professional development of over 3,000 individuals in PE and school sport. Particularly challenging for colleagues was the need to return to their own organisation or agency and sell the message that the Partnership had agreed. District council SDOs have been instrumental in several developments, including taking a lead on the Annual Youth Games in their own areas.

The Active Sports Manager has developed county-wide leadership skills with governing bodies and others. Individual governing bodies, like Basketball, have taken positive action for countywide developments. The Sport Through Education Project Officer (the second author) has been central to monitoring and evaluating programmes.

As already stated, just as important has been political leadership, in issues like establishing the School Sports Association Federation and developing the new County Sports Partnership. There is also the danger that political support may wane as local elections come and go. In 2003, for example, we had to reinvent the strategy for new officers and politicians alike.

The pace and complexity of changes in the educational landscape also presented problems in keeping up with new developments. Examples included having to implement the Millennium/County Youth Games; the advent of the New Opportunities Lottery Fund and its programme for new school buildings; the government's policy for school sport in *Game Plan* (DCMS, 2002); the reorganisation of Sport England; the introduction of Specialist Sports Colleges; and most recently the introduction of the *Physical Education, School Sport and Club Links* strategy (DES, 2003) and the extended school agenda. All had to be fitted into the emerging structures and plans.

Partnerships

Partnership working is key to all sports development. Planning for the School Sports Coordinator initiative, for example, had to be done in the knowledge that PE and school sport will, in the future, be delivered through partnerships, each comprising a cluster of schools around a Specialist Sports College hub. It means a fundamental review of the roles and responsibilities of local authority SDOs and LEA advisers. No longer were they controlling training/development and delivering activities, if they ever did. Their role now is in enabling – facilitating and providing much-needed strategic leadership. STE's latest challenge is to ensure it is a major player in the DfES's Extended Schools agenda, the latest reincarnation of community use of schools, which was first promoted in a circular *A Chance to Share* in 1965. The government has declared that it wishes to develop schools (ultimately every school) as centres of their communities, 'extended' to provide a wide variety of activities including adult and family learning, sport and leisure, social and health services. The need for coordinated planning has never been so crucial.

Over the period 1998 to 2004, STE worked with a wide range of partners, with greater and lesser degrees of success. One of the most effective partnerships in the early stages was SDOs working in local authorities and for specific sports. It was quickly established that STE and local sports development had similar aims and objectives, focused on young people and sport. The success of some partnerships has been excellent, with long-lasting outcomes – for example the development of a local School Sports Forum in Melton (Case study 4.1), which became the framework for School Sports Coordinators programme in that district. But in instances where staff turnover in a district has been high, there has been less success.

It must be remembered that at the outset some district councils viewed working with schools as solely the role of the county council. However, through successful partnership working, the STE strategy has been able to demonstrate that local authority objectives can be achieved by working directly with schools. Probably the best example of this is the Youth Games which include a wealth of school-based competitions, more than many other county games in England. However, opportunities for joint staff training and development in important areas like community leadership and partnership working were limited – an issue not foreseen, perhaps. This was a weakness in our long-term planning.

MELTON SCHOOL SPORTS FORUM

Having established a common aim of working with local schools to develop PE and Sport, the borough council set up the School Sports Forum in conjunction with the STE. Over the last five years it has become a model of best practice in developing joint working with local authority sports development, local schools, clubs and other sports organisations. The Sports Development Officer and STE strategy staff worked very closely on developing the forum, and succeeded as a result of common target-setting, clear division of roles and responsibilities and mutual respect for each others' work.

HEALTH AUTHORITY PARTNERSHIP

This was established as early as 1999, but has had little success. Physical activity for young people was established as a common area of work but, instead of joint working, duplication developed, including training for primary school staff. One of the problems was a lack of clarity about roles and responsibility and another was the turnover of staff from the health authority, as well as a lack of experience in partnership working between education and health. Fortunately, as a result of the development of the Healthy Schools programme delivered through education but in partnership with health professionals, more experience is accruing in joint working. Primary Care Trusts are now active members of the STE steering group.

In the initial stages it could be quite difficult to determine the bounds of common areas of work with some partners, often relying on the quality of the people involved to make them work. In the field of health, for example, STE has struggled to develop effective partnerships for various reasons, but primarily because the health authorities staff involved had little experience of working partnerships in a sports arena, and underwent rapid turnover which impaired the consistency of relationships (Case study 4.2). This was complicated by the dissolution of the Health Promotion Agency, replaced by six or more Primary Care Trusts in Leicestershire.

78

As more organisations have formulated their own development plans and are now sharing them, it became much easier to identify joint targets, particularly in the case of the School Sports Coordinator (SSCO) Programme. This utilises experienced secondary school staff released off timetable to plan and develop PE and sports projects, within a development plan for each 'family' of schools. By 2004 there were 222 partnerships with 8,105 schools. The first monitoring of the SSCO programme (IYS, 2006) showed that:

- 62% of pupils spend at least two hours a week on high quality PE and school sport within and beyond the curriculum, reaching 80% at Key Stage 3. Pupils in the longest-established partnerships spend the longer time on PE, showing that partnerships are making a difference.
- Schools devote 100 minutes curriculum time each week to PE on average.
- Each school provides, on average, more than fourteen sports, notably football, swimming, basketball, canoeing and badminton.
- 96% of schools held at least one sports day last year.

The *PESSCL* strategy set a target that, by 2006, three-quarters of pupils would be spending at least two hours on high-quality PE and school sport, in and beyond the curriculum. Overall the government is investing over £1 billion to improve many aspects of PE and school sport.

Figure 4.1 outlines the first partnership in Leicestershire, based at Lancaster Sports College in Leicester. As with all Phase One partnerships, it was established

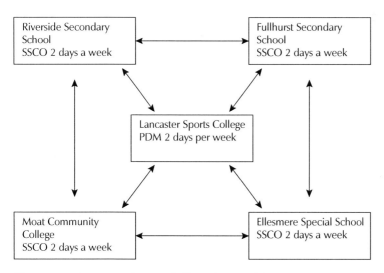

Figure 4.1 Lancaster Sports College Partnership

in a very short period and, moreover, only one term after the school had started as a specialist sports college.

Nevertheless, as with the STE strategy, the success of the SSCO partnerships will depend on the effectiveness of joint working, and in turn on the quality and consistency of people in the programme. The majority of staff are not familiar with working outside their own school and with the issues facing primary school staff in delivering PE and sport. Indeed the second Leicestershire partnership, based at Burleigh Specialist Sports College in Loughborough suffered initially from the limited ability of primary schools to comprehend the benefits of being involved. The local early partnerships have also struggled because of rapid staff turnover, especially in the secondary schools. Additionally, in the early days staff roles were less clear, with some secondary school staff assuming they were in post to deliver PE on behalf of primary schools, rather than helping them to develop their capacity. Furthermore, the training was patchy and not quality assured or consistent.

Working in partnership with STE as enabler, rather than a direct deliverer, SSCO partnerships have helped raise the profile of PE and sport in Leicestershire, something the STE strategy was unable to do.

It was evident very early that local authority SDOs could play a major role in helping STE achieve its goals. At the outset in 1996 only just over half the districts in Leicestershire had established such a post, and the hours available for such work varied enormously. The STE strategy was instrumental in helping establish a sports development framework across the county.

Much work was spent on developing an understanding of the stresses and constraints on PE and Sport school staff. Previously, simple mistakes had been commonplace, such as trying to contact primary school staff with a full timetable, between 9.00 a.m. and 3.30.p.m. In establishing the SDO infrastructure, not only were existing staff much better placed to work effectively with schools, but also new staff were taken on by some authorities with a particular brief to work with schools. Bearing in mind that district councils have no direct funding to work with schools, this was a very effective development.

Over the last eight years the STE worked more strongly and effectively with schools within a wider county sports strategy, not only via SDOs and the Lottery-funded Youth Games but also via the Disability Federation through the setting up of initiatives like the Leicestershire Special Schools Sports Federation.

Progression

Judgement of not only the STE strategy's success but also of the Leicestershire and the 44 other County Sports Partnerships will be on how effective they are in establishing progressive sporting pathways for youngsters that are clear to participants, teachers, coaches, SDOs and parents alike.

For the first time, there is now a national *Physical Education, School Sport and Club Links* strategy, which is properly funded (see Chapter 2). Locally, however, the STE strategy has so far established a communication framework and structure for some coordinated development. For example, the highly successful Alliance & Leicester Tag Rugby programme in primary schools was built up from scratch with exit routes to local clubs. Over the last four years, 90 per cent of primary schools have taken up the scheme, with 10 per cent at least linked to local clubs for extension activities.

The Leicestershire School Sports Federation was set up to provide a support structure to a wide range of associations (including little-known ones) to encourage and improve their competitive sports activities for young people. They are based primarily on teachers as volunteers, who have been unrecognised so far in the PE and sport infrastructure of the *PESSCL* strategy.

HIGH-QUALITY PE AND SPORT

Until quite recently there has been very little quantitative or qualitative research measuring the standard of PE and sports provision or projects. In 1999 the STE group undertook an evaluation of the TOPs Programme across Leicestershire in terms of how helpful the training had been in supporting non-specialist staff in delivering PE in primary schools. While not the most scientific of evaluations, with a follow-up in 2001, this was the only known research carried out on the TOPs programme. Results from a good response of 44 per cent, showed several interesting points: one was that TOPs had a positive effect in raising the profile of PE in the curriculum, even after the introduction of the national Literacy and Numeracy programmes.

The Coaching for Teachers (CFT) scheme is a training programme developed for specialist and non-specialist PE staff, linked to national governing body awards. It was run in Leicestershire from 1998, and in 2000 an evaluation highlighted the benefit staff felt in terms of developing their confidence and teaching skills. It is in two parts, one delivered through LEA partnerships, and the other centrally by sports coach UK, at locations across England, twice a year. The latter part is monitored and evaluated by sports coach UK, but until 2000, no local evaluation had been done other than identifying numbers and attendances. In summary, a substantial majority (75 per cent) of participants agreed that the courses were very useful in helping them deliver PE and sports activities more effectively.

Besides Ofsted reports on inspections, in Leicestershire an analysis was conducted in 1992 on the quality of PE lessons as part of the LEA's Education Development Plan process, and at that stage PE was not highlighted as a subject for concern, with the rating of most Key Stage teaching as satisfactory or better. But people in the profession have some questions about the validity of some Ofsted findings about PE, because of inconsistency of PE expertise in Ofsted teams and the marginalisation of PE inspections compared to other subjects. The new Ofsted framework has gone some way to addressing these issues, and now includes specific reference to inspecting PE and school sport.

The Qualifications and Curriculum Authority (QCA) has been coordinating some projects investigating the impact of PE and school sport, and it chose Mount Grace secondary school in Leicestershire and one of its feeder primary schools (Case study 4.3).

CASE STUDY 4.3

MOUNT GRACE QCA PROJECT

What did they do?

The teachers at Mount Grace secondary school (MG) noticed that, although more than a quarter of its annual intake of Year 7 pupils came from Holliers Walk primary school (HW), few took part in after-school clubs and teams. They were also aware that HW pupils tended to have a negative attitude to PE. During a pilot year, MG's Head of PE visited HW school every two weeks. He taught some lessons, supported teachers in others, and got to know the pupils. Some activities for Year 6 pupils took place, and a celebration event was held at the end of the summer term. The Head of Girls' PE also visited HW school on five occasions in the year. Staff used these visits to develop a scheme of work for MG that they could build on with incoming pupils.

What difference did they make?

Following the pilot year, significantly more pupils from HW got involved in teams and squads when they arrived at Mount Grace. Data from club registers, teachers' assessments and observed behaviour changes combined to show success. Year 7 teams showed that the number of pupils in each rugby, soccer, netball and hockey squads from the targeted school almost doubled (Table 4.1).

Table 4.1 Former Holliers Walk pupils in the Mount Grace squads

Year	Rugby	Soccer	Netball	Hockey
9	5 of 20 = 25%	5 of 17 = 29%	4 of 16 = 25%	4 of 11 = 36%
8	6 of 18 = 33%	4 of 18 = 22%	6 of 14 = 43%	6 of 11 = 55 %
7	15 of 32 = 47%	11 of 16 = 69%	9 of 15 = 60%	6 of 13 = 46%

Moreover, the behaviour of some of the lowest achievers from HW also improved dramatically after the pilot year, with two-thirds of referrals in Year 9 coming from that school, and 65 per cent in Year 8, but none in Year 7.

Why did they succeed?

The regular contact between HW pupils and the MG PE department meant that the pupils knew what was expected of them when they started at secondary school. This helped them to settle in more quickly, and gave them the confidence to get involved in out-of-hours sport.

A number out-of-school-hours learning (OSHL), PE and sports projects have been developed and implemented in the STE strategy partnerships (Case study 4.4).

One of these was the *Playing for Success* programme, which uses sport as a 'hook' to develop improved learning in Numeracy, Literacy and ICT by getting pupils with poor learning records to attend study centres based at professional clubs – in this case at Leicester Tigers (rugby), Leicester Riders (basketball) and Leicester City FC. The national fourth year evaluation has contributed to improved achievement, for example, in numeracy where pupils made substantial and significant progress. On average, primary pupils improved their numeracy scores by about 17 months, and secondary pupils by about 24 months, much greater than is experienced in conventional schooling – but aided by dedicated mentors, apart from the attractions of the club venue. Attendance and attentiveness also improved. These results were reflected locally in Leicestershire.

OUT-OF-HOURS LEARNING AND MINI-LEADERS

This eight-week after-school programme uses leaders to support primary children, to develop their self-confidence and their communication and social skills through sport.

In Leicester, a pilot was developed with Leicester Tigers RFC, and delivered by some of its coaches at Sacred Heart School. It proved so successful that twelve other city schools took the programme from September 2002.

In Leicestershire, eight primary schools were involved, but the programme was delivered by a local coaching company, in two sports. Again, the programme proved hugely successful, so much so that it was identified in an Ofsted report as making a significant contribution to raising standards across one school being inspected. In another instance, in a report on a school in 'special measures', it was highlighted as a key tool in helping it move back to normal operating.

Achievements

In summary, the achievements to date are:

- All primary schools TOPs trained.
- 7,000 staff trained in PE and Sport.
- Over 800 community staff TOPs trained.
- Over 40,000 pupils coached by professional clubs.
- 25,000 children in Youth Games.
- LSSF recognised as National Exemplar.
- 7,000 students at County Hall presentation events.
- Over 200 successful school A4A bids, totalling over £300,000.
- Three schools achieved Specialist Sports College status.
- Over £30m secured for school capital sports projects.

These achievements can be unpacked for the first five years under the three strategic aims (LCC, n.d.).

Curriculum

Aim: To ensure that the PE curriculum is balanced, broad and is relevant.

- Over 6,000 staff on training courses.
- Every primary school involved in the training of the youth Sport Trust's TOPs programme, with all special schools trained in Sportability.
- Over 600 staff involved in school cluster follow-up meetings for planning and training.
- More than 40 per cent of secondary schools involved in the Nike-sponsored Girls PE and Sport project.
- More than twenty schools awarded Sportsmark for good curricular and extra-curricular sport and community links and four awarded the Gold award.
- Three county STE conferences and three for teachers.
- Lancaster School given SSCO status in 2000 and Burleigh School re-accredited.

Community sports links

Aim: To develop progressive programmes linking schools with local sports groups, clubs, and voluntary organisations.

- 15,000 children involved with various activities, leading to 4,500 in the County Games.
- The county Federation of School Sports Associations recognised as a leading example in England, with 70 affiliates and over 30 sports, a termly newsletter and annual handbook, and presentation evenings with 5,000 youngsters.
- Every special school and some units supported by the Special SSF.
- 500 community TOPs bags for use by 800 trained staff.
- Two School Sports Coordinators involving nine secondary and thirty-two primary schools (including four special schools).
- 40,000 children trained by professional clubs, including Leicester Tigers' tag rugby for 10,000 children in 200 schools.
- Two study support centres at Leicester FC and Leicestershire CC for *Playing for Success*, and one to come at the Tigers.
- Four school sports forums, including Melton (Case study 1).

Facilities and resources

Aim: To provide quality support and training to increase community use of facilities on education sites, and to secure funding to expand provision.

- With one-third of the East Midlands Awards for All small grants, Leicestershire the most successful county (£256,000 in 1997–2002).
- Two LTA community tennis partnerships and over 100 schools with mini soccer goals from the FA.
- 200 staff in training sessions on increasing community use.
- Four primary projects worth £2m via Space for Sport and the Arts funding.
- Twenty-eight bids for New opportunities Lottery funding, totalling £8.5m (£4.9m in Leicester, £3.3m in the county, and £0.2m in Rutland).
- £115,00 for ten schools to improve their grounds via Learning through Landscapes.

CONCLUSIONS

Counties in England where the LEA leads provision are rare. The STE strategy allowed us to revisit decades of under-investment and lack of management structure and training. The Strategy for 2003–2008 (LCC, 2003) highlighted things still to be done:

- Get more designated SScs.
- Introduce TOPs2 to primary schools and extend to other sports and dance.
- Review the condition of all school PE and sports facilities, many of them ageing.
- Try to improve low take-up of INSET training.
- Address social exclusion, especially of ethnic minorities.

Lessons from Sport Through Education: our assessment

Strengths

- A strategic planning process – involving all stakeholders.
- Strong political support and leadership.
- Continuous review of roles and responsibilities.
- Partnership working.
- Developing pathways and links to sports clubs.

Weaknesses

- A lack of joint training and development across agencies.
- A dependence on specific individuals.

86

- The basic and incomplete collection of evidence concerning impacts.
- Failures in communication across a complex landscape.
- Finding sufficient staff time and resources for partnership working.

But the STE strategy was overtaken and rolled into a wider County Partnership which involves club and municipal provision (see Chapters 3 and 5) and takes the programmes into meeting the cross-cutting issues of improving jobs and environment, making communities more cohesive and safer, improving health and lifelong education and reducing crime. The strongest legacy of much effort by hundreds of people from scores of organisations may not be the individual projects and the £23m spent in capital and revenue, but the lessons of working out real partnerships by hard experience.

REFERENCES

Department for Education and Skills (2003) *Learning Through PE and Sport: A Guide to the Physical Education, School Sport and Club Links Strategy*, London: DES.

Department for Culture Media and Sport (2002) *Game Plan*, London: DCMS.

Fairbairn, A.N. (1979) *The Leicestershire Community Colleges and Centres*, Nottingham: Nottingham University.

Institute of Youth Sport (2006) *School Sport Partnerships: Annual Monitoring and Evaluation Report for 2006*, Loughborough University: IYS.

Jennings, B. (ed.) (n.d.) *Community Colleges in England and Wales*, Leicester: National Institute of Adult Education.

Leicestershire County Council (1997) *The Strategy: Sport through Education*, Leicester: LCC.

Leicestershire County Council (2003) *Sport through Education: Strategy 2003–08*, Leicester: LCC.

Leicestershire County Council (n.d.) *Sport through Education – the Strategy: Five year Review 1997–2002*, Leicester: LCC.

Mason, S.C. (1960, revised 1963) *The Leicestershire Experiment and Plan*, London: Councils and Education Press.

Penney, D., Houlihan, B. and Eley, D. (2002) *Specialist Sports Colleges National Monitoring and Evaluation Project: 1st Year National Survey Report*, Loughborough: Loughborough University, Institute of Youth Sport.

Sharp, C. et al. (2003) *Playing for Success: An Evaluation of the Fourth Year*, Report RR 402, London: Department for Education and Science.

CHAPTER 5

A NEW ACTIVE SPORTS PARTNERSHIP

Lancashire Sport

Tony Charlton

> *The 'vision' [to] be the class leader . . . the benchmark for sports partnerships nationally.*
>
> *(Lancashire Sport, 2003: 6)*

INTRODUCTION: SPORT AND PARTNERSHIPS

County Sports Partnerships (CSPs) were introduced by Sport England in 2000, to try to address the perennial problem of fragmentation in delivering sporting opportunities – between schools, clubs and their national governing bodies of sport (NGBs), and local authorities. Such fragmentation was particularly prevalent in large counties like Lancashire with two-tier local government, and numerous NGBs all operating their own approaches. It was the intention of CSPs to combine the efforts of all providers under a single umbrella (Sport England, 2001: 1), following the prevailing ethos of 'joined-up provision for joined problems', and they were defined as partnerships of 'key agencies and providers committed to establishing a sustainable infrastructure to provide a single system for all young people to benefit from sport and physical activity' (CSPN, 2003).

Previous attempts at holistic approaches had not proved successful because one or more of the actors was unable to fulfil their obligations, either due to funding issues, pursuing individual agendas, setting incompatible goals or expecting different outcomes, as illustrated by Houlihan's (1991) study of the British sports policy process. The CSPs were intended to overcome such difficulties in that they would:

- actively contribute to increasing participation and widening access to sport and physical activity and the achievement of sporting success;
- be pivotal to delivering the 1 per cent per year participation target set by government, with a particular focus on:

- developing more community sports opportunities for young people by supporting the delivery of the *PESSCL* strategy;
- helping to develop more opportunities for hard-to-reach groups and those not already engaged in community sport (Sport England, EM, 2006).

As Enoch (Chapter 3) explains, the Active Sports (AS) programme had been designed to provide a bridge between young people displaying some talent for a sport, their schools, the governing bodies of their sports, and the local voluntary clubs, to ensure that such young people are not lost to the sporting system, and are able to progress to the limit of their desire or their talent. Such a framework could not be provided then, because local authorities, governing bodies, voluntary clubs or schools could not individually manage such a programme. In 1999 Sport England encouraged the formation of forty-five CSPs as vehicles to deliver the ASP (Sport England, 2000). This meant each individual actor devolving some authority to the Partnership, to ensure that the ASP was delivered logically and equitably.

This chapter examines the evolution of a large CSP during the first six years of its development and operation. It seeks to highlight the mechanics of partnership and to demonstrate how the challenges of meeting the demands of political, cross-cutting agendas were met, and incorporated in an entity recognised by Sport England and DCMS as a model of good practice. It is based on participant observation and in-depth interviews with a Head of Department, six Heads of SDO teams, and six single SDOs (Charlton, 2008). These were analysed using social and story network analysis (Boje, 2001). Such partnerships 'sit at one remove from, but also intersect both elected and appointed bodies, as well as community, voluntary and business sectors' (Skelcher, 2000).

Lancashire had a history of collaborative working based on the work of Lancashire Cultural and Leisure Officers Group (LCLOG), which provided a network for strategic discussion and planning, and of the Lancashire Sports Development Officers Forum which offered SDOs an opportunity to professionally share, exchange and network, but with no decision-making powers. However, some traditions do not necessarily give the right strengths to maximise future sporting opportunities for the county, as mentioned above. This was made clear in a 2000/1 baseline assessment of the infrastructure's readiness to engage low-participant groups that identified weak structures, sporadic resource allocations, programmes often not joined up to exit routes or sustainable pathways, developed over periods too short to make a lasting difference.

Lancashire is a large area over which to deliver any policy locally, housing 1.4 million people. AS was adopted as part of a county sports strategy, and the CSP was an attempt to provide the voluntary sector with the necessary support for it both to deliver sport-specific programmes and to meet the demands of other agency agendas. Lancashire Sport (LS) is a partnership formed as a separate new organisation, suitable for long-term working and where staff and resources would be needed (Audit Commission, 1998). LS comprises all fourteen local authorities in the county, the county council, ten governing bodies of sport, sports coach UK, the English Federation of Disability Sport, Sport England (a main funder), and Myerscough College (host agency). It has the largest number of CSP partners outside London, and embraces the largest range of partners from outside sport. To meet its objectives, LS sought to gather some thirty-four representatives of the main partners, acting as the catalyst for linkages in the form of development groups to promote and deliver various programmes. These linkages should demonstrate the shared responsibilities and negotiated roles of a partnership and its dynamic, responsive nature, and whether it achieved 'collaborative advantage' (Huxham, 1996).

EVOLUTION OF THE LANCASHIRE SPORT PARTNERSHIP

To provide a sequential account of LS's evolution, this section is organised into four main parts, adapted from Lowndes and Skelcher's (1998) framework of partnership development. These are designated as:' Build-up' (2000), 'Preparing for launch' (2001–2003), 'Operations' (2003–2005) and 'A new role' (2006).

Build-up, 2000

At the outset, LS sought to interpret the political imperatives of its local authority partners, and align its strategy to support them in meeting HMG's requirements of providing and demonstrating Best Value. The process was geared to Sport England's vision for the ASP – 'Changing the way sport is delivered forever' – and to entice partner organisations to combine their efforts to make LS the Active Sport benchmark, the 'class-leading' CSP in England.

Developing the organisational infrastructure and capacity

Effective partnership is very difficult, time-consuming and, certainly during the outset, costly to achieve (Carley et al., 2000). Cooperation is obtained and then sustained, through establishing relations premised on solidarity, trust, loyalty and mutual support, rather than through hierarchy or bargaining. The structure selected to achieve synergy in LS combined and adapted two traditional formats of relationships – a 'federation' and a 'hub network'. A federation is formed of, recognition of mutual needs . . . based on relational (rather than transactional) contracts, developing out of personal relationships built between individuals in two or more organisations, rather than 'arms length' relationships, which are defined by legal and binding contracts. Federations are born out of pre-existing networks.

(Hutchinson and Campbell, 1998: 31)

A hub network is where a core partner coordinates and integrates the activities of the others, having a 'complex role acting as a broker between the other organisations, and it is the hub which creates the network' (Hutchinson and Campbell, 1998: 32). LS's core partner is the Chief Executive Officer (CEO) and his staff.

The Service Team comprised the CEO, officers for Information and Communications, Coach Development, Partnership Development, Club Development and Volunteers Development and 'activators' for swimming, girls' football, basketball and athletics. This provided information and resources for the clusters as 'communities of practice' (Wenger, 1999).

Thus, the adapted model of the LS partnership comprised:

- The Hub, with a core membership of fourteen, providing the executive management function, but introducing additional members such as NGB officers at key points in the business cycle.
- Three 'clusters', combining the resources and experiences of the three areas Lancashire was divided into for strategy purposes – east, central and coastal – to embody coordination over a large area and focus on local community impact. Each cluster Chair was part of the Hub.

This structure is shown in Figure 5.1.

Leadership

The CEO had to exert a charismatic influence on SDOs and NGB officers of varying experience, professional calibre and power to overcome historic prejudices and competitiveness. Previously an experienced local government officer, he 'put himself about' in local meetings, seeking to get partners to sign up to the LS slogan 'Join the Sporting Revolution', exuding energy, empathy, optimism and imagination.

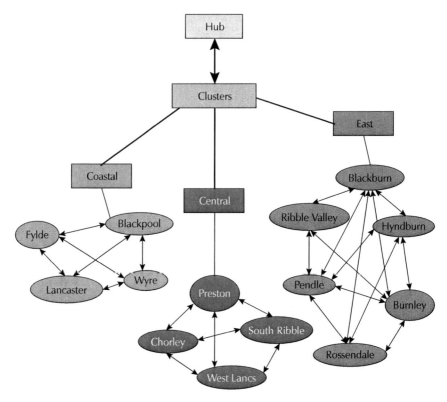

Figure 5.1 Lancashire Sport's hub and cluster structure

Empowering partners

The CEO organised a Vision Day in March 2000, a drip feed of detailed information, to help partners 'move at a deliberate and careful pace' (Charlton, 2008: 225) without overloading them, and then a regional conference Planning to Succeed in June, before submitting the business plan for funding to Sport England in December.

Preparing to launch, 2001–2003

2000 had introduced the style to develop capacity within a fairly loose collaboration, giving ownership to partners, combined with a direction to satisfy Sport England's bidding process. The roll-out required development groups for each sport (rugby, swimming, girls' football and cricket) and for coaching/coach training, responsible for producing the development plans for submission to the Hub and for costing within the Lottery bid. The CEO initially supported each

92

group, to ensure consistent planning and identify common difficulties requiring executive action to meet deadlines.

At this time, there were no tangible benefits to be gained, no working hierarchy in which to work, nor any powers delegated to the CEO. The driving factor at the grassroots was a belief in the idea of AS and the future benefits that could materialise for their communities. For the Hub, selecting the various portfolio holders generally reflected the members' 'day jobs', bringing their expertise to bear on the engine of the partnership.

For this approach to succeed, much depended on the ability of the SDOs to fulfil the requirements of the coaching and sport groups in demonstrating a deep skill and experience to perform outside rigid, hierarchical approaches typical of local authority bureaucracies. Variations in attitudes, abilities and methods of working led to several planning deadlines having to be amended, and consequent frustration for the CEO that tested his management style. Once the bid was accepted, a period of concentrated effort to determine the working details of the sports development plans, the coach development plan and the essential policy documents were completed for a launch planned for September 2001. The CEO reported:

> We are now at the verge of delivering the most comprehensive sports development programme in the country. In total it looks like a huge task, but with a well organised collective effort, clear arrangements for delivery and the extra resources (financial and human) we will succeed and become a benchmark for good practice – the class leader we aspired to become on 9 March 2000.
>
> (Internal correspondence to partners, 2001)

Figure 5.2 shows the complexity into which the structure had evolved.

The launch in September 2001, under the slogan 'Join the Sporting Revolution' set initial targets of 1,600 children participating, of training and employing 160 coaches, and assisting 56 clubs to achieve Clubmark accreditation. In addition, the first major links with the Invest to Save project for disaffected young people, 'Beyond Sport', were coming to fruition, notably with Lancashire Constabulary.

It became apparent, however, that not all partners were keeping pace with the 'revolution'. After the launch the 'feel-good factor' was lost, with reports of slipping deadlines, equipment not materialising, and services promised to the voluntary sector not being met. Inequity in provision by NGBs became obvious, increasing dissatisfaction being voiced to the Partnership Services Team. Strategic gaps appeared. Yet there were positive aspects: the cluster arrangements proved

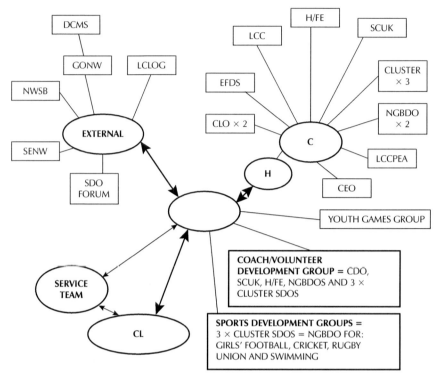

Figure 5.2 Lancashire Sport's structure at launch

successful in encouraging and aiding cross-boundary working and developing trust; and LS had provided a new identity that reinforced the status of the work and helped to share resources and good practices.

Operations, 2003–2005

This next phase required the CEO to move from charismatic 'Pied Piper' to transformational leader, to seek to 'raise one another to higher levels of motivation and morality' (Bass and Avolio 1994: 20). The first Executive Summary in 2002 reported a need to integrate AS and the Beyond Sport social inclusion work, because it appeared that separate names and programmes continued to discourage real joining up of those pathways. But the CSP structure had proved effective in managing geographical and political boundaries, consultation and empowerment processes, and in demonstrating an ability to reach local communities. All this reinforced the relationships with the intervention agencies, particularly Lancashire Constabulary. It was apparent

tony charlton

from the interviews, however, that deeper consultation with each partner was needed to identify and allow variations in support, because it was obvious that 'one size did not fit all'. These evidences helped to plan the second year of operation, when three sports (athletics, basketball and tennis) would be launched, and three more (hockey, rugby league and netball) incorporated in the Year 3 bid.

By 2004, LS had significantly increased the capability of clubs, coaches, schools and intervention agencies to work together. Over 1,600 coaches and volunteers were supported, with 76 achieving the national minimum operating standard and 200 working towards it, of whom 33 per cent were women, 2 per cent from Black and ethnic minorities and 1 per cent disabled. In addition, 241 young volunteers were recruited, with 96 achieving 200 hours input.

Over the three years, 162 clubs were introduced to Clubmark accreditation, to raise their standards to support the 2,000 participants involved in their programmes. Three-quarters of their participants were women (against a target of half), 15 per cent were disabled (target 11 per cent), and 4 per cent from Black and ethnic minorities (target 7 per cent). To meet the original targets for widening participation, 27 per cent of the programmes and associated clubs were in Priority Areas against a target of 32 per cent (compare those figures cited by Enoch for other areas on p. 59, Table 3.5). In addition, ten clubs were supported to provide sporting opportunities to 25 young people referred through the Beyond Sport service, demonstrating to many intervention agencies the value of sport as an effective diversionary tool to divert young people from crime and anti-social behaviour. Following a pilot, these services were extended to all fourteen local authorities, employing seven Community Sports Facilitators, enabling 299 young people to access mainstream sporting opportunities, a significant achievement in partnership working.

But the three-year mark (2003) proved to be a turning point in the fortunes of LS. Following publication of the first progress report to Lancashire's sporting community, *Playing for Keeps* (LS, 2003), the CEO announced his resignation to take another post, which happened after the inaugural AGM, in July. LS was at a pinnacle of delivery, had gained recognition from peers and government (the Minister for Sport having quoted it as the benchmark), and provided Sport England with a model of good practice for developing the concept of CSPs.

The Service Team continued to support the partners on a day-to-day basis, and the PDM assumed the leadership mantle for what was expected to be a short period. But there was the beginning of a loss in strategy-building terms because high-level regional and external contacts were not sustained with the lack of a recognised leader. This was compounded by Sport England going through yet another reorganisation, so capacity for guidance from that quarter was curtailed. Sport England's CEO even admitted that it was 'an organisation living in the past ... trying to use nineteenth-century organisational structures to implement a twentieth-century approach to providing sporting opportunities to a twenty-first-century nation' (Draper 2003: 104).

Even though the core business was able to continue relatively smoothly, participant observation showed that developing the partnership slowed to a halt, exacerbated by the pressure to find funding, for instance, to sustain some of the Team and the Beyond Sport facilitators on short-term contracts. Only partial success meant turnover of staff, with those remaining having to assume the missing roles in addition to their own work, leading to overstretch at the centre and in clusters. Some decisions appeared to be made by the Acting CEO, the Hub Chair and the Sport England representative and reported to others. One of Charlton's (2008) interviewees, Head of an SD team, with ten years' experience, commented:

> I always found it better when I was on the Hub – I knew exactly what was happening. I came off that and I found myself being more distant – found myself not being as proactive on the partnership.

A new CEO with no local sporting experience was appointed in February 2004, but by the publication of the Annual Report, *Life: Game On – 2003/4* (LS, 2004) was on sick leave, and resigned after eight months, with the PDM taking over again. The Hub Chair resigned after four years' work; at the same time, the revamped Sport England announced a review to ensure that CSPs' founding principles still held good, and that they were 'fit for purpose', to use Minister for Sport, Richard Caborn's favourite phrase (Sport England, NW 2004). A new Chair was elected, and it was decided to defer appointing a CEO until Sport England's review was completed. Contact with LCLOG continued and more Chief Leisure Officers appeared in the Hub, perhaps to ensure the machine still ran.

A new role, 2006

After the Carter report (2005), HMG's review of Sport England was that structures needed to be simplified (in the case of grant aid from seventy-five to two!), with more freedom for partners once strategy had been agreed, and this impacted on CSPs. They were still seen as central to the 'single system of delivery' (as again in 2008, when yet another minister had rearranged Sport England's purposes and another national strategy had appeared). Three principles of access to all; top-down policy and bottom-up delivery; and effective local alliances of education, community and sports bodies, were to be enshrined in the operational ethos.

Also in 2006 a new self-assessment tool for CSPs was produced – *Towards an Excellent Service (TAES)* (Sport England/IDeA, 2006). This had been developed for local authorities when it was made clear that they were not to be disciplined by Audit Commission inspection, but to demonstrate their strengths and weaknesses transparently to government and the public. *TAES* was then extended to NGBs and CSPs. Most of the eight main themes of *TAES* relate directly to our narrative about LS:

1. leadership;
2. policy and strategy;
3. community engagement;
4. partnership working;
5. use of resources;
6. people management;
7. standards of service;
8. performance management and (organisational) learning.

LS clearly showed (like SAZs – see pp. 206–7) how important strong leadership is, and how an organisation can lose its way, especially when it needs financial and human contributions from its partners.

QLM's (2005) independent review of *TAES* for CSPs recommended some changes to content, and more support from Sport England in implementation and validation. Most, if not all CSPs had undertaken *TAES* evaluations in 2006/7, and were rated fit for purpose, most on a fair/good score, including LS.

A new CEO was appointed for LS in February 2006 with the brief to re-energise the 'communities of practice', to join up the network and demonstrate to external links that LS could continue to produce the required outputs. In July the Hub group was dissolved and replaced by a 'Management Board', with the emphasis for the new core team and existing cluster structure to be more on strategic delivery and less about direct delivery as had previously been undertaken.

The 2006–09 strategy, *Changing Lives* (LS, n.d.) identified core themes:

- enhancing the sporting infrastructure;
- developing the workforce;
- creating stronger and safer communities;

- health and wellbeing;
- young people;
- benefiting the economy;
- performance measurement and intelligence;
- strategic planning and coordination;
- marketing and communications.

The first five were seen as desirable outcomes of increasing participation in and widening access to sport, the last three as crucial support functions.

A new planning cycle was developed, and theme groups set up for sporting infrastructure and workforce development, the latter a new area of work overseen by a group of eleven partners. In 2007/8:

- Several training courses were run.
- Over 400 volunteers were recruited for Step into Sport, Positive Futures and Millennium Volunteers programmes.
- A project for University and FE volunteering was set up.
- Strategies and Action Plans were developed for all fourteen Sport and Physical Activity Alliances (one for each local authority – CSNs elsewhere in England) under an SPAA Leading Members' forum (LS, 2008a).

At this point the core team comprised: a Sporting Infrastructure group of six staff (three appointed in 2007 for the area clusters); a Workforce Development group of five; two staff for communications; two staff for business support; and a hockey Development Officer. With the CEO, this made a total of seventeen. Each group produced an annual delivery plan, together with one for the Partnership, which had its own Advisory Board. Particular opportunities here were seen as a legacy for London 2012 and Building Schools for the Future (LS, 2008b).

CONCLUSIONS

The literature offers several versions of 'partnership'. Not all partnerships are equal, and LS's experience in the phase without a substantive CEO, was that some of the smaller LAs were suspicious that their larger, more powerful neighbours were dominating decision-making, often without open discussion. One lesson might be that an adequately experienced and trained deputy is a necessary insurance for such overview agencies. Thus it might have been easier to sustain an ideological consensus and the transformational mission. The latter, however, may not be fully possible in this model of partnership governance, where most partners put their local missions, timetable and priorities first, finding LS's agenda easiest to support when it coincided with their own. Charlton (2008: 365) came to the conclusion that LS perhaps was more a 'consortium' (Prior, 1996).

The CSP developed its vision and business model on the 'sport for good' agenda related to the cross-cutting issues in public services, especially social inclusion and cohesion, and the sporting performance pathways traditionally associated with NGBs. LS's emphasis was roughly equal on the two pathways, seeing them as mutually reinforcing rather than separate. The CSP exercise demonstrated that no one agency can deliver SD across the sports continuum, nor indeed across the large areas, counties or regions, that are the NGBs' units for their sports.

Evidence of the impact on SDOs suggests that existing workloads are being over-stretched, especially in small SD teams or for lone workers – a consistent motif, for example, in feedback on the annual County Youth Games. This is particularly problematic regarding sustainability, unless support is forthcoming from LS's central resources. Unitary authorities and larger departments are better equipped to act as drivers for the Partnership, and to satisfy LS's demands while still meeting their employers' obligations. This raises the delicate issue of returns on investment – in creating a database of coaches, for example, where larger partners questioned 'subsidies' for less well-resourced authorities. A mechanism to ensure continuity has been to move from an informal, relational system to one formalised via Service Level Agreements (referred to within LS as 'Joint Action Plans') to overcome problems of delivering agreed programmes.

Since inception, the CSP role has moved beyond ASP to meet wider social policy demands necessitating links to other agencies and networks. In 2005 CSPs were subjected to a fit-for-purpose review to determine their responsibilities in the emerging Single Delivery System, revolving around NGBs' Whole Sport Plans, involving links with Primary Care Teams in striving to meet to increase physical activity for health (see Chapter 13), and affected by changing LA management structures for sport or culture. The CSP was seen as a strategic resourcing function, one level down from Sport England, rather than a delivery agent. For instance, LS can use the example of the introduction of an ICT referral network (Beyond Sport) with the potential to link referrals from health professionals, offer volunteering possibilities, and work placements for students. However, there cannot be a one-size-fits-all outcome because not all forty-five CSPs are at the same stage of development.

For the present, the focus is on producing a smoother player pathway from participation to performance, club development, coach development and

linkages to schools. Inclusion remains central to the work, and all the pathway and development processes operate in the context of an inclusion policy and equity targets. The Partnership provides strategic links at many levels and successfully brings together a range of key agencies employing sport to positively benefit young people's lives.

McDonald (2005: 587) suggested that, of four modes of governance identified by Newman (2001), CSPs fell within the rational goal mode, but dominated by national agencies and policies, with room for manoeuvre only on tactics rather than strategy. They have only really just bedded in as organisations when their remit is being changed, so evaluating impact is difficult. Houlihan and Lindsay (2008) quoted KKP (2005) as commenting that some of their club work was limited by the uneven distribution of clubs, and their credibility is affected by whoever is their host – if it is a particularly large local authority, it may be seen as having disproportionate influence.

The switch from sport for good to sport for sport's sake, and especially partici-pation, with a limited budget for each CSP from Sport England of £300,000 (plus a national contribution of £1m from DoH for health-related work) means that some CSPs will not be able to continue posts in some social policy spheres when short-term contracts come to an end, while others have developed extensive funding partnerships which makes them less vulnerable.

POSTSCRIPT

After this study was completed, the advent of a new Secretary of State led to a reverse out of 'sport for good' (Coalter, 2007) to 'sport for its own sake' (Sport England, 2008) with action focused, for both participation and performance, on NGBs. So far as the CSPs are concerned this does not greatly affect their main objectives of coordinating delivery through the CSNs, and should increase the nature of the partnership, particularly in areas of workforce and volunteer development, to support their local sporting infrastructure. Table 5.1 sets out the core services agreed with Sport England for £200,000 p.a., some enhanced services for Sport England and NGBs, and some coaching services which will be introduced in 2009/10 and 2010/11 for an estimated £40,000–£50,000 p.a.; the PA work for DoH mentioned above will be in addition.

tony charlton

Table 5.1 Sport England's specification for services from County Sports Partnerships

Business objective	Services	Measurement
Core services		
1. Cross-sport, to NGB priorities	1.1 Connect NBGs to CSP area	NGB satisfaction
	1.2 Align to NGB needs for coaches, volunteers, club investment	Agreed numbers, Clubmarks
	1.3 Promote *PESSYP* to NGBs	
	1.4 Broker money for Building Schools for Future and others	Agreed facilities, £ inward
	1.5 Advise Sport England on grant bids	£ inward
2. Strategic alliances, local networks	2.1 Networks for LAs, SSPs, facilities, clubs and others; advocate for Sport England, sport in LAAs	Stakeholder satisfaction; LAA objectives
	2.2 Knowledge base	Stakeholder satisfaction
3. Sound governance, compliance as sub-regional partnership	3.1 Effective governance structure/decision-making processes; maintain Safeguarding and Equality standards	Meet Sport England's governance measures, as with NGBs
Enhanced services		
Coordinate YP services for Sport England NGBs	Deliver Sport Unlimited to youth, grow volunteering, begin Recruit into Coaching	Deliver contracted numbers
	Services as agreed in 2009–13 Whole Sport Plans	To be defined
Coaching delivery		
1. System	County Coaching Support Network and 4–7 Plan	
2. Frontline delivery	Ensure coaches register and are deployed in national, school, LA programmes	
3. Support	Promote PDPs for coaches, SkillsActive bursaries, School Sport and Recruit programmes and publicise jobs, courses	
4. Qualifications, CPD	Develop Coach Management Information System, promote assessment of practice, minimum operating standards	
5. R&D	Support sports coach UK R&D	

Source Sport England, 2009 documentation.

Endnote

Since this chapter was written, some significant policies have been introduced which could enhance PE and Sport facilities and curricula. One is 'Extended Schools', providing for community use in the early morning, evening, weekend and holidays (a twenty-first-century version of 1965's 'A Chance to Share'). A second is 'Building Schools for the Future' (BSF), a 15–20 year programme for rebuilding 3,500 schools across England. BSF is an ambitious programme for change, offering a once-in-a-generation opportunity to transform educational provision. It is intended to act as a catalyst and enabler, by providing flexible twenty-first-century facilities for an innovative curriculum, and an inspiring setting for teachers and pupils alike. PE and Sport have a key part to play, and there is a requirement for local authorities to establish a PE and Sport 'Stakeholder Group' of which the local CSP is a key member (Sport England/YST/PfS, n.d.). This reinforces the role of CSPs in representing the views of a wide range of partners, developing a strategic overview, and communicating this to BSF project teams.

REFERENCES

Audit Commission (1998) *A Fruitful Partnership,* London: Audit Commission.

Bass, B.M and Avolio, B.J. (1994) *Improving Organisational Effectiveness through Transformational Leadership*, London: Sage.

Boje, D.M. (2001) *Narrative Methods for Organisational and Communication Research,* London: Sage.

Carley, M., Chapman, M., Hastings, A., Kirk, K. and Young, R. (2000) *Urban Regeneration through Partnership*, Bristol: Policy Press.

Carter, P. (Lord) (2005) *Review of National Sport Effort and Resources*, London: Sport England.

Charlton, A. (2008) The trials and tribulations of joined-up working: an example of a sub-regional partnership from the sports sector, unpublished Ph.D., Ormskirk: Edge Hill University.

Coalter, A. (2007) *A Wider Social Role for Sport: Who's Keeping the Score?* London: Routledge.

County Sports Partnership Network (2003) *Briefing Note*, London: Sport England.

Draper, R. (2003) The modernisation of Sport England, in S. Campbell and B. Simmonds (eds) *Sport, Active Recreation and Social Inclusion,* London: The Smith Institute.

Houlihan, B. (1991) *Government and Politics of Sport,* London: Routledge.

Houlihan, B. and Lindsay, I. (2008) Networks and partnerships in sports development, in V. Girginov (ed.) *Management of Sports Development*, Oxford: Butterworth-Heinemann.

Hutchinson, J. and Campbell, M. (1998) *Working in Partnership: Lessons from the Literature*, London: Department of Education and Employment.

Huxham, C. (1996) *Creating Collaborative Advantage*, London: Sage.

Knight, Kavanagh & Page (2005) *Active Sport/CSP Impact study: Year 3, Final Report*, Bury St Edmunds: KKP.

Lancashire Sport (2003) *Playing for Keeps,* Preston: Lancashire Sport.

Lancashire Sport (2004) *Life: Game On – 2003/4*, Preston: Lancashire Sport.

Lancashire Sport (n.d.) *Changing Lives: Lancashire Sport Strategy 2006–09*, Preston: Lancashire Sport.

Lancashire Sport (2008a) *Core Delivery Plan 2008/9*, Preston: Lancashire Sport.

Lancashire Sport (2008b) *Partnership Delivery Plan 2008/9*, Preston: Lancashire Sport.

Lowndes, V. and Skelcher, C. (1998) The dynamics of multi-organisational partnerships: An analysis of changing modes of governance, *Public Administration*, 76: 313–33.

McDonald, I. (2005) Theorising partnerships: Governance, communicative action and sport policy, *Journal of Social Policy*, 34(4): 579–600.

Mackintosh, M. (1992) Partnership: Issues of policy negotiation, *Local Economy*, 7(3): 210–24.

Newman, J. (2001) *Modernising Governance: New Labour, Policy and Society*, London: Sage.

Prior, D. (1996) Working the network: Local authority strategies in the reticulated state, in H. Davies (ed.) *Quangos and Local Government*, London: Cass.

QLM (2005) *Independent Evaluation of TAES for County Sports Partnerships*, Executive summary www.sportengland.org accessed 26 August 2008.

Skelcher, C. (2000) Changing images of the state: overloaded, hollowed-out, congested, *Public Policy and Administration*, 15(3): 3–19.

Sport England (2000) *Active Sports Development Framework for Partnership Services*, London: Sport England.

Sport England (2001) *The Sports Partnerships: Building for the Future: A Discussion Paper*, London: Sport England.

Sport England, NW (2004) *Evolution of County Sports Partnerships in the NW: Guidance Notes*, Manchester: Sport England.

Sport England, EM (2006) *County Sports Partnerships Briefing Note 2/06*, Nottingham: Sport England.

Sport England (2008) *A Strategy 2008–11*, London: Sport England.

Sport England/Innovation and Development Agency (2006) *Towards an Excellent Service – County Sport Partnerships*, London: Sport England/IDeA.

Sport England/Youth Sport Trust/Partnerships for Schools (n.d.) *PE and School Sport in Building Schools for the Future* (leaflet), London: PfS/Sport England.
Wenger, E. (1999) *Communities of Practice: Learning, Meaning and Identity,* Cambridge: Cambridge University Press.

tony charlton

CHAPTER 6

SPORT AND HIGHER EDUCATION

Participation and excellence

Rod Thorpe and Mike Collins

INTRODUCTION

It is the first author's intention to focus on the university (Loughborough) that he worked at – first as a lecturer, and then as Head of the Sports Development Centre from 1997 to 2003. Whilst Loughborough is not wholly typical of Higher Education Institutions, in that it has an exceptional commitment to sports development, most HEIs can contribute to elements of sports development, as the second author's work with Universities UK (Collins, 2004a) showed.

The 'potted history' box below gives a summary of events in the evolution of Loughborough as a Mecca for student and elite sport.

Sport at Loughborough: A potted history

1909   Dr Herbert Schofield establishes the Loughborough Technical Institute – four colleges in the town, for education, art and design, and engineering.

1920   This becomes Loughborough Technical College.

1930s   Athletics school established, and short courses in teacher/coach training.

1940s   Teacher Training College established, first for men and later for women, with lunch-time sessions for local PE teachers.

1950s   Continued development of Schofield's four colleges.

1960s   ▪ Starts offering B.Ed. in PE.
        ▪ In 1966 becomes a College of Advanced Technology.
        ▪ Sport England grant aids sports science research.
        ▪ In 1969 offers UK's first M.Sc. in Recreation Management – with some ribald press coverage. (Now an M.Sc. in Sport and Leisure Management, in its 36th year.)

1970s	College of Education and University merge, as do Student Unions.
	A wide range of separate and joint honours degrees develop.
1980s	Sport gains credibility as a degree subject and a research field.
	Campus becomes base for a branch of the National Coaching Foundation.
	Sports Council grant aids Institute for Sport and Recreation Planning and Management.
1990s	Department gains 'International' ranking in three successive national Research Assessments; Institute for Youth Sport established.
	Postgraduate teaching becomes specialised, with nine Masters degrees.
	Hosts Youth Sport Trust.
2000s	Department becomes a School, hosts ISRM and several governing bodies of sport, and gains Queen's Anniversary Prize 2003.
	Lottery grants and partnership schemes bring £340m worth of world-class training facilities in ten sports.
	Olympic Studies centre and special programme for research in disability sport founded.

(See Cantor, 1990; Wallace, 2004)

On the campus the School of Sport and Exercise Sciences teaches over 1,000 students – at undergraduate and Masters or Postgraduate Certificate in Physical Education level. The portfolio of specialist Masters degrees now encompasses physiology, nutrition, psychology, biomechanics, physical education, coaching, and sport and leisure management. It hosts over 60 Ph.D. students, and has over 40 academic staff and over 50 support staff. The Sports Development Centre (SDC) has also grown to over 150 staff to service the student, elite and community sport, and another 100 work for professional and national governing bodies. Others sporting bodies would like to come, drawn by this growing centre of strength – a 'SportPark', a concept already approved (York Consulting/KKP, 2004) and then being built at the western edge of the campus. The Estates Department spent £340,000 (5 per cent of its budget) on maintaining the University's share of facilities, with a contribution from the EIS and interest, and depreciation on £5m of University investment of £400,000 (Wallace, 2004). But as the potted history shows, while the pace of change has been hectic in the last twenty years, the roots go back half a century.

In 1997 Loughborough decided to use the title 'Sports Development Centre' to describe the unit responsible for supporting most of the sport experience, beyond teaching and research. Other HEIs use different terms – Sport Centre,

Physical Education Centre – to describe such a unit, but we will use Sports Development Centre (SDC) as a generic term. The nature of the sports development work in an HEI with a commitment to sport is influenced by the chosen focuses of the sport experience. Again, Loughborough is different from most in having:

- major teaching programmes that embrace the biological sciences, social sciences, leisure management, teacher education and, in another faculty, manufacturing engineering;
- a commitment to high-level research across this range of subject areas;
- a commitment to providing exceptional performance opportunities from beginner to World-Class levels, and an environment for performance improvement;
- most importantly, a commitment to develop people in the wider context of sport, a point central to this chapter.

Most HEIs have a paid member of staff with responsibility for the students' sport experience but this can vary from a Director of Sport Development with professorial status, as at Loughborough and a growing number of other HEIs, to a single person identified to oversee sport, in some cases employed by the Student Union rather than the HEI itself. The SDC's resources have to support teaching, fundamental and applied research, student fitness, recreational and competitive sport, sport opportunities for staff, training programmes for the resident and some visiting national and regional representative senior and youth squads, and use by local schools, clubs, groups and individuals, as well as televised professional athletic events and, for example, the matches of Leicester Riders professional basketball team, 'exiled' for several years by the obsolescence of their hall in the city.

Thus, with the largest number of hosted governing bodies of any of the branches of the English Institute of Sport (EIS), a student sporting population larger than that of its small (50,000 people) host town, and the range of other users of space, the staff and community groups may not have as much space as in HEIs with fewer specialist demands. The Lottery-funded facilities at the Universities of East Anglia, Central Lancashire and Hertfordshire can provide more time for local users, and the balance of management tasks is different.

It is not the purpose of this chapter to define sports development (SD), rather the authors will work from the premise that this is a commitment to provide either the environment and/or the people in which development of sport and people in sport can occur. Simply it is the authors' contention that many HEIs could provide the environment to do this, and all will have the sort of people that one looks for to aid sports development. In addition HEIs can add massively to the development of sport in the host community.

In the remainder of this chapter we will look at how Loughborough seeks to serve three groups of clients – the students, elite sportspeople and the community – and how it does so through developing strategic partnerships with other agencies. These partnerships range from junior soccer camps with the local borough council, to World-Class Performance programmes with the national governing bodies and the English Institute of Sport. To reflect this commitment to partnership, a brand name 'Loughborough Sport' with a strapline 'developing people, developing sport' was produced to indicate this approach. A student from another East Midlands HEI who trains regularly at Loughborough may enjoy the association with 'Loughborough Sport', but not feel an affinity with Loughborough University. The fact that 'developing people' is the first phrase in the strapline is important. It is a major premise of this presentation that to really develop sport we have to look first to the human resource.

SPORTS DEVELOPMENT FOR STUDENTS

An HEI provides a privileged context for young people who are passionate, not to say mad, about sport – a reasonably flexible timetable, good facilities and coaching and paramedic/science support on site, free or cheap. Not surprisingly, full-time students are the most active cohort of the population, 72 per cent taking part once a month or more often in 1996 (Sport England/UKS, 2001). It is recognised that there is so much more to a 'higher education' than merely the teaching and research experiences; one of Loughborough's objects in its 1966 Charter was 'to develop the character of its students by virtue of its corporate life', and its 1999 strategic plan mentions an ethos characterised by 'a unique contribution to the development of a wide range of sports, allowing exceptional opportunities for participation and achievement at every level'. At Loughborough, the Athletic Union (AU) was grant-aided by £140,000 from the University (19 per cent of the total subvention to the Student Union, which LSU more than doubled through its commercial activities in shops, bars, a night club, and rents (Wallace, 2004)) and operates as an independent organisation. Thus sabbatical, elected AU presidents have responsibility for fifty-five to sixty clubs, depending on the interests of current cohorts (compared to an average of thirty-five for English HEIs (Collins, 2004a)), and some 4,000 students who are subscribing members of the AU. All clubs have to have a constitution requiring an elected committee, and typically about eight people would be given responsibility. Committees vary, but active ones achieve amazing feats –

rod thorpe and mike collins

organising overseas tours, raising money for major pieces of equipment, supporting local community clubs, fulfilling major league commitments; and some operate six-figure budgets. It does not take a giant leap to see that HEIs can be real training grounds for the people who will make a difference in the broader sports development or business worlds.

Loughborough has won the British Universities Sports Association (BUSA, now merged with University and College Sport to form British Universities and Colleges Sport (BUCS)) championships continuously for more than two decades. These championships involve some 46,000 students in team sports and 50,000 in individual sports. To come to Loughborough and win is considered a major achievement and cause for a celebration by other HEIs. In addition, there is intra-mural sport; Loughborough has possibly the largest programme in the UK, with each of the fourteen halls of residence playing the others at fourteen sports. Sport England data (2004a) suggested that half or more of HE students play intramural soccer (53%, plus 81% playing 5-a-side) badminton (53%), and basketball (49%). Then there are also casual running, swimming and fitness activities.

In addition, students volunteer in increasing numbers to work in schools, clubs and local communities as coaches and mentors and assistant sports develop-ment officers. As part of a wider study of volunteering based on twenty HEI interviews, Sheffield University for Sport England (Taylor et al., 2003) estimated that student volunteering involved some 18,000 students in 1.5 million hours worth £17.4m a year, but this excluded intramural sport. A more detailed study by De Souza (2004) suggested that this was a gross underestimate – his figures being 43,000 students giving 7.7 million hours worth £90.1m (Table 6.1).

Table 6.1 Volunteers in sport in HE in England, 2002 and 2004

	Sport England 2002	de Souza 2004
Average number of sports clubs per university	47	36
Average number of volunteers per sports club	4.7	4.8
Average number of volunteers per university	157	371
Estimated number of volunteers in HE in England	18,212	43,067
Average number of hours per volunteer per year	81.7	179.1
Estimated number of hours all volunteers per year (m)	1.488	7.712
Estimated value of volunteering in HE in England per year (m)*	£17.394	£90.152

Sources: Sport England, 2002 focus group questionnaire, n = 308; De Souza 2004 surveys: qualitative questionnaire 1, n = 69; qualitative questionnaire 2, n = 115.
Notes *Using the average wage for all industries of £11.69 (used by Sport England, 2003).

Students volunteered in sport because they enjoyed it, but also because it provided evidence on their CVs that they had practical and personal skills. The government has tried to stimulate student volunteering of all kinds by offering the Higher Education Active Communities Fund.

Data on twenty-one HEIs suggested that 49% of volunteers were active in supporting student clubs, 41% in intramural sport and 10% in their local communities. More and more had a member of staff responsible for training, placing and supporting volunteers, and an average budget for student sport outside such salaries was £12,000, though 11% had more than £45,000 a year. The average number of volunteers per HEI was 54, but over one-fifth had over a hundred. Time offered averaged 40–60 hours a year, two hours a week in term time (see www.ucsport.net/downloads). Beneficiaries from eighteen schemes totalled over 8,500; at a cost of between £50 and £100 per volunteer, this is very high leverage and value for money. Collins (2004a) included examples of Durham, Hertfordshire, Leeds and South Bank students working in schools. Southwark teachers said 'the scheme improved sporting performance and interest in sport' and it 'contributed to improved behaviour and pupil performance'. Loughborough shares these experiences with, conservatively estimated, 500 students – having (and mostly enjoying) significant roles in operating and developing sport.

Students running sport is very valuable, but not without its problems, given the annual turnover of the population. At Loughborough, coaches – some paid, many volunteers, some full-time, many part-time – occasionally question the wisdom of the Sports Development Centre vesting control of the clubs with the students, particularly when operating within national structures. In reality, the Centre acts as a major support system. In addition, students in the clubs and the Athletic Union realise the value of vesting some responsibility with the coach, or manager, particularly when playing in 'open' national leagues, but it is their choice to do so. It is quite apparent that major national sporting organisations will not sign long-term agreements with student unions, and so major developments rest with the HEI, usually guided by its sports development centre.

This partnership of AU and SDC differs considerably between HEIs. A number of HEIs decided to form federations of their SDCs and their AUs as a genuine partnership. There are many advantages, but perhaps a disadvantage is that inevitably the permanent, professional Director of SD and other HEI employees can dominate decision-making. In other HEIs the students have voted for the SDC to run student sport, recognising that they do not have the skills or time commitment to do so; a disadvantage here is that students will not have the opportunity to gain organisational/managerial experience, commitment and skills. Such a decision about the structure of student sport depends on both circumstance and philosophy. It was always the first author's philosophy that a major role of an SDC in a place like Loughborough was to maximise the potential and realise the aspirations of students, and that leadership development was important to communities, national governing bodies and the nation. Perhaps this explains why Loughborough alumni are found in leadership roles across the UK and worldwide. The skill is to do this without detrimentally affecting individuals' sport performances and careers.

DEVELOPING SPORT FOR STAFF

Loughborough University has 3,000 staff, of whom about a third are 'blue collar', mainly in residential and estates workforces. The permanent primacy of student sport and the recent additional focus on elite sport with all the new EIS partnerships had meant that provision for staff had to be put on hold. Despite working at a sporting Mecca, staff were scarcely more active than the English population as a whole, with 37% doing more than 2.5 hours of moderate exercise a week, compared to 32% on average. There were a number of staff development courses encouraging a healthy lifestyle, space in the 50 metre pool and the fitness centre, and sessions in other facilities, but a survey showed that many did not know about them, did not realise that they were subsidised and generally cheaper than sessions in the town's Leisure Centre or private clubs. Moreover, some were sure they did not want to share sessions with students (either because they would meet their own students or because they did not want their fitness and body shape compared).

Thus there were four challenges in establishing a 'Healthy Campus' programme: to raise awareness of existing offers; to extend these especially at lunchtime and weekends; to ease the difficulties of having almost all facilities at the east end of a 2-mile-long campus; and to get a corporate concern as a good employer involving personnel, estates, residential and staff development services. Two-thirds of twenty-eight HEIs responding to a survey had some such programmes, with major thrusts at Bath, Brighton and Sussex (Collins, 2004b). Workplaces assume a new importance as a setting for promoting sport and physical activity in Sport England's new *Framework* (2004b), and with the BHF Centre for Exercise and Health also on campus, the University is now progressing this work through its Strategic Plan.

PARTNERSHIPS IN DEVELOPING HIGH-PERFORMANCE SPORT

Support for elite sport is an increasing feature of government policy worldwide. In Europe, nine out of ten states provide support services and half have sports scholarship schemes (Amara *et al.*, 2004). In any partnership, honesty and clarity of purpose and responsibility are key from the start (Carley *et al.*, 2000). There were three years of shenanigans about an English Institute of Sport based on the Australian model by two governments over whether there should be a single large HQ at Sheffield or Loughborough. In the event, New Labour chose a devolved regional network with a small London base (Theodoraki, 1999). The first author thinks EIS officers were surprised that rather than just telling them what Loughborough could do for them, he made it clear that any initiative had to benefit the University and the students, whilst listening carefully to their agenda. Then it was possible to see how the UK's largest HE sports science base – and good if old and basic facilities – could be improved to help governing bodies, nine of whom had longstanding links (which they had made clear they wished to retain and develop (DNH, 1996)). Then a 'win–win' situation could be negotiated.

The second principle of partnership is what we call the 'fall out' principle. Agreements should be based on the fact that partners *may* fall out, and what contingencies and procedures then operate; SD links often depend on personalities agreeing, but long-term agreements and budgets cannot depend on this. For example, Loughborough's relationship with the Lawn Tennis Association is that the 'Academy' (school-age youngsters) will have access to four of the original indoor courts and the University will have access to the other four indoor courts at certain times; in reality the coaches discuss needs and share both courts and players, e.g. LU tennis scholars hit with academy players. Such a relationship, with clear written agreements which are then softened at the edges by the people on site, operate for many of the high-level performance ventures at Loughborough – in athletics, badminton, cricket, cycling, gymnastics, netball, rugby, swimming, triathlon and cycling.

The HE sector is a major reservoir of World-Class potential performers (those not quite world-class, but who, in a positive supportive environment, can reach the very highest level). Sir Roger Bannister (1996) predicted that by 2010 a third of the UK's World-Class athletes would come through HEIs rather than clubs. Lottery funding, sports scholarships, HEIs' investment, and the EIS (notably through the Talented Athletes Sports Scholarships scheme (TASS)) has accelerated this trend, and it is likely that this share has been surpassed. In Beijing, 26 of the 47 British medal winners were HE students or recent graduates. Loughborough, hosting permanently or regularly 22 NGBs and having 16 National Performance Directors on site, was the only university mentioned in the London 2012 bid as a base for acclimatisation camps and pre-competition training (see www.London.2012.com), though of course others would be used for smaller numbers of sports. HEIs feature largely in the lists of venues in each region identified as potential training camps.

PARTNERSHIPS IN LOCAL SPORTS DEVELOPMENT

As mentioned above, those who play and enjoy their sport in HEIs may be more likely to move into community clubs on leaving (though not always in the same sport). As many ex-students report, however, few can find the same 'club experience' in the community. This chapter is not intended to look at what the authors consider the most critical weakness in UK sport, the 'club' system – see Chapter 9 regarding swimming – but it is important to note that a university must take great care when entering any local community relationship, which most HEIs have the facilities to do, even if they cannot support World-Class performers. Sport England (2004a) recorded that 88% of HEIs in England had partnerships with community clubs, 74% with NGBs, 69% with local authorities, 42% with Specialist Sports Colleges and 58% with other schools.

To take a local example: in the early 1990s Loughborough began negotiating with the Lawn Tennis Association (LTA) and its Leicestershire branch (the LLTA) to build a 4-court indoor centre, to act as a national and county resource as well as one for the University. The LLTA made it quite clear it preferred a centre in Leicester, which might yet also appear (the LTA then had a nationwide Indoor Tennis Initiative). This honesty ensured that the University, responsible for funding and running the facilities day-to-day, knew the risk. Clearly an income from the local community on a pay-as-you-play (PAYP) basis was an obvious partial solution. The University did not choose to do this.

Some years previously, a senior member of the Badminton Association of England impressed the first author by saying that whilst the numbers of (fairly casual) badminton players had risen in the wake of provision of public leisure centres, club memberships had dropped. The implication was that, without a balance in club development, PAYP might be detrimental (though demographic trends, time squeeze and other factors were also operating). In the 4-court indoor tennis centre that LU opened in 1996 the evening sessions for community use were offered to local clubs, and were wholly taken up. Hence, several local clubs were able to increase their attractions by advertising that, besides their outdoor courts, they had access to, for example, two hours on four indoor courts. In this way LU helped strengthen local clubs rather than poaching players only. The fact that students also coached in these clubs, has been a bonus.

At other times a community club or the local authority may approach the HEI for a partnership scheme based on a sports facility. At Loughborough the 8-lane 400m synthetic track is a specialist facility. Charnwood Athletics Club has a clubhouse on site and shares it. But now, flanked by the indoor athletics hall, it can provide a base for many elite athletes worldwide and yet serve the Youth Sport Trust's children's courses and the Leicestershire Youth Games and a televised athletics meeting each June. Likewise the SDC has always offered local cricket clubs access to the University's indoor nets and has protected this allocation when developing the National Cricket Academy.

As part of the EIS developments, the University built dedicated netball and badminton centres. These sports are usually played in multi-purpose halls, and so there was a real danger that activities would be 'sucked' away from such less 'ideal' facilities. To avoid this, the University met local, county and regional BAE and EN officials to resolve how the facilities could enhance badminton and netball, yet avoid disadvantaging existing local SD work.

Again, while apparently an attractive offer giving students daytime access, there is need for caution. Unlike schools, where most extra-curricular activity is over by 6 p.m., evenings form the peak demand of students, like working adults. Of course there are major differences between a campus site like Loughborough and city HEIs, and links are affected by size. Loughborough is located in Charnwood Borough which, with 150,000 people, is a large district and should provide most of its needs for community facilities.

The Amateur Swimming Association and the School of Sport and Exercise Sciences both require lane swimming for training, teaching, and research. Staff and citizens who are 'splashers' can use the Leisure Centre pool in town. However, an opportunity was missed to operate joined-up thinking. The Lottery grant was for a purely performance training pool; but providing a 25m x 50m pool with two booms rather than a 20m x 50m pool with only one would have provided an amenity for the citizens of the town and a source of income, should lack of success or the vagaries of Lottery ticket sales reduce the World Class income via the ASA. As it is, before a year was out every minute of space was taken up.

A different approach was used when addressing Association Football. The University bought a long-term lease of a local football ground, on the basis that the money would be spent on developing a new pitch and surrounds. The local club now has a floodlit stadium and excellent pitches with 50 per cent use and priority at weekends, while the University has 50 per cent use, with priority in midweek. In addition, but separate from the usage agreement (the 'fall out' clause), the University Student Football Club decided that they would play as a

114

student side midweek, but join with the local club for league matches. University coaches would look after the playing aspects, community club officials would run the business side, and so the University would not become involved in player payment etc., as the team rises through the leagues. The community can now take pride in an improving football facility serving community and University needs.

In reality this proved too idealistic, and whilst a relationship remains, the University Student Football Club decided to go it alone, not least because of local football politics.

CONCLUSIONS: FROM RESEARCH TO PRACTICE

Some aspects of HE research directly affect practice, but in many cases it is the more general knowledge that resides in a HEI that can give insights to help in sports development as in other aspects of society (Duff and Suthers, n.d.). The key is how to transfer this knowledge at a time when researchers are increasingly pressured to allocate major elements of their time to satisfying the demands of Research Assessment and Teaching Assessment exercises. One way of liberating this knowledge base is to bring researchers and practitioners together with an appropriate intermediary. This can be done occasionally, but it is the authors' experience that this occurs in 'Houses of Sport' or 'Institutes of Sport', when both interests are co-located and share the 'coffee table' experience of informal day-by-day dialogue. On return from a fact-finding tour of Institutes of Sport around the world, Dr Henryk Lakomy, then lecturing in the School of Sport and Exercise Sciences (SSES), commented that one major omission from most plans for athletes' support in branches of the EIS was a room where athletes, coaches and support service staff could 'chill out' together.

At Loughborough this concept was taken a step further by developing a building, the Sir John Beckwith Centre for Sport (SJB), in which the SSES and its Institutes and the Sports Development Centre share spaces with tenant partners like the Youth Sports Trust (YST), the Institute of Sport and Recreation Management, sports coach UK, and several sport-specific bodies. A major driving force for the concept was the need for better information on which to base the develop-ment of children's sport, and co-locating the independent YST (focusing on implementation) next to the SSES' teacher training, sports sciences, and the Institute of Youth Sport (focusing on frontier research, evaluation and dis-semination) was obvious, but there are many more linkages.

The SJB building sits adjacent to the Performance Centre where the sports medicine, sports science, and conditioning services for the EIS and the University are sited. The agreement for this building is based on 50/50 usage, and while some staff are employed by the EIS with specific roles to service World-Class performers, and some by the University to service staff and students, when joined by national governing body staff, the whole resource is immense. The nature of World-Class performers' needs for services is spasmodic and seasonal. The willingness to cross boundaries means large numbers of World-Class performers can be served at one time, in exchange for contributing to University needs when elite demands are low and (importantly) sharing costs. Their aspirations for an even more ambitious 'SportPark' will soon be realised.

This synergy was a significant factor in Loughborough being able to record in 2002 its contributions:

- Elite/professional performance sport – 200 national/international repre-sentatives in 22 sports.
- Leadership – in leisure management (and over a thousand managers in UK and worldwide), local government, national governing bodies and the sports industry (manufacturing, retailing, media, and with a spin-off company with Reebok in Progressive Sports Technologies Ltd).
- 4,000 Physical Education teachers.
- Professors and Directors of Sport in at least twelve UK and nine overseas universities.
- Partnerships with scores of companies, NGBs and institutes at home and twenty-three HEIs overseas (LUSSES, 2002).
- This led to it being awarded the Queen's Anniversary prize, the first for a university school in this field.

The development of the physical environment that allows better interaction of the human resources is a major underlying principle of developments at Loughborough. Compromises have had to be made because this was not a blank sheet, a clear site, but principles of partnership and increasing knowledge and skill flow were used throughout development. The Vice Chancellor calculated the total cost of sport at around £1.75m a year (or under 1.3 per cent of total LU expenditure), asking whether this is good value for money (Wallace, 2004). In a regional economic impact of sport study for the East Midlands Development Agency (York Consulting/KKP, 2004) Loughborough was seen as the centre of a sports industrial cluster that could link to other clusters on food, textiles, engineering and the creative industries, as well as tourism.

Other campuses have begun to develop similar, if smaller nexuses. The government certainly seeks such arrangements developing (DfES, n.d.). The Association of SDCs, University and College Sport aims to 'pursue excellence in

providing, managing and developing sport in Higher and Further Education'
and to 'support UCS members in increasing the strategic role of sport within
universities and colleges across the UK' (www.ucsport.net). Sport was accorded
importance and had a recognised strategy document in 43% of English HEIs
(Sport England, 2004a); it was given priority in campus development because
it can attract students (38%), provides health benefits (21%) and it strengthens
relations with external bodies (23%). This is perhaps a belated recognition of its
role as a major economic factor in a post-industrial society (Cambridge
Econometrics, 2003; Bennett et al.,1999) without getting sucked into the US-
style professional sport/TV/sponsorship complex with its pressures to perform
(Bowen and Levin, 2003).

POSTSCRIPT

As part of its *Strategic Framework*, Sport England (2004b) developed relationships
with HE in every region. After a review of resources in the region's eight HEIs
and twenty-eight FE colleges, Sport England, East Midlands (n.d.) in a review:

- confirmed that students were by far the most active group (with 36 per cent
  taking three 30-minute sessions of moderate or vigorous PA a week
  compared to 21% by England's population in general);
- confirmed the features above of facility provision (2,577 in the region)
  with the majority used by local communities, training and coaching for
  recreational and elite sport, and volunteering in the community.

In terms of developments and action, it noted:

- the likelihood of 2012 training camps at Loughborough and other sites;
- the work of the new FE/HE education unit Podium, funded by the HE/FE
  funding council and Local Skills Council;
- the development of training via the National Skills Academy and its regional
  branches;
- the £18m provided for posts of FE Sports Coordinators to drive achieving
  3 hours each term-time week of quality PA outside the curriculum, but
  regretted that no links had been made with their school equivalents (SSCOs);
- and affirmed that each county had an action plan and that in 2008/9 it
  would link each institution with its CSP and CSN.

After the formation of BUCS, and with its new 2008–2011 strategy for increasing
participation, Sport England (2008) noted that the sporting estate of HEIs was

worth £20bn, and it had recently invested £73m in grant-aiding HEI facilities; and that, apart from the external offers, 967,000 full-time and 700,000 part-time students formed a market of huge potential (and perhaps more ready for change) towards attracting 300,000 new participant by 2012. It is appropriate to end with a quotation from Ed Smith, 2008 chair of BUCS:

> I firmly believe that universities are a vital part of the community in which they are located and sport plays a vital role in creating those community connections through students acting as volunteers and coaches. All of this is a key part of delivering Sport England's strategic goals.
>
> With the formation of BUCS and the emergence of the Sport England new strategy, we have an exciting set of opportunities to engage more effectively with key parts of the sports 'system' in England. Sport helps to develop 'life skills' and sport in higher education is very significant for the individual, for the university and for many of our national governing bodies as our higher than average participation and our Olympic success demonstrates.
>
> (Sport England, 2008: 17)

REFERENCES

Amara, M., Aquilina, D. and Henry, I. with PMP Consultants (2004) *The Education of Elite Young Sportspersons: A Review of Policy in the 25 European Member States*, Loughborough University: Institute of Sport and Leisure Policy.

Bannister, R. (1996) *Raising the Game: Report of the Working Group on University Sports Scholarships,* London: Department of National Heritage.

Bennett, O., Shaw, P. and Allen, K. (1999) *Partners and Providers: The Role of HEIs in Providing Culture and Sport Facilities for the Public,* Bristol: Higher Education Funding Council.

Bowen, W.G. and Levin, S.A. (2003) *Reclaiming the Game: College Sport and Educational Values,* Princeton, NJ: Princeton University Press.

Cambridge Econometrics (2003) *The Value of the Sports Economy in England,* London: Sport England.

Cantor, L. (1990) *Loughborough University of Technology: Past and Present,* Loughborough: Loughborough University.

Carley, M., Chapman, M., Hastings, A., Kirk, K. and Young, R. (2000) *Urban Regeneration through Partnership,* Bristol: Policy Press.

Collins, M.F. (2003) *Sport and Social Exclusion,* London: Routledge.

Collins, M.F. (ed.) (2004a) *Participating and Performing: Sport in Higher Education in the UK,* London: Universities UK.

Collins, M.F. (2004b) *A Healthy Campus for Loughborough? A study for the Sports Development Centre,* Loughborough: Loughborough University.

Department for Culture Media and Sport (1996) *Report of the Working Group on University Sports Scholarships*, London: DCMS.

Department for Education and Skills (n.d.) *A Sporting Future for All: The Role of Further and Higher Education in Delivering the Government's Plan for Sport* (mimeo), London: DfES.

Department for National Heritage (1996) *The British Academy of Sport: Prospectus,* London: DNH.

De Souza, A. (2004) An investigation into the role of Higher Education in the development of volunteering in sport, unpublished M.Sc. Sport and Leisure Management dissertation, Loughborough: Loughborough University.

Duff, I.D. and Suthers, W. (n.d*.) Employment and Income Generation Effects of HEIs: The Town and Gown Interface* (mimeo), Middlesbrough: Teesside Business School.

Loughborough University School of Sport and Exercise Sciences (2002) *First for Sport, First for People in Sport* (portfolio for Queen's Anniversary Prize), Loughborough: SSES.

Sport England/UK Sport (2001) *General Household Survey: Participation in Sport,* London: Sport England/UKS.

Sport England (2004a) *Higher Education and Sport in* England (executive summary of TNS audit report), London: Sport England.

Sport England (2004b) *The Framework for Sport in England: Making England an Active and Successful Sporting Nation: A Vision for 2020,* London: Sport England.

Sport England (2008) *Higher Education and Community Sport*, London: Sport England.

Sport England, East Midlands (n.d.) Coordinating developments in HE/FE, PowerPoint presentation by E. Compson, Nottingham: Sport England.

Taylor, P. *et al.* (2003) *Sports Volunteering in England*, London: Sport England.

Theodoraki, E. (1999) The evolution of an English Institute of Sport, *Managing Leisure*, 4: 187–200.

Wallace, D. (2004) *Universities in the Market Place: Where's Loughborough?*, www.lboro.ac.uk/adnmin/vc.

York Consulting/Knight, Kavanagh & Page (2004) *The Economic Impact of Sport in the East Midlands*, www.sportengland.org/eastmidlands, accessed 27 September 2009.

CHAPTER 7

SPORT IN A DEVOLVED SYSTEM

The Scottish experience

Ian Thomson

INTRODUCTION

This chapter reflects on the experience of devolution in Scotland since 1999, with a specific focus on the development of sport. The chapter is divided into two sections, covering events on either side of the election of a Scottish Parliament in May 1999. Devolution is intended to provide Scottish solutions to Scottish problems, and, it is claimed, the creation of a Scottish Parliament brings to bear a more informed judgement on purely Scottish issues. The evidence is that devolution has not produced a noticeably distinctive version of sport in Scotland. The Scottish government is becoming more interventionist in sports policy, but there is a remaining gap between local and national strategies for sport. None of the three administrations elected since 1999 has made the kind of investment in school sport that has driven up standards and performance in England. To that extent it appears that divergence in policies is not benefiting sport in Scotland.

DEVOLUTION

In July 1997 the newly elected Labour government published a White Paper on devolution which stated that the Westminster Parliament, without in any way diminishing its powers, was choosing to exercise sovereignty by devolving legislative responsibilities to a Scottish Parliament. There are powers reserved to Westminster such as foreign policy, defence and national security, macro-economic monetary and fiscal affairs, employment and social security. The Scotland (1998) Act assigned to the Scottish Parliament all matters not reserved (Cooney and Fotheringham, 2002: 120). In 1998 the Scotland Act was passed by the Westminster Parliament. Its historic first sentence stated 'There shall be a Scottish Parliament'. Elections were held on 6 May 1999. Labour won 56 of the 129 seats, narrowly short of an overall majority, and had to negotiate with the Liberal Democrats with 17 seats to form a coalition government. The Scottish National Party (SNP) emerged as the official opposition party, with 35 seats. In 2003 the coalition government retained power, albeit with a reduced majority. Then the elections held in May 2007 gave the SNP one more seat than the Labour Party, and the Parliament agreed that the SNP should take power as a minority government.

Devolution was strongly opposed by the Conservative governments under Margaret Thatcher and John Major. John Major was convinced that granting Scotland legislative self-government would lead to the break-up of the UK. He described devolution as 'one of the most dangerous propositions ever put before the British nation'. That line of argument led to the Conservatives being regarded in Scotland as an essentially English party. They paid the price in the 1997 General Election, when they lost every seat in Scotland. What they had under-estimated was how far people born in Scotland perceived themselves first as Scottish and only secondly as British. The proportion of people who claimed to feel more Scottish than British grew from 65 per cent in 1974 to 75 per cent in 2004 (Adams and Schmueker, 2005: 15). Devolution allowed the electorate to express this in political terms:

> The history of devolution is that of a people who increasingly believed they had a particular national identity and wanted that identity expressed in political form. It is a history of political response, not political initiative.
>
> (Taylor, 2002: 21)

In 2000 the ESRC launched a 5-year research programme on 'devolution and social change' which aimed to explore the implementation and consequences of devolution. One of the main themes was how far devolution fostered convergence or diversion in social policies. In some areas, such as free care for the elderly, Scotland has diverged from England. In others, such as Higher Education, there is an integrated UK-wide policy community which helps to contain political pressures for divergence. Of the spate of books on devolution, only one of 97 essays in four volumes edited by Hassan and Warhurst (1999, 2000, 2002a, 2002b) was on sport, and that was limited to football. It can be argued that, apart from school sport, there has been convergence in policies for sport across the UK. The Sport Council and governing body structures which link the four territorial countries in the governance of sport, funding and selecting British teams all encourage convergence. There are signs of change, however, stemming from the election of an SNP government in 2007. As long as there was a Labour government in power both at Westminster and in Scotland, national pride was not a threat to the union of the parliaments. The SNP has promised to conduct a referendum on independence in 2010. If successful, it could achieve one of its most cherished ambitions, namely for Scotland to compete as a separate nation at the Olympic Games in London in 2012.

Devolution has opened up debates about identity (Craig, 2003: 22; Bromley et al., 2006: 141). Jarvie (2006: 114–15) pointed out that politicians from various political parties have used the emotions associated with different sports to rally support for the nation. He quoted Jim Sillars, SNP Deputy Leader, who complained that the electorate were '90-minute patriots', meaning that football supporters could show an affinity for the nation through sport without necessarily voting for the policies of the SNP. Bairner (2001) suggested that sport has played an important role in the quest for a separatist national identity. After a searching analysis of football, golf, rugby and shinty, however, he concluded that none of them is a truly distinctive national game. Nevertheless, sport provides something of a vehicle for negative national sentiments. He commented: 'Scottish sporting nationalism is most cohesive when it is most clearly characterised by anti-English sentiment' (Bairner, 2001: 65).

Scottish athletes perform at the Olympic Games as members of a British team, whereas Scotland participates as a nation at the Commonwealth Games. This led the First Minister of the Scottish Parliament, Jack McConnell, to make the following comment during the Manchester Games in 2002: 'In terms of national interest and government priority, the Commonwealth Games should now rank higher than the Olympics' (Scotsman, 1 August 2002: 21). During debates about setting up UK Sport and its scope, there was animosity between Sport England and what its Director General, David Pickup (1996) called the Councils of 'the Celtic fringe'. The issue of the twenty-three sports that receive funding from UK Sport and their home Sports Councils remains unsolved.

He did qualify this with the statement that we should avoid some sort of flag-waving, tub-thumping Scottishness. Therein lies a particular dilemma for sport. Political support may stem from a nationalist source that is essentially negative, anti-English and parochial, or it can rely on legitimate attempts to develop a distinctive brand of Scottish sport. This is compounded by the need to engage in global sports structures, whatever the political will.

DEVELOPMENTS BEFORE 1999

Historically there has been a cross-party consensus that government should not impose its will on sport. Successive Conservative governments from 1979 to 1997 showed no great interest in sport in Scotland. They were happy to transfer responsibility, genuinely 'at arm's length', to a quango – the Scottish Sports

ian thomson

Council (SSc, now known as sportscotland). Prior to devolution the ministerial team at the Scottish Office consisted of the Secretary of State for Scotland and four Under-Secretaries, all of whom spent most of their time at Westminster. Each had a full portfolio of duties, and sport was not a major responsibility. It was not expected that Ministers should be expert in this area. This was reflected within the civil service where the Sports Policy Unit in the Scottish Office comprised only three middle-ranking civil servants. Sport has been a very small part of larger departmental budgets and responsibilities. In 1999, when sport came under the heading of Health, its budget was £9.8m compared to the total Health budget of £4.6bn (Jarvie and Thomson, 1999: 90). All of this ensured that until 1999 the Scottish Sports Council had a fairly free rein over sports policy, albeit within a small budget. The one exception was in 1987 when Minister Michael Forsyth promoted a Team Sport Scotland programme.

Local government

In Scotland the legislative base for local authority provision of sport, recreation and leisure services imposed, and continues to impose, a statutory duty to make 'adequate provision' (Local Government (Scotland) Act, 2003). This can mean anything the authority chooses to do. It also means that the government cannot compel local authorities to invest in new facilities or upgrade existing ones. Without compulsion, provision has been uneven and uncoordinated across Scotland. The level of spend on leisure services per head of population by local authorities varies widely. In 2005/6 the average spend by the thirty-two authorities was £83 per head of population, ranging from £36 per head in Edinburgh to £136 in East Lothian (Audit Scotland, 2008: 11).

Between 1980 and 1995 there was steady growth in local authority investment in leisure and recreation as indicated by figures for net revenue expenditure, which grew from £87 million in 1980/1, to £120 million in 1985/6, £232 million in 1990/1, and £317 million in 1995/6 (Pringle and Cruttenden, 2001: 18). Gross capital expenditure also increased gradually, peaking at £81 million in 1995/6. However, investment was insufficient to maintain, much less enhance, existing facilities. A study of public swimming pools in Scotland concluded that the cost of upgrading them could amount to £540 million over the period 1999–2019 (Kit Campbell Associates, 2000: 15). The situation had not improved six years later according to a national audit of facilities commissioned by sportscotland (Kit Campbell Associates, 2006: 4). The audit covered 6,000 outdoor and indoor facilities, including swimming pools and golf, and found that the cost of upgrading and maintaining all of them over twenty-five years would be equivalent to £110 million annually.

The Conservative government in Westminster was deeply unpopular in Scotland throughout Mrs Thatcher's reign as Prime Minister. The Labour Party dominated local councils across Scotland, and the Strathclyde Regional Council accounted for nearly half of the population – it was almost an alternative government. The government decided to reorganise local government, getting rid of regional councils, changing it from a two-tier system of twelve large regional councils and fifty-three smaller district councils to a new system of twenty-nine unitary, all-purpose district councils and three islands authorities. This resulted in a wholesale restructuring of leisure services departments and staffs, which in turn led to a loss of experienced and knowledgeable senior staff. There was a slump in local authority spending on sport, particularly in capital expenditure, which fell from £81 million in 1995/6 to £44 million in 1999/2000. The National Lottery Act was passed in 1993, and the Scottish awards programme began in December 1994. The Scottish share of the UK Lottery Sports Fund was 8.9 per cent, equivalent to about £25 million per annum, initially restricted to capital projects. The injection of new funds from the Lottery came at the very moment when local government was cutting back on the kind of developments that might well have qualified for Lottery support.

The aspirations of *Sport 21*

The SSc (1994) had published *Achieving Excellence*, and proposed a system of classifying/carding athletes for grant aid, and raising the profile though major events, as had been done in Canada, while the Scottish government (1995) produced a White Paper focusing narrowly on school, college and university sport, in contradistinction to the breadth of *Sport, Raising the Game* from Westminster.

Then sportscotland undertook a wide national consultation process between 1996 and 1998 before publishing a national sports strategy, *Sport 21: Nothing Left to Chance* (SSc, 1998). *Sport 21* was issued just over a year before the first elections for the Scottish Parliament. It identified three visions for sport in Scotland:

1. A country where sport is more widely available to all.
2. A country where sporting talent is recognised and nurtured.
3. A country achieving and sustaining world-class performances.

Sport 21 set out four main challenges, each accompanied by ambitious targets. These were: the establishment of a Scottish Institute of Sport; the appointment of a National Physical Activity Task Force; publication of integrated strategic

124

local plans by every local authority; and improved management of governing bodies of sport. These seemed to be reasonable goals to be achieved within its 5-year timescale.

The new strategy included ambitious targets for new sports facilities. The projected requirements for community facilities were daunting, even if spread over ten years. Some proposals seemed unrealistic – for example, 160 community sports centres, 38 indoor bowling centres and 300 turf pitches. It was also hard to believe that Scotland, with more golf courses per head of population than any other country, needed another 47 courses or, taking account of the weather, that there was a need for another 900 outdoor tennis courts. In addition to these new facilities, the need to maintain and upgrade existing community facilities would have imposed an almost unbearable burden on local authorities.

The estimated cost of the strategy was £222 million, which included £175 million for facilities. It was proposed that local authorities should contribute £108 million over the following four years towards the capital costs, with the balance coming from the National Lottery and the commercial/voluntary sectors. Most of the revenue costs would have to be met by the Lottery and the Scottish Sports Council. If local authorities had not been experiencing an unprecedented period of financial stringency, the ambitious plans might well have come to fruition. Facility requirements were removed from all future versions of *Sport 21* and in due course a separate national/regional facilities plan was introduced.

DEVELOPMENTS SINCE 1999

The Scottish government's initial agenda for sport was set in May 1999 when senior members of the Labour and Liberal Democrat Parties met to hammer out an agenda for a coalition administration. They produced a 24-page document, *A Partnership for Scotland*, that made only brief references to sport, like offering support for the *Sport 21* strategy. It was intended that much of the work of the new Parliament would be done by sixteen standing committees, one of which was for Education, Culture and Sport. Over the next eight years sport was separated administratively from education, and was moved between the Environment Committee, the Tourism Committee, and finally the Health and Sport Committee. The contribution of physical education to sports development, if any, was not clarified. Indeed, when the Minister for Education set up a Physical Education Review Group in 2002, the chairman declined requests from members that the remit should include school sport. School sport would be left to School Sport Coordinators.

The low status of sport was demonstrated when only 14 of the 129 MSPs bothered to attend the first debate on the subject in the Scottish Parliament. They were outnumbered by those in both the press and public galleries. This did not prevent the Minister for Education, Sam Galbraith, from opening the debate with a very up-beat evaluation of sport. Echoing comments by his English counterparts, he referred to its contribution in solving health problems, giving young people positive lifestyles, and combating youth crime (Meetings of the Parliament, 9 November 2000). He announced a one-fifth increase in the annual grant to sportscotland, an extra £3 million a year for sport from the Lottery, £87 million from the New Opportunities Fund, plus £10 million to support the Ryder Cup bid. He asked sportscotland to use the additional funds for a major expansion of the Active Primary Schools programme and the secondary School Sports Coordinator programme. In addition, there would be a substantial investment in the 48 Social Inclusion Partnerships areas to increase the number of people participating in sport who lived in economic and social disadvantage.

In 1998, *Sport 21* had identified two main challenges to be achieved by the end of 1999. The first challenge had effectively already been met, namely that a Scottish Institute of Sport and a network of Area Institutes should be established. The £20 million budget for the Institute which had been identified in *Sport 21* was confirmed 1998–2002, met from the Lottery Fund. The Institute was linked to the UK Sports Institute. Scottish athletes who met entry standards came under the auspices of the latter, and frequently moved south to train at national centres like the velodrome in Manchester or the canoeing course at Nottingham. This ensured that at the elite sports level there was convergence of Scottish and British policies.

Nine sports were selected for the Scottish Institute programme, and within twelve months an Executive Director and national coaches had been appointed for seven of them, and Stirling University was selected as the site for the Institute's headquarters. The structure and location of six Area Institutes was also agreed. 116 athletes were inducted into the Institute and a Talented Athlete Programme provided support for them. Investment in the programme remained high in 1999 at £2.63 million, but it was much more focused. The number of athletes in the network programme was reduced from 705 in 1998/9 to 493 in 1999/2000. Of the Scottish team of 198 athletes for the 2002 Commonwealth Games in Manchester, 66 were Institute athletes, who accounted for 20 of the 29 medals won.

The second challenge was to appoint a National Physical Activity Task Force. During his term as Health Minister prior to devolution, Sam Galbraith (a neurosurgeon before entering politics) had presided over a White Paper,

Towards a Healthier Scotland (Scottish Executive, 1998). It was a coherent attack on health inequalities and it provided a focused programme of initiatives aimed at improving children's health. Ministers from six departments signed up to its proposals, one of which was that a Task Force should be set up to develop a National Physical Activity Strategy. It was appointed in June 2001 and reported in *Let's Make Scotland More Active* (Scottish Executive, 2003) making a powerful case for a permanent full-time physical activity team within the Scottish Executive, including a national coordinator. It recommended that all children should take part in at least two hours of PE a week, and that a group should be appointed to review the content and status of the subject. The Executive appointed a National Coordinator for physical activity, established a PE Review Group, and allocated £24 million for a substantial increase in the Active Primary Schools programme. Increasingly, health took over as the focus for the government's investment in physical activity and school sport.

In its first year of operation the Education Sport and Culture Committee was heavily committed to scrutinising a major Education Act, but time was found to report about school sport to the Parliament (Scottish Executive, 2000). It argued that sport had: positive effects on the personal qualities of young people, a social role in promoting social inclusion, and national benefits through elite level achievements. It recommended considering piloting Specialist Sports Colleges (SSCs), its author being impressed by results achieved at an SSc she had visited in Cheshire, particularly that sport was used creatively across the curriculum in all departments. She suggested the English model would be more suitable, being uneasy about attaching a unit catering for a few talented young athletes to a secondary school, as had happened at Bellahouston Academy in Glasgow, the only sports school in Scotland. Local authorities in Scotland are uneasy about any form of selection, and there is only one national School of Dance and only two for Music. The Scottish government did offer incentives for local authorities to pursue the recommendations.

The appearance of this report coincided with the publication of a comprehensive sport policy document from the Department for Culture Media and Sport, *A Sporting Future for All* (DCMS, 2000). This was where policies for PE and school sport in Scotland and England began to diverge. The Minister for Sport in England, Kate Hoey, described *Sporting Future* as 'the most significant sporting manifesto ever seen in the United Kingdom'. Over the next few years, the Blair government invested £1.5bn in a *Physical Education, School Sport and Club Links* strategy (*PESSCL*, now *PESSYS*) aimed at improving the quality of teaching, coaching, learning, and delivery in PE and school sport. It involved creating 400 SSCs, 400 primary–secondary School Sport Partnerships, 400 school sport Competition Managers, 3,200 secondary School Sport Coordinators and 18,000 primary or special school Link Teachers. It was a revolution in support for PE and school sport in English schools. There was no parallel investment in Scotland.

Failure of *Sport 21*

Shortly after Jack McConnell was elected as First Minister in 2001 it was announced that another review of *Sport 21* would begin, this time under a ministerial forum chaired by the Deputy Minister for Tourism Culture and Sport, Elaine Murray. The results would be published in 2003, and subsequent reviews would occur every four years in line with the cycle of Parliamentary elections. Murray discussed with sportscotland representatives the extent of the Scottish Executive's involvement, arguing that there could be benefits in terms of ownership and possibly increased resources if *Sport 21* became a government strategy. She gave in to arguments that it should continue as a strategy owned by Scottish sport, however, on the grounds that it would encourage sports bodies and political parties to take ownership of it (*Sport 21* Ministerial Forum, 8 May 2002, sportscotland).

The revised new strategy, *Sport 21 2003–2007: Shaping Scotland's Future* (sportscotland, 2003), set a key challenge, namely that 60% of adult Scots should take part in sport at least once a week by 2020. There were eleven specific targets to be achieved by 2007. Three years later, sportscotland had to admit that only one of these had been met (monitoring data, sportscotland, 2006). In an interview with Jack McConnell, a journalist suggested that the *Sport 21* targets were wildly optimistic: 'with the exception of those aged 45–64, the numbers participating in sport each week have actually fallen since 1998, in some cases dramatically' (*Scotland on Sunday*, 1 October 2006).

Some targets were not even close to being met. For example, the proportion of adults taking part each week, at 46%, was the same in 2005 as in 1994, but it was well adrift of the 2020 target. The proportion of 13–17 year olds taking part more than once a week fell from 79% in 1998 to 69% in 2005, and there had been a 5% drop in participation by 17–24 year olds. In view of the government's commitment to social inclusion, the failure to meet the target for those aged over 14 living in Social Inclusion Partnership Areas had been particularly disappointing: the very ambitious target was of 49% taking part each week, and the actual figure in 2005 was 39%. McConnell accepted that targets had not been met, but made a distinction between setting goals and implementing them: '*Sport 21* had all the right aims but did not have the clarity about who would deliver the actions that would lead to its implementation' (*Scotland on Sunday*, 1 October 2006).

When the 4-year targets for *Sport 21* were set, there was debate about the relative utility of national and area-based targets, but a lack of robust data. Consequently, the Scottish Executive provided funding for a large-scale survey of participation in 2003/4. This report (Coalter and Dowers, 2006) compared participation at least once a week in all thirty-two local authorities. The highest participation rate was 65% and the lowest, in Glasgow, was 34%. Thus some areas were already exceeding the national target of 60%. At the other end of the scale, six authorities in the West of Scotland, with a third of the Scottish population, had participation rates of 40% or less. Seeking explanations for these differences, the authors concluded that authorities with high levels of participation had a 'culture of participation'. They also concluded that sports development was much more important than facility development, and that the greatest differences between males and females tended to be in areas of generally low participation. The report demonstrated that a one-fit-for-all approach would not work. If it was to succeed, a national strategy would have to be aligned with regional and local strategies, and major on reducing the gender differences.

Growing centralisation

By this time it must have been obvious to McConnell that the existing structures in Scotland were not delivering government objectives for sport. There was a need for greater government investment and intervention in sports policies. One of his first official visits outside Scotland as First Minister was in 2002 to the Commonwealth Games in Manchester. He wrote afterwards that he was surprised to discover how little government money had gone into the Scottish teams over the years, and he set up an endowment fund of £2.5 million (*Sunday Herald* supplement 'Glasgow 2014', 12 March 2006). Interest from the fund is used to part-fund team training and preparation for and participation in Commonwealth Games and Commonwealth Youth Games. The combination of financial support from government and technical help from the Scottish Institute of Sport had a positive impact on Scottish results at the Games. Scotland improved from ninth in the medals table in 2002 to a best-ever placing of sixth in Melbourne in 2006, increasing the number of gold medals from six to eleven.

McConnell became a passionate advocate for a Scottish bid to host the Games in Glasgow in 2014. He persuaded Cabinet colleagues to underwrite four-fifths of the estimated public sector commitment of £298 million for the Games – the largest offer ever made by government to Scottish sport. He not only attended the 2006 Games, but was heavily engaged in lobbying support for the Scottish bid for 2014. On his return, McConnell announced his intention to hold a summit to engage those key to the development of Scottish sport. The First Minister's Sport Summit was held at Stirling University in September 2006.

Two months later, McConnell was reported to have come up with the idea of a dedicated Scottish University for Sport and he intended to present it for approval at the annual Scottish Labour Party conference later that month (*The Herald*, 4 November 2006). It was widely assumed that Stirling would be awarded the title. Some of the other Scottish universities took umbrage at the idea of a coronation for Stirling, and it was not until May 2008 that Alex Salmond could formally announce that Stirling would henceforth be known as Scotland's University for Sporting Excellence (Scottish Executive news release, 8 May 2008). The Scottish Funding Council allocated an initial £600,000 to Stirling to recognise its pre-eminent position in elite sport and education. The intention was that future generations of athletes and coaches would be able to study at a government-backed university in Scotland, instead of applying for scholarships abroad or training at centres in England such as Loughborough University.

A steering group was appointed to review *Sport 21* and to produce a national delivery plan for sport. Most unusually, it was chaired by a civil servant – head of the government's Sports Policy Unit – and as well as the Chief Executive of sportscotland, it included influential representatives from COSLA (the Chief Officers for Sport and Leisure Association), selected local authorities and governing bodies of sport. A draft document was approved by ministers in August and discussed at the First Minister's Sport Summit in September; the finished version was published in February 2007, to fit with the run-up to the elections for the Parliament in May. The Scottish Executive stamped its authority on the new strategy, *Reaching Higher* (Scottish Executive, 2007). This process was widely interpreted as a damning indictment of sportscotland. The earlier report of the Sport Summit included the following:

> While the strength of *Sport 21* lay in its ownership by Scottish sport, the absence of clear leadership had by 2005 become a weakness. Scottish Ministers believe that if we are to progress towards our sporting goals, leadership and direction is essential and that this should be the role of the Scottish Executive.
>
> (Scottish Executive, 2007)

This criticism was expanded in a briefing paper for the Enterprise and Culture Committee (March 2007) which identified the following weaknesses of previous attempts to implement *Sport 21*: failure to tackle major issues, a lack of clear leadership, a lack of clarity regarding the roles of stakeholders and a consequent absence of accountability, the setting of ambitious targets and a lack of monitoring systems.

Audit Scotland was set to conduct a review of how sport was organised and funded to deliver policy objectives in Scotland. It presented a depressing account of lack of coordination and insufficient investment (Audit Scotland, 2008), concluding that the country had a national strategy for sport, but with no clear links between local and national strategies. Targets for young people's participation were not being met, and adult participation was falling. Also, while some steps had been taken to adopt a strategic approach to facility planning following publication of the national audit, there was no associated strategy for nationwide investment. Public bodies spent more than £558 million a year on sport, of which local authorities were responsible for £511 million. The budget was falling behind what was needed. Over the three years from 2004 to 2007 local councils spent an annual average of £74 million on capital projects compared to the target of £110 million set by the national audit. The provision of facilities and services was fragmented, with neither any clear link between the government's national strategy for sport and councils' investment of money in local facilities and services across Scotland, nor any clear link between levels of spend and levels of participation. The expenditure by sportscotland was in line with the *Sport 21* priorities, namely £11.5m on widening opportunities, £6.6m on developing potential and £ 0.1m on achieving excellence.

While targets for increasing participation were not being met, the audit revealed indications of improvements in elite performance. On a more positive note, the report noted that Scotland's adult participation levels compared favourably with other European countries: the Eurobarometer 2004 survey collected data on fifteen European countries, including the UK which came sixth, with Scotland's performance similar to the UK as a whole.

A reconstructed sportscotland

The SNP had stated in every manifesto from 1997 that it would abolish sportscotland (SNP, 2007: 41) and the criticism in *Reaching Higher* provided some justification for that stance, but the new Minister for Communities and Sport had to explain publicly what would replace it. He had been persuaded through extensive consultation that there was a need for a national agency for sport. An earlier commitment to include sport in a Ministry for Arts and Leisure was dropped in 2007. In a statement to the Scottish Parliament ('Future of sportscotland', Scottish government press release, 9 January 2008) he announced that sportscotland would merge with the Scottish Institute of Sport under a single Board, a new structure claimed as fit for purpose and without the layers of bureaucracy of the previous one. Although he argued that the new body would be functionally different from sportscotland, it would retain the name as an established brand. The Institute would become the performance arm of sportscotland, reporting to its chief officer and the sportscotland Board, and this high-performance arm would remain in Stirling. Otherwise, the key to the new system was decentralisation. The headquarters of sportscotland would move to the new Clydeside indoor arena in Glasgow, and the staff would also be spread around four 'hubs' – in Aberdeen, Edinburgh, Glasgow, and Stirling – to assist with delivering frontline services. He argued that the decentralised structure would mean that staff in the hubs would be in a better position to work with the six Area Institutes of Sport.

As a consequence of the new structure, the chairs of sportscotland and the Institute were sacked. The new chair was Louise Martin, the Secretary of the Commonwealth Games Federation of Scotland, who had worked tirelessly to bring the Games to Scotland. The post of Executive Director of the Institute was downgraded to 'Director of High Performance' and the incumbent was appointed to the post. The SNP could certainly claim that they had tackled the issue of leadership, but they had not 'abolished' sportscotland.

Implementing *Reaching Higher*

The SNP government was committed to implementing *Reaching Higher*, even though it originated under the previous Labour administration. The strategy aimed to build on the 'legacy opportunities' available from the successful bids for the 2012 London Olympic Games and the 2014 Glasgow Commonwealth Games. It sought to deliver two key national outcomes, namely increasing participation and improving performance. It set out four interdependent national priorities to build and sustain a sporting infrastructure which would deliver the outcomes – improving the pathways, well-trained people, strong organisations and quality facilities. The identified barriers were familiar, and there was little new in the agenda for change. The fresh thinking was contained in the sections about delivery and roles and responsibilities.

At local level, responsibility should lie with local authorities and their community planning partners, who should provide leadership and accountability. The report made a strong plea for regional planning and delivery. Local authorities had shunned this idea, presumably because they feared another restructuring of local government. *Reaching Higher* emphasised the role of the six Area Institutes and the two pilot Regional Planning Partnerships in Central and Fife in strengthening the player pathway. It advocated more partnership working, including regional development strategies, concordats between partners, and joint funding for sport-specific programmes. At national level, national governing bodies were seen unequivocally as responsible for delivering their sports, but the Scottish Executive would provide leadership and support in delivering the overall strategy. There was a considerable expansion in the role of the Executive within wider government agencies, such as for health and education. There was a fresh emphasis on monitoring and evaluation at every level, and policy alignment across the Executive, and it was made clear that it would assume this responsibility: 'we will develop a framework which will allow everyone involved in developing and delivering sport to monitor and evaluate progress' (*Reaching Higher*, 2007: 54).

Soon after its publication, there was a wide-ranging discussion of *Reaching Higher* at a round table discussion by a relevant Parliamentary committee (Scottish Executive, Enterprise and Culture Committee, 13 March 2007), where more than one member pointed out that the strategy was essentially a traditional, supply-led approach, when what was needed was a demand-led one. The consensus of those invited to that meeting was that it was a useful roadmap for all agencies. There has been no indication of additional financial investment on the back of the strategy.

CONCLUSIONS

Scottish sport, like its English equivalent, has been under constant scrutiny during the last ten years. Plans have been laid and approved at various levels of government. The national agency for sport, sportscotland, has played a pivotal role in producing strategies for developing sport in Scotland, but like Sport England and the Australian Sports Commission, has failed to deliver increased participation. The ambitious targets it set out in *Sport 21* have almost all failed, and the idea of setting targets for specific groups has been abandoned. Consequently, the Scottish government has pulled together a more pragmatic plan restricted to achieving two national outcomes of increased participation and improved performance. From the available evidence, this will only succeed if local authorities can overcome persistent problems of low levels of participation in areas of social inequalities. Local authorities provide nine-tenths of the public investment in sport, but there are no clear links between their localised approaches and the government's national strategies for facilities and services. The government can only seek to persuade, but not compel local authorities to increase their investment in sports services. There are signs that staging the

Commonwealth Games in Glasgow in 2014 may provide a focus for a more coordinated approach to the development of sport.

There has been no coherent voice for sport at Cabinet level. It is not helpful when sport and PE are located in different departments of government. Jack McConnell was only able to achieve significant progress because he had six uninterrupted years as First Minister. It was he who created a fund to support Commonwealth Games athletes and teams, and it was he who delivered nearly £300 million of public funds for the Games in 2014. McConnell was also the person who conceived the idea of Scotland's University for Sporting Excellence at Stirling (Scottish Executive news release, 8 May 2008). Thus he was a significant champion and policy broker.

The SNP government elected in 2007 stopped short of its manifesto pledge to absorb sportscotland into a government department. Time will tell if the recent restructuring of sportscotland will be beneficial in the longer term to the development of sport. Many have argued that the strength of the Scottish Institute of Sport was that it did not allow its vision to be diluted, and was totally committed to world-class performance. No evidence was submitted by the minister to suggest that it will flourish within an organisation which frequently has been branded as bureaucratic. The decentralisation of much of sportscotland into regional hubs is another unproven initiative. The Area Institutes have been successful at nurturing and promoting talented regional standard athletes into national teams. The two regional pilot projects have not yet overcome the problems of uniting governing bodies of sport and developing regional versions of national plans. It is not yet clear how the sportscotland hubs will strengthen these two structures.

The overall conception of sports development has changed in the past ten years, and irrespective of which party is in government, it has to serve national outcomes, such as reducing childhood obesity, people leading healthier lives, improved well-being and building supportive communities. Such a conception of sport can accommodate nation-building and showcasing Scotland on the international stage. Sport has to be included in a cross-cutting agenda alongside other services. At local level it has to be an integral part of community planning. This is the rationale for public sector investment in sport in Scotland.

It had been feared that devolution would lead to divergence in social policies. However, there is much continuity of policy and purpose, and remarkably little change. It is only in PE and school sport that England has diverged significantly from Scotland. There is no equivalent of the *PESSCL* programme which has benefited from massive government investment. The SNP government has increased central control of sport, without as yet providing increased investment.

134

Sport has become even more nationalistic since 1999 – not necessarily in the sense of fuelling the idea of independence from the UK, but more to do with the idea of nation-building. The Commonwealth Games have become a focus for Scottish athletes and national pride. It has been possible for a First Minister to persuade colleagues to make the largest ever investment in sport in Scotland without reference to the United Kingdom Parliament.

REFERENCES

Adams, J. and Schmueker, K. (2005) *Devolution in Practice 2006*, London: Institute for Public Policy Research.

Audit Scotland (2008) *A Performance Overview of Sport in Scotland*, Edinburgh: Audit Scotland.

Bairner, A. (2001) *Sport, Nationalism and Globalisation*, Albany, NY: State University of New York.

Bath, R. (2006) A Question of Sport, *Scotland on Sunday*, 1 October, 26–7.

Bromley, C., Curtice, J., McCrone, D. and Park, A. (2006) *Has Devolution Delivered?* Edinburgh: Edinburgh University Press.

Coalter, F. and Dowers, S. (2006) *An Analysis of Regional Variations in Sports Participation in Scotland*, Research Report 105, Edinburgh: sportscotland.

Cooney, F. and Fotheringham, P. (2002) *UK Politics Today*, Fenwick: Pulse Publications.

Craig, C. (2003) *The Scots' Crisis of Confidence*, Edinburgh: Big Thinking.

Department for Culture Media and Sport (2000) *A Sporting Future for All*, London: DCMS.

Hassan, G. and Warhurst, C. (eds) (1999) *A Different Future*, Edinburgh: Centre for Scottish Public Policy.

Hassan, G. and Warhurst, C. (eds) (2000) *The New Scottish Politics*, Edinburgh: The Stationery Office.

Hassan, G. and Warhurst, C. (eds) (2002a) *Tomorrow's Scotland*, London: Lawrence & Wishart.

Hassan, G. and Warhurst, C. (eds) (2002b) *Anatomy of the New Scotland*, Edinburgh: Mainstream Publishing.

Jarvie, G. and Thomson, I. (1999) Sport, nationalism and the Scottish Parliament, *Scottish Affairs*, 27: 82–96.

Jarvie, G. (2006) *Sport, Culture and Society*, London: Routledge.

Kit Campbell Associates (2000) *The Ticking Time-bomb*, Edinburgh: sportscotland.

Kit Campbell Associates (2006) *National Audit of Sports Facilities: Summary Report*, Edinburgh: sportscotland.

Pickup, D. (1996) *Not Another Messiah: An Account of the Sports Council 1988–1993*, Edinburgh: Pentland Press.

Pringle, A. and Cruttenden, T. (2001) *Sport and Local Government in the New Scotland*, Research Report 79, Edinburgh: sportscotland.

Scottish Executive (1998) *Towards a Healthier Scotland: A White Paper on Health*, Edinburgh: Scottish Executive.

Scottish Executive (2000) (Education Culture and Sport Committee) *Sport in Schools*, Sp 91, Edinburgh: Scottish Executive.

Scottish Executive (2003) *Let's Make Scotland More Active: A Strategy for Physical Activity*, Edinburgh: Scottish Executive.

Scottish Executive (2007) *Reaching Higher: Building on the Success of* Sport 21, Edinburgh: Scottish Executive.

Scottish Government (1995) *Scotland's Sporting Future: A New Start*, Edinburgh: Scottish Government.

Scottish Government (1999) *A Partnership for Scotland*, Edinburgh: Scottish Government.

Scottish National Party (2007) *Manifesto*, Edinburgh: SNP.

Scottish Sports Council (1994) *Achieving Excellence*, Edinburgh: SSc.

Scottish Sports Council (1998) *Sport 21: Nothing Left to Chance*, Edinburgh: SSc.

sportscotland (2003) *Sport 21 2003–2007: Shaping Scotland's Future*, Edinburgh: sportscotland.

Taylor, B. (2002) *The Road to the Scottish Parliament*, Edinburgh: Edinburgh University Press.

PART C

CASE STUDIES OF SPORTS DEVELOPMENT PROCESSES AND OUTCOMES

CHAPTER 8

BUILDING A LEGACY FOR YOUTH AND COACHING

Champion Coaching on Merseyside

Barbara Bell

INTRODUCTON

This chapter outlines and analyses the impacts and outcomes of Champion Coaching (CC) in St Helens and Knowsley, which ran from 1996 to1999. One purpose is to demonstrate the complexity of sports development interventions and the problems of evaluating their impacts over time. It also reinforces the need, indicated in the Cabinet Office research review (Collins et al., 1999) and subsequently (Coalter, 2007) for clear, measurable objectives and indicators for programmes, so that their successes or failures can be clearly attributed and tracked.

As a programme intended to develop both opportunities for youth sport and coaching development, Champion Coaching also demonstrated potential conflicts between those responsible for designing and implementing programmes. Diverse objectives and the involvement of different stakeholders can result in outcomes differing from the original 'blueprint', or impacts unintended or unforeseen. Consensus is often assumed, and yet implementation can vary widely across different sites, as a result of varied interpretations of programme intentions.

This evaluation required examining the aims, objectives and theory behind CC, using a 'theory-based' or 'program logic' approach (Weiss, 1998). A brief summary of the research and its findings is preceded by a brief examination of Champion Coaching's aims and objectives and a short description of its key features. More details can be found in NCF publications (1992, 1993, 1997). The chapter goes on to outline the lessons learned from the Merseyside cases and to examine CC's legacy to its successors, the Active Sport programmes and the County Sport Partnerships, examined by Enoch, Lindeman and Conway, and Charlton in Chapters 3, 4 and 5.

139

The National Champion Coaching Scheme

Champion Coaching operated from 1991 to 1999 in England, Wales and Northern Ireland (Scotland having its own youth-oriented coaching programme). This made it one of the largest and longest-running sports development programmes in the UK. The scheme had a national template, though it was delivered locally by partnerships, usually led by local authorities. The then Chief Executive of the NCF, Geoff Cooke, described Champion Coaching as 'the success story of the decade' (NCF, 1997: 1). Initially a pilot of just twenty-four schemes, it grew to involve more than 145 local authorities, and over 8,500 coaches. In 1997/8, 14,000 children were taking part in sports courses offered across England and Wales (Table 8.1).

The mission of Champion Coaching was to:

> Promote quality-assured youth sport coaching for performance-motivated children, within a coordinated community structure.
>
> (NCF, 1996: 3)

Its purposes (NCF, 1996: 3) were to:

- recruit and develop coaches to work with junior performers;
- create quality coaching opportunities which enable keen and interested 11–16 year olds to become more confident and competent in sport;
- support the development of junior clubs and their coaches;
- raise the national and local profile of coaching and youth sport development.

The concept behind Champion Coaching was encapsulated by the slogan in the NCF's (1996) *Champion Coaching: The Guide* – 'Better coaching . . . better sport for young people'. By providing structured and good quality coaching for young people after school, the scheme aimed to close the gap to club-based sport through 'exit routes' or pathways into local clubs or county development squads. Crucially, being managed by the NCF, it was clearly seen as an important tool in meeting the development needs of coaches as well as of performers. NCF funding enabled coaches to be paid an agreed rate and to access training according to their needs, as indicated by 'profiling' meetings with the responsible SDO.

While CC was a major scheme, supported by the Sports Council through an annual grant to the NCF, its final costs are almost impossible to estimate. The NCF estimated that by 1995/6 various national agencies, including the

Table 8.1 Champion Coaching outputs, 1991–1999

	1991/2	1992/3	1993/4	1995/6	1996/7	1997/8*	1998/9*
Schemes	24	44	65	76	90	45	54
Local authorities	27	83	103	130	145	136	n/a
Sport programmes	110	450	553	700	850	600	464
Coaches involved	330	1,350	1,650	2,100	3,000	1,608	1,387

Source NCF, 1997.
Note *NCF annual reports.

Foundation for Sport and the Arts and the local authorities, had invested over £1.5m since 1992 (NCF, 1996); clearly, by the end of the scheme the final figure was much greater.

A particular convergence of work in different policy streams, in Physical Education, coaching and youth sport, CC's programme design was clearly influenced by the work of the *Coaching Matters* review (Sports Council, 1991). Also, as indicated by Collins (1995), CC's growth was mirrored by the increase in employment of Youth Sport Managers and Development Officers, many of whom had a coaching background. Despite its growth, the scheme was not adopted by all local authorities, which had to bid for funding to the NCF, against specific 'readiness criteria'. Not all were successful in their applications – for example, despite being one of the original twenty-four pilots in 1991, Cheshire County Council failed to achieve funding for subsequent programmes.

In 1996, Champion Coaching became absorbed into the new National Junior Sport Programme (NJSP), together with the BT TOPs programmes of the Youth Sport Trust. Relaunched and redesigned, the scheme gained impetus, support and funding, though it remained under the auspices of the NCF.

One of CC's important features was that local authorities selected the sports they wished to target for development from a list of seventeen sports. Selection was based on local audits and evaluations of development needs and resources (such as existing junior clubs). As a result of this local decision-making and interpretation, local schemes varied in sports, size and scope, a diversity recognised in *Recipes for Action* (NCF, 1992). This diversity contributed to challenges in evaluating scheme impacts.

Though the original report (NCF, 1992: 6), said CC should be 'available to all young people', there was little in the guidance for local schemes to meet specific equity targets. Those from deprived socio-economic groups were not mentioned in guidance on evaluation (NCF, 1996): local schemes were required to report only on the number and gender of participants and young people with a disability.

No national report was completed when CC was terminated in 1999, so evidence of success or lessons learned were never widely disseminated. In the review of coaching in 1999, culminating in *The UK Vision for Coaching* (UK Sport, 2001), a dearth of research into the impacts of 'quality coaching' was reported. Later, despite the size and significance of CC, it was not mentioned in the Coaching Task Force's report (CTF, 2002), nor in the review completed by MORI for sports coach UK (MORI, 2004).

OUTCOMES AND IMPACTS: THE PROBLEMS OF EVALUATING A MOVING TARGET

While evaluation of CC nationally was problematic, as a result of a lack of resources and agreed outcome measures, these issues were compounded locally by the diversity of implementation models and the speed of new policy initiatives. The aims, objectives, scope and outcomes of each local CC scheme depended on the priorities, concerns and inputs of the authorities and individuals responsible. This made any evaluation of outcomes much more complex and multifaceted, since without consistent baseline data on the selected measures, any improvements or benefits claimed are very difficult to trace. For this reason, selecting a small number of cases for evaluation appeared to be the only viable solution.

After some problems in identifying suitable cases and obtaining the necessary cooperation, St Helens and Knowsley were chosen (along with Flintshire, though these results are discussed elsewhere (Bell, 2004)). This enabled the author to do an in-depth analysis of the contexts, mechanisms and outcomes achieved, and it is hoped, a better understanding of 'what worked', for whom and in what circumstances. This is advocated in the 'realist' approach to evaluation of Pawson and Tilley (1997). Evaluation problems were further compounded by the lack of resources available for extensive before-and-after studies or cohort comparisons. Research was completed single-handedly, and there were significant personnel or management changes in the local authority departments concerned, which contributed to a loss of relevant data. Thus though only modest cohort studies were achieved, they were deemed worthwhile, given the significance of the sports development intervention they represented.

A growing demand for more robust evidence of long-term outcomes for sports development interventions, was highlighted by Collins (2003) and Coalter (2000, 2001). The lack of local baseline data for this study remained, with no possibility of a selecting a 'control' cohort to compare results with a comparable cohort of those in Knowsley and St Helens. Consequently, results from the National Survey of Young People (Sport England/MORI, 2000) were used for key indicators, like club membership, regular sports participation and the number of sports played in and outside school by participants.

Another comparison with young peoples' participation in performance-oriented courses was with a large-scale study of a county CC scheme in Nottinghamshire (Collins and Buller, 2000, 2003). Though this study found good exit routes after participation in CC, it had limited scope to explain some of its results or to trace longer-term outcomes. However, it found participation across that county was related to the level of deprivation of an area, indicating barriers to participation that were 'more structural than circumstantial' (Collins, 2003: 93). The coaching development aspects of the Nottingham scheme were not addressed, and there were few comparative studies of coach development, though Lyle *et al.* (1997) had considered recruitment and motivation of coaches and a Team Sport Scotland evaluation had considered some aspects of coach development (Allison and Taylor, 1997).

The mechanisms of CC were the essential aspects of the process as outlined by the NCF and subsequently adapted by the authorities. These comprised:

- an audit of local sports opportunities and resources for young people;
- a Youth Sport Manager responsible for CC;
- local sports-specific coordinating groups;
- based on the audit, the selection of sports for development;
- junior club development – helping clubs to establish a suitable exit route;
- coach development – the enhancement of individual coaches' knowledge and skills;
- coach profiling, through one-to-one meetings and support for training (scholarships);
- delivery of sport programmes, at relatively low cost to participants;
- development of a coaching community (leading to creation of a local coaching development plan);
- monitoring and evaluation, albeit on a limited range of factors, reported to NCF;
- governing body templates for each sport, identifying CC's role in player development.

The impacts of these mechanisms were investigated through a variety of methods, outlined below, but since the research was retrospective, they were partly determined by the data available, rather than what was ideal. A lack of clear, unambiguous and agreed outcome measures meant that each local authority had different systems for recording participant data and monitoring its scheme. As the NCF emphasised, output-oriented management information – the number of courses, coaches and participants – was what the authorities recorded and reported. According to Rossi et al. (1999) 'distal' outcomes are longer-term behavioural changes arising from an intervention, as opposed to such immediate outputs. 'Intermediate' outcomes of CC included the enjoyment level of children or improvements in coaches' knowledge or experience. Based on extensive experience, Collins et al. (1999) suggested that, ideally, up to seven years should be allowed before policy outcomes can be said to be sustained.

This is not a problem unique to sport – Sanderson (1998), Alcock et al. (1998) and Davies et al. (2000) noted the difficulties of many public programmes in obtaining evidence of 'what works'. Of course, outcomes can also be influenced by factors other than the scheme itself. In this case, membership of clubs and regular sport participation (at least once a month) from two to five years after the sports course were used as outcome measures for participants. Outcome measures for the coaches were the self-reported extent of youth and per-formance coaching since CC, involvement with CPD activities, as well as the retention of coaches by local authorities. The visible outcome of an increased profile and status for coaching was represented by the development and implementation of a local coaching strategy. Club membership also served as a measure of the effectiveness of local pathways in converting interest into performance-oriented engagement with sport, once CC ended.

RESEARCH METHODS AND APPROACHES

The research started late in 1999 and ran until 2003, utilising a social rather than a 'scientific' realist approach (Obare and Nichols, 2001) which recognised that the complex nature of the social aspects of the programmes was best understood by using both qualitative and quantitative methods. In this way, differences in the local contexts, the mechanisms employed and the results achieved in each borough were analysed to achieve as complete as possible an appraisal of the impacts (Bell, 2004).

The qualitative method of in-depth interviewing was useful in arriving at a better understanding of 'how' programmes worked, particularly in dynamic and changing situations over the elapsed period, considering the range of factors recognised as influencing the sport participation of young people (Kremer et al., 1997; de Knop et al., 1996).

The summary of the local outputs is shown in Table 8.2, from reports submitted by the local authorities to the NCF.

Table 8.2 Champion Coaching in St Helens and Knowsley, 1996–1999

	St Helens	Knowsley
Sports	Girls' football, hockey, netball, cricket, basketball, girls' rugby	Girls' football, netball, hockey, cricket, water polo, badminton, basketball
Sport programmes	17	21
Registrations*	336	752
Coaches	20	20

Note *Figures based on reports from Sports Development Units (incomplete data – estimated for 1999).

The methods used were:

1. survey of pupils and their parents, using questionnaires;
2. survey of coaches, using questionnaires;
3. interviews with coaches and SDOs;
4. visits to schools for interviews with teachers and group discussions with pupils.

Different approaches to registrations meant that sample groups differed in their composition, limiting direct comparisons – for example, it was possible to survey participants in St Helens for 1996–1999 but only for 1999 in Knowsley. A gap of two years between surveys in St Helens (late 2000) and Knowsley (2002), covered a similar time lapse, but may have contributed to a lower response from the latter. Surveys of coaches were completed in 2002 in both case study areas and of a sample from the national register of coaches. Follow-up interviews with coaches and SDOs and visits to schools took place in 2003.

1. Survey of pupils and parents

A questionnaire to participants and their parents was mailed to addresses supplied by the relevant authorities. Largely based on that used by Collins and Buller (2000), it was designed to allow comparisons on selected variables with their larger sample. Participants were asked about their enjoyment and benefits they perceived from their coaching, their participation in sport – in and out of school, their exit route from CC, and their experience of club membership. Parents were asked to rate aspects of CC about which they might be expected to have concerns, namely the organisation and accessibility of the courses, the information they received about progression opportunities for their children, and their contact with the coaches. Given the lapse of time and problems of missing, duplicate or incomplete registrations, response rates of 40% and 26% were considered acceptable for St Helens and Knowsley respectively.

2. Survey of coaches

A questionnaire was posted to all case study coaches for whom addresses were available, including a small group in Flintshire, and a national database sample of 105. Only 50 usable answers were received initially, a response of 34%. Additional responses were obtained by telephone with all who could be contacted, increasing the sample to 67, including a good proportion of the coaches in both Merseyside programmes (about 25%).

Coaches were asked to identify how their involvement with CC had impacted on the level and amount of their current coaching, their relationship with the local authorities, and their subsequent use of continuing professional development (CPD) services, particularly any provided by sports coach UK (scUK).

3. Interviews with coaches

Social and personal factors appeared to be central to coaching motivations (Lyle *et al.*, 1997; Lyle, 2002), so they were explored through the interviews both in person and on the telephone. In interviews lasting from 30 minutes to an hour, five coaches from Knowsley and four from St Helens, across six sports, were interviewed face to face, in a semi-structured format based on the mail questionnaire, but allowing in-depth examination of concepts and amplification of key points. A further five Merseyside coaches were contacted in more limited telephone interviews. Interviews were taped and transcribed, or notes taken, if taping was impractical or objected to.

The main themes explored with coaches were:

- CC's impact on the level and volume of coaching they subsequently did;
- the impact of paid employment as a coach and their subsequent careers;
- attitudes to and influences on their professional development.

Interviews were also conducted with SDOs in each local authority, the Acting Director of the Merseysport Partnership (who had been the St Helens SDO), the Regional Coaching Development Officer of SCUK, the Adviser for PE in St Helens, and the PE Curriculum Leaders group in Knowsley.

4. Visits to schools and group interviews

Visits to schools in both areas followed up issues raised in the participants' questionnaires, and children and teachers were interviewed. Group interviews focused on what young people in the same age groups (Years 10 and 11) felt about local sporting opportunities, and examined their perceptions of current pathways for people interested in sport. Teachers were asked about their perceptions and recollections of CC, and their current relationships with SD units.

'Low' and 'high' referring schools were identified by analysing the registrations provided by the local authorities, though there were some problems in schools agreeing to take part. The size and composition of the groups varied, but they included 74 children and two staff in two schools in St Helens and 57 children and four staff in three schools in Knowsley.

BRIDGING GAPS? THE IMPACTS ON PARTICIPANTS AND PATHWAYS

The characteristics of the samples from each borough were slightly different, as shown in Tables 8.3 and 8.4. However, when compared to all registrations, these groups were considered representative by gender and sport. Children had all completed their CC courses between one and four years earlier. As Knowsley registrants were from one year only, the levels of repeat registrations could not be determined, except for some children who attended more than one sport. It was clear that in St Helens, the sample included several children who attended each course over the three years that it operated. They had progressed in age groups as the coaches had changed the target groups for coaching and they had developed their own expertise.

As in Nottinghamshire, there was clear evidence that CC was successful in providing enjoyable and worthwhile courses for young people. Children said they enjoyed their course – 94% in Knowsley and 90% in St Helens, with similar

Table 8.3 Characteristics of the participant samples

	St Helens (n = 78)	Knowsley (n = 54)
Mean age	15.7 years	14.8 years
Girls	70%	59%
Boys	30%	41%

Table 8.4 Champion Coaching courses attended

	St Helens (n = 77)	Knowsley (n = 53*)
Hockey	25	1
Netball	14	17
Cricket	12	8
Basketball	8	10
Girls soccer	21	10
Badminton	n/a	10
TOTAL	80	56

Note *1 missing case; about 6% took part in more than one course in both schemes.

proportions stating that they had benefited from their courses. Children were likely to identify that improving performance and learning more skills was the thing they most enjoyed. This confirmed that CC courses were perceived as appropriate and of good quality for performance-oriented children. Encouraging rates of club membership and regular sports participation in the respondents was also found, as shown in Table 8.5.

The pattern of club membership showed no clear relationship to the time elapsed, or the particular course, though girls were less likely to be club members

Table 8.5 Current club membership

Currently member of a club?	St Helens (n = 74)	Knowsley (n = 53)	Sport England national survey*
Yes	70%	58%	46%
No	30%	42%	54%
Mean time since course	2.0 years	2.2 years	n/a

Note *Sport England/MORI, 2000; club membership aged under 16.

Table 8.6 Current rates of club membership, by gender

Scheme	% of girls	% of boys	% of girls and boys
St Helens (n = 74)	66	81	70
Knowsley** (n = 53)	47	76	59
Sport England national survey*	36	56	46

Notes *National average for all (boys and girls) aged under 16 (Sport England/MORI, 2000); **Pearson Chi-Sq 0.291, signif. at 0.05.

than boys in Knowsley. As shown in Table 8.6, rates of club membership were still higher than the England average for both groups of girls and boys. It must be recognised, however, that children were selected to take part or referred to the courses because they were interested (mostly by teachers) and in the case of Knowsley, over 70% were already in some form of club at school. So, higher rates of club membership might be expected than for 'typical' 15–16 year olds. Participants enjoyed a range of exit routes as can be seen in Figure 8.1.

A key exit route for these schemes was the well-established Merseyside Youth Games (MYG). This was part of a deliberate and planned approach of integrating CC into existing youth sport opportunities through district-based training and county-based competition. This engagement allowed young people to extend their sport involvement beyond the CC courses, and may have contributed to the extent of sustained participation and club-based sport later. As confirmed in later discussions, whether young people joined a club was clearly not due solely to their CC experiences. Essentially, children relied on clubs being accessible and this was clearly not always the case, particularly in Knowsley.

But, the clubs that young people joined often met 'youth-friendly' criteria (de Knop et al., 1994). As shown in Table 8.7, these were: a welcome from the club, an active junior section, organised matches and competitions, friendly coaches and leaders, and low fees and charges. However, only a minority of participants indicated that they had found out about their club from the CC course, as displayed in Table 8.8.

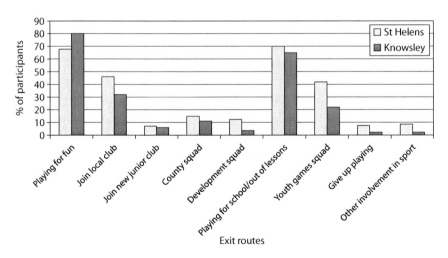

Figure 8.1 Exit routes from Champion Coaching in Knowsley and St Helens

Table 8.7 Sports club characteristics

What the club did (% indicating 'yes')	Knowsley (n = 27)	St Helens (n = 26)
Had organised matches/competitions?	78	82
Welcomed you into the club?	67	75
Had low fees?	56	71
Had friendly coaches and leaders?	78	71
Had a junior section?	30	50

Table 8.8 How children found out about the club

Source (%)	St Helens (n = 55)	Knowsley (n = 34)
Friend	41	32
Teacher	24	44
CC course	21	21
Parent	5	3
Already a member	3	0
Advertisement	3	0
Other	3	0

This reproduced the findings of Collins and Buller (2000), who discovered that the level of information to children about opportunities to follow CC was generally poor, and how children understood and acted on it varied.

Parents' views and impacts on pathways

Parents rated characteristics of the courses on a scale from 1 (poor) to 5 (excellent). The highest mean score was for the enjoyment of the children and the lowest was for the coaches' contact with parents. This is also consistent with Collins and Buller's (2000) findings and appears to show that CC tended to neglect communication with parents by coaches. The small number of children who had found out about their club from their parents, as shown in Table 8.8, could indicate that these children were from families where sports club membership was not traditional.

High parental ratings were not apparently influential on whether children went on to join a club. Due to the small samples, there was little pattern to the ratings of parents of the sports concerned.

150

Table 8.9 Parents' ratings of Champion Coaching courses

Score, on a scale from 1 (poor) to 5 (excellent)	St Helens (n = 78)		Knowsley (n = 53)	
	Mean	SD	Mean	SD
Standard of coaching	3.89	1.04	4.18	0.89
Organisation of sessions	4.04	1.18	3.98	1.01
Parental contact by coach	2.87	1.87	3.06	1.32
Administration by centre	3.38	1.75	3.30	1.42
Enjoyment of child	4.55	1.18	4.60	0.64
Cost of the course	4.05	1.42	3.90	1.47
Information about progression	3.06	1.66	3.24	1.33
Accessibility of the venue	4.21	1.26	4.06	1.10

Geography and participation

The distribution of children showed clusters in certain parts of both boroughs, reflecting the venues, schools and population characteristics. Postcodes from home addresses were converted to wards, to see if there was any relationship to the degree of social deprivation, as measured by ward scores for the Index of Multiple Deprivation (DETR, 2000). The higher this score, the more deprived the ward. Figures 8.2 and 8.3 show that in Knowsley some of the most deprived wards achieved higher participation rates than wards in St Helens. This participation was proportional to the 2001 population aged under 16 in the most deprived wards, as shown in Table 8.10. Most significantly, in Knowsley these wards are amongst the most deprived in England. Analysis of participant postcodes also showed some overlap of registrations between the boroughs, with some courses clearly accessible to children from the neighbouring authorities, including some from deprived wards in Liverpool. This was a positive impact of cross-boundary working and planning.

As highlighted by the schools visits, transport and mobility remains an issue for young people, still too young to travel extensively alone. Without adequate public transport, young people rely heavily on parents' willingness and ability to chauffeur them to sport opportunities. In Knowsley, courses were provided at both ends of the borough, to enable easier access, or transport was provided from schools to alleviate the pressure on parents. This may account for a more even spread of enrolments across Knowsley wards. The St Helens distribution was clearly skewed to its more affluent wards, despite many venues being centrally located.

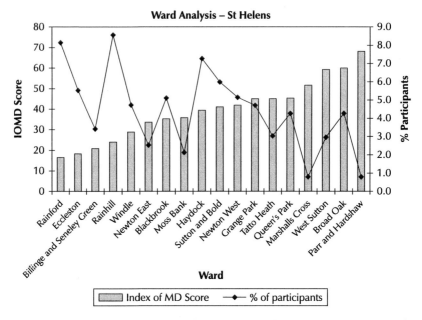

Figure 8.2 Ward deprivation and Champion Coaching participants in St Helens

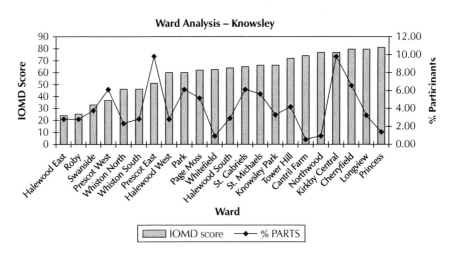

Figure 8.3 Ward deprivation and Champion Coaching participants in Knowsley

Table 8.10 Participants and populations compared

	St Helens	Knowsley
% of population aged 5–16 living in most deprived wards*	26.5	20.8
% of CC participants living in most deprived wards	13.3	21.1

Note *Population data from 2001 Census.

The views of teachers and children on pathways and opportunities

Since more than three years had elapsed since the end of CC, it was difficult to find school staff who had been directly involved. However, some were able to give their views on the current relationship with the SD Unit, on links established with clubs, or on opportunities available.

In low-referral schools in both boroughs, Year 10 and 11 children's attitudes towards sport after school ranged from very positive to very negative. Children knew of local opportunities but were often not interested in taking them up, and very few were in clubs or any organised sports, in or out of school. These opportunities were also in sports not involved in CC, like boxing, dancing or boys football. Girls were often more critical than boys of local opportunities. Many children from both high and low referral schools cited transport and distance as being big factors in whether or not they took part, even if they were interested in the sport on offer. Children, whether active or not, blamed lack of involvement in sport on a lack of interest or motivation, though they also criticised the standard of the facilities available to them.

The main role fulfilled by 'low referral' schools was to communicate the sports opportunities through distributing information on noticeboards or in assemblies, but they provided little else by way of direct links to clubs. Some low referral schools were trying to do more, but were hampered by poor facilities or lack of time. Teachers also pointed to problems, not confined to low-referral schools, of getting children to after-school clubs or competitions outside school hours where both parents were working, or unable to provide transport.

Schools' relationship with the SD Unit also varied: high-referral schools had regular meetings with SD staff, discussing plans and joint initiatives. But success appeared to vary, depending on the priority afforded to links with community sport by the school and the enthusiasm of individual teachers. The notion that only affluent areas got involved with CC could be refuted by looking at the referrals from Knowsley schools, several of which were in very deprived wards.

In Knowsley, communications were enhanced by regular meetings of the PE Curriculum Leaders group, attended by SD Unit staff, which gave both interests a chance to highlight any issues or concerns, either with the schools present or through minutes of meetings. Though there was no equivalent group in St Helens, the SD Unit was very proactive in planning and working with the Education Department on borough-wide approaches or specific projects (Sports Development, Leisure and Education were in one Department after a reorganisation in 1999). The St Helens schools with highest referral rates in CC continued to be heavily involved in council-led initiatives, but others were also clearly doing more joint schemes than in 1999. One school with only moderate referrals to CC had become a Specialist Sports College, and with new impetus to after-school sport, involvement with the SDU was now clearly very important to staff and much more fruitful in offering opportunities to pupils.

A positive aspect of CC noted by many teachers was the opportunity it gave to children who had been unused to such a level of attention from coaches, or in a sport the school could not offer to the same level. There was no indication from any teachers of any philosophical objections to CC or its selection process, as suggested by earlier research (Edwards, 1993). Concerns about elitism were raised by the PE adviser, but based on the teacher interviews, CC was not seen as elitist. On the contrary, teachers indicated it was good experience for the children who had taken part.

The relatively poor state of school sports facilities was particularly striking, except for Sport Colleges, where there had been recent refurbishment. Low-referral schools, despite being designated as 'community sports facilities' were particularly poor in both boroughs. This cannot help attract children seeking to take part in after-school activity, an issue raised by children in all schools. Sport and PE in low-referral schools were perceived to have lower priority than other subjects, despite the efforts of staff. In contrast, high-referral schools, even if they had problems with their facilities, gave PE a high priority and encouraged the provision of a range of after-school participation opportunities.

The lack of referrals from some schools was attributed to various factors:

- a combination of poor communication and lack of consultation from the SD Unit to school in CC's planning phase;
- lack of interest by children in the sports offered;
- selection of venues and timing of courses making access more difficult;
- lack of enthusiasm by some staff to actively promote external courses perceived to compete with existing after-school programmes or commitments.

154

THE LEGACY AND IMPACTS ON COACHING AND COACHES

The survey of coaches provided some background against which to examine the experiences and impacts of the coaches in the case studies. Most (59%) of the respondents were Head Coaches, who had been involved with CC from one to five years. The majority, therefore, were well qualified and experienced. Only 23% were assistant coaches, who may have been gaining their first experience of coaching young people. As shown in Figure 8.4, 93% were already coaching young people, and 57% had taken the opportunity to gain an additional coaching award as a result of being involved with CC. Only 19% of respondents were teachers, though slightly more indicated that they had delivered coaching in schools since their CC involvement.

Only 43% reported receiving scholarship support, suggesting that this mechanism was not as widely used by local authorities as the NCF recommended. In fact, none of the Knowsley or St Helens respondents recalled having the scholarship support they had in fact received, according to the SDOs' reports to the NCF. This suggested responses were affected by lack of recall or awareness that their training had been subsidised.

The impacts of CC on their subsequent work varied, as Table 8.11 shows. Though the amount of paid work seemed to have reduced, few coaches were doing less coaching, and many coaches were doing more, particularly work with young people.

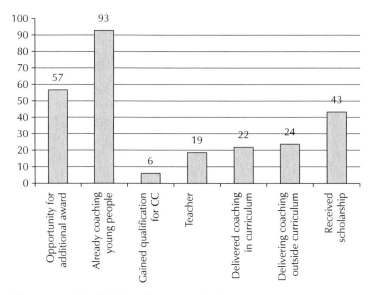

Figure 8.4 Key findings from coaches' survey

Table 8.11 Exit routes for coaches from Champion Coaching in Knowsley and St Helens

Variable	Less (%)	Same (%)	More (%)	n/a (%)
Time spent coaching (n = 64)	11	42	47	0
Work with young people (n = 65)	14	42	42	2
Performance-oriented coaching (n = 53)	13	36	38	13
Club involvement (n = 60)	12	53	32	3
Paid work as a coach (n = 62)	23	29	37	11

Impacts on subsequent professional development were mixed, with only one in three coaches having experienced updates or training from their governing bodies after CC (Figure 8.5).

One aspect of good practice that had clearly not continued was the annual profile meeting, as only 14% had met with their SDO since CC ended. As shown in Figure 8.6, just over half of the coaches felt they were more effective as a result of CC. 26% of the respondents were involved in an Active Sport programme, and 53% were members of Sport coach UK. Despite the emphasis on coach development by the local authorities and the NCF, the aspect of the CC scheme

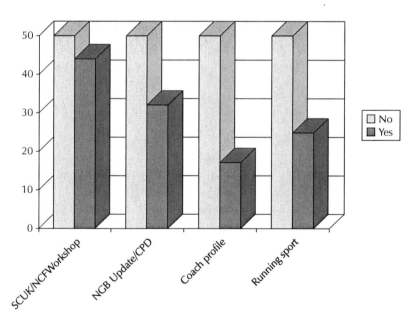

Figure 8.5 Coaches' Continuous Professional Development since Champion Coaching

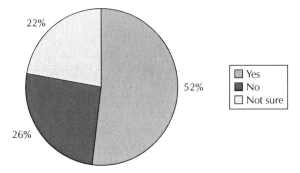

22%

52%

26%

Yes
No
Not sure

Figure 8.6 Improved coach effectiveness as a result of Champion Coaching

that coaches thought most valuable was the development of youth sport opportunities, and the provision of coaching for young people.

Coaches and their experiences – key findings from coach interviews

The coaches' interviews revealed interesting contrasts and issues that reinforced the difficulties of demonstrating sustainable outcomes from sports development initiatives. Although CC sought to embody 'good practice' in coach management and development, there was some evidence in the survey, reinforced in interviews, of what Rossi et al. (1999) termed 'process failure' – that is, not all the coaches experienced the CC process in the same way, or how it was intended to operate. On the other hand, there were coaches who had a very positive experience, very much according to NCF guidelines, but were no longer involved in coaching for reasons nothing to do with CC.

Coaches also varied in how they saw coaching in relation to their lives and careers. For some, usually the head coaches, it was absolutely central and very important, even if not their career. For others, often the assistant coaches, it was simply a phase, a brief interlude, something to do to help out at their club or school, or part of their own education (degree). They didn't see themselves as a 'coach', more of a 'helper', so in the long term, training and development was of less importance:

> Getting access to awards, and all that, wasn't really relevant to me at the time . . . I was busy enough.
>
> (Girls' football coach, St Helens)

At the other extreme, several coaches were very committed and heavily involved, and had found the CC experience to be an important phase in their development. One of the St Helens coaches had become a full-time, self-employed coach since CC ended. Although this was not directly attributed to his experience, working in CC was undoubtedly an important catalyst to a career change, due to the help with training and encouragement from the SDO:

> What helped with putting me on courses . . . different things . . . got me pushed on to the next level . . . don't remember getting any funding for it as such, but I did sort of get pushed in the right direction. It was all done through [St Helens SDO] and [Knowsley SDO] and the [Cricket] CDO got involved, to make sure I got on the right course.
>
> (Cricket coach, St Helens and Knowsley)

One of the less encouraging things to emerge from the interviews was the lack of support coaches received once CC finished. Though the situation varied between sports, governing bodies were heavily criticised by many coaches for offering little or no support, encouragement or guidance. The most criticised, particularly by female coaches, were hockey, netball and football. Indeed, most coaches, except some in voluntary positions with their governing body, had had no personal contact at all since, or even during the CC scheme. More positively, most coaches pointed out the satisfaction experienced through working with the young people – particularly those who had done only limited or ad hoc work previously. Working to well-defined and structured NGB development schemes (even if they didn't always follow them) had helped develop experience and confidence.

The SDOs were often praised by the coaches for their personal support during and immediately after the scheme, as they offered positive reinforcement and in some instances, encouraged them to go further in coaching. Indicative of the problems of maintaining a coaching workforce once funding and priorities changed, was that about one in five coaches was uncontactable, due to out-of-date or incomplete records. An example of positive support was from another cricket coach in Knowsley:

> I've got a really good relationship with Sports Development and they've helped me a lot, and we did talk about it [his development] a bit and I do a bit of work with them these days . . . I'm on the development group for Knowsley . . . so I see them quite a bit . . . I mean they've advised me and I've only got good words to say about Knowsley.
>
> (Cricket coach, Knowsley)

He was the only coach interviewed currently employed directly as a coach by the borough SD Unit concerned. Several others were still coaching in their sport, but in a voluntary capacity, or were doing other coaching not paid for by the borough. For some this was because their sport was not selected for Active Sport; for others it appeared that they were simply no longer required by the SDOs, though they had not been informed why. The SDOs indicated that other coaches from CC were still being used where possible, but they were either unavailable, uncontactable or declined an interview.

THE LEGACY OF CHAMPION COACHING

More recent youth sport initiatives – such as Active Sport, the work of the Coaching Task Force and the emergence of Youth Sport Trust-led PE, School Sport and Club links strategies – have significantly changed the environment for coaching and development work with young people of school age. New funding streams, new organisational structures and partnerships, and a renewed impetus for after-school coaching and club links have emerged in the new strategy for PE and after-school sport (DES, 2003), renamed the *Physical Education and Sport Strategy for Young People (PESSYP)* (YST/SE, 2008), and slightly extended. Meanwhile, the implementation of the Coaching Task Force recommendations (CTF, 2002) have also seen significant changes in the approach to developing coaches and their employment in the youth sector. So, what is the answer to the central question posed by this analysis – Did CC develop a legacy for both youth and coaches? The response to this can be summarised in three key areas – people, processes and practice.

First, in people or the impacts on individuals, the above results suggest successful impacts for young participants – through increased rates of club membership and regular sports participation. Young people were clearly enabled through CC mechanisms to remain engaged in organised and regular sport participation, which was more likely to be sustained.

The increase in confidence and expertise reported by coaches was very important, though what this represented as a legacy in more active and effective coaches is less clear. Various other factors influenced whether or not coaches have continued to coach and at what level, over which CC had no influence. Similarly, though some coaches were developed, the ensuing gap before the Active Sport systems were fully developed meant that some coaches lost momentum in their development, so were no longer as engaged as previously.

Second, in terms of the process of sports development, an extensive network of opportunities and exit routes, linked to the Youth Games in particular, may have emerged at the time of CC, but in many of these selected sports it is difficult to see that any were sustained. Gains made in opportunities for youth in clubs were not always sustained because there was insufficient time to become established, before funding was withdrawn as attention shifted to other priorities. School–club links and after-school work in general has been heavily influenced by subsequent schemes and funding streams, but CC nevertheless contributed to highlighting where gaps and deficiencies remained. Gains were more clearly sustained in areas with existing sporting capital and established infrastructure, and where NGBs had sufficient resources to continue their development work, even if Active Sport was no longer supporting their sport directly.

Processes for coach and club development had benefited from the use of countywide approaches through Merseysport partnership working. The coaching development strategy on Merseyside was directly linked to the growth of coaching experience, not only in these boroughs, but across the county. This is likely to have been replicated across the areas involved in CC, due to the links with NCF, and later sports coach UK planning and support.

And finally, in practice, perhaps one of the most important legacies of CC is the development of expertise by the boroughs' SD officers, in managing these processes and implementing complex schemes. This can clearly be seen in Merseyside, where SD officers with experience of working on CC continued to contribute to the implementation of Active Sport and other school sport initiatives, building on the good practice which emerged through CC implementation.

Many of the current systems and procedures for coach development and management are legacies of CC – though with experience, changes have been made. Though Active Sport was a more complex and all-encompassing scheme than CC, they shared many similarities:

- referral of young people by schools and a selection process for entering coaching programmes at different levels;
- sports-specific development groups to advise on local implementation;
- promotion of a coach development strategy;
- phased selection of specific sports for development;
- assistance to clubs to develop junior sport opportunities.

Lessons from Champion Coaching and the emerging policy in youth and coaching

As indicated at the outset, though the youth and coaching objectives of CC may have appeared compatible, they contained potential for conflict and this affected the results achieved. In St Helens a more explicit emphasis on coach development resulted in more repeat registrations and a focus on a narrower range of sports and courses. Effective pathways were established by integration with existing development programmes, like the MYG. In coach development, despite successes at the time, CC did not always achieve the long-term development of individual coaching careers, as personal factors also influenced whether coaches continued to coach and develop, and both individual and sporting priorities inevitably changed over time.

Knowsley's approach of targeting schools, 'pay as you go' pricing and offering courses district-wide was successful in recruiting children from deprived areas. But there were similar problems in maintaining the development of coaches and pathways once CC funding ended. Knowsley's lack of local clubs limited its ability to maintain pathways for young people, though now this is gradually being improved. Knowsley was also successful in achieving significant funding in improving school sport facilities through the New Opportunities Lottery programme.

For developing coaches, the important factors appear to be long term, and individual contact with SDOs and local authorities, together with the support of the sport governing body, which was often missing. An emphasis on often expensive and time-consuming qualifications or courses does not necessarily lead to more effective or active coaches, as reinforced by recent research on coaches for sports coach UK (MORI, 2004). Often, changes or improvements to coaching practice or knowledge are assumed, rather than monitored or measured, once coaches return to their coaching positions. More direct proactive approaches, which take into account individual needs, differences and personal circumstances of coaches, may be more appropriate, though they can be costly in staff resources and difficult to sustain without NGB cooperation. There has clearly been some confusion over where the responsibility lies for such support. Recent developments in the North West of an online coaching registration and deployment service may yet demonstrate a more coach-friendly approach.

Therefore, while announcements of increased funding to support a coach development role (DCMS, 2003) seem geared to closing this gap, only time will tell whether this funding was sufficient when spread across forty-five county partnerships, eleven sports and over 3,000 'new' community coaches and existing volunteers. Subsequently, sports coach UK have instigated a more extensive research-led approach to the implementation of the new Coaching Framework and Coaching Certificate. However, monitoring and supporting individual coaches in their long-term development, whether as full-time workers or volunteers will be crucial to the success of similar schemes. Building on the baseline data provided by MORI will be a key area of future research.

Clearly, the lessons learned in practice by both the SDOs and coaches involved in CC were invaluable in developing both competence and confidence. Communication and planning with schools, targeting and management information systems have all improved, as CC highlighted specific needs. Targeting participants, for example, was recognised as even more important by the SDOs, when Best Value and other reviews of performance demanded results linked to corporate or societal objectives (Audit Commission, 2002). Perhaps most tellingly, more recently set targets related to youth sport are explicit in the need to address the groups most likely to be not participating and to work in more appropriate ways with those who are already showing some interest and aptitude for sport (Sport England, 2004).

A key lesson from CC is the need to have sport-specific development groups driving the opportunities for both coaches *and* participants, to ensure that limited resources are effectively implemented and appropriately targeted. Gaps in opportunities for young people will remain, however, where there continue to be problems affecting the sustainability of clubs – which may not be 'youth-friendly'. Clearly SD units are not resourced to overcome long-term and deep-rooted deficiencies in local sporting infrastructures, or make up for the limited human and financial resources in many clubs.

Therefore, though CC represented a major step forward in developing systems for both youth and coaching, it is clear that SD units cannot alone solve all the problems relating to youth sport and coaching in any given area. CC was undoubtedly a major catalyst for youth and coaching work in local authorities, but a 3-year implementation programme was not long enough for its legacy to be sustained in these Merseyside boroughs.

It remains to be seen whether AS, and the CSPs, supported by Lottery funding, when evaluated, will eventually demonstrate more success. They have been under great pressure to develop new structures since the end of Active Sport funding, with redesigning of their remit in relation to youth in particular – as the Youth Sport Trust developed more influence on programmes for school-age children, both in and out of schools. Local authorities also now have to contend with the extension of after-school sport in the new '5-hour offer' announced by Gordon Brown in 2007 (DCMS, 2007). School Sport Partnerships now cover most schools, with the government claiming its objective for participation levels has been met, with over 85% of children receiving at least 2 hours of PE and sport a week (DCSF, 2007). In relation to more performance-oriented children, clubs and coaching, a new set of targets and strategies has been set for Sport England, to support the 5-hour offer, and to reduce drop-out, as well as contributing to enhanced talent identification systems for young people (Sport England, 2008). Alongside this, SCUK is working hard to implement a new, more professional coaching framework, with more funding directed to employ extra paid coaches, rather than relying on enthusiastic volunteers.

All these developments of policy point to a continued focus on improving sporting opportunity and the quality of young people's sport experiences. There remains however, an apparent lack of attention to monitoring both the quality and the equality of such experiences, even though underrepresented groups are now more closely targeted (Sport England, 2004, 2008). Rather than tracking participants along their sporting pathways, there remains an emphasis on targeting and counting the proportion of young people taking part at a club.

Despite the newer programmes, Champion Coaching remains the only sport development programme which employed significant numbers of coaches (over 3,000), and operated over a sufficiently long period to permit (but *not* officially commission) evaluation of its overall impact or longer-term outcomes. More research, particularly longitudinal, is needed into the impact of club-based participation on the sports careers of young people into adulthood. For coaches and coaching, we also need to track the progress since the implementation of the Coaching Task Force recommendations, of the Active Sport coaches and those employed in communities, to see whether these mechanisms have had the desired impacts on coach retention and effectiveness. Thus over time, practice in sports development can be better informed through better evidence and greater understanding of 'what works' in different contexts.

REFERENCES

Alcock, P., Barnes, C., Craig, G., Harvey, A. and Pearson, S. (1998) *What Counts: What Works? Evaluating Anti-poverty and Social Inclusion Work in Local Government*, Sheffield: Sheffield Hallam University/Improvement and Development Agency.

Allison, M. and Taylor, J. (1997) *Team Sport Scotland 1994–97 Evaluation*, Research Report 53, Edinburgh: Scottish Sports Council.

Audit Commission (2002) *St Helens MBC, Sport and Leisure Best Value Review*, London: Audit Commission.

Bell, B. (2004) An evaluation of the impact of Champion Coaching on youth sport and coaching, unpublished Ph.D., Loughborough: Loughborough University.

Coaching Task Force (2002) *The Report of the Coaching Task Force*, London: Department for Culture Media and Sport.

Coalter, F. (2000) Managing for outcomes, unpublished presentation at NW Sport Federation Conference, Wigan, 12 September.

Coalter, F. (2001) *Raising the Potential of Cultural Services: Making a Difference to the Quality of Life*, London: Local Government Association.

Coalter, F. (2007) *A Wider Social Role for Sport: Who's Keeping the Score?* London: Routledge.

Collins, M.F. (1995) *Sports Development Locally and Regionally,* Reading: Sports Council/Institute of Leisure and Amenity Management.

Collins, M.F. (2003) *Sport and Social Exclusion,* London: Routledge.

Collins, M.F. and Buller, J. (2000) Bridging the post-school institutional gap: evaluating Champion Coaching in Nottinghamshire, *Managing Leisure*, 5: 200–21.

Collins, M.F. and Buller, J.R. (2003) Social exclusion from high performance sport: are all talented young people being given an equal opportunity of reaching the Olympic podium?, *Journal of Sport and Social Issues,* 27(4): 420–42.

Collins, M.F., Henry, I., Houlihan, B. and Buller, J. (1999) *Research Report: Sport and Social Exclusion: A Report to Policy Action Team 10*, London: Department for Culture Media and Sport.

Davies, H.T.O., Nutley, S.M. and Smith, P.C. (eds) (2000) *What Works?* Bristol: Policy Press.

Department for Children, Schools and Families (2007) Government hails 'quiet revolution' in school sport, http://www.dcsf.gov.uk/pns/DisplayPN.cgi?pn_id=2007_0189, accessed 20 October 2007.

Department for Culture Media and Sport (2000) *A Sporting Future for All,* London: DCMS.

Department for Culture Media and Sport (2002) *Game Plan: A Strategy for Delivering Government's Sport and Physical Activity Objectives,* London: DCMS.

Department for Culture Media and Sport (2003) *Coaching Task Force Position Statement*, http://www.culture.gov.uk/coachingtaskforcerecommendations.pdf, accessed 5 April 2003.

Department for Culture Media and Sport (2007) Five hours of sport a week for every child, http://www.culture.gov.uk/reference_library/media_releases/2211.aspx, accessed 20 July 2007.

Department for Education and Skills (2003) *Learning through PE and Sport: A Guide to the Physical Education, School Sport and Club Links Strategy,* London: DES.

Department of Environment, Transport and the Regions (2000) *Regeneration Research: Summary Indices of Deprivation 2000* (No. 31), London: DETR.

Edwards, P. (1993) Champion Coaching: a case study, in Whittall, R. (ed.) *Pathways to Excellence: The Growing Child in Competitive Sport,* British Institute of Sports Coaching Conference 1992 Leeds: National Coaching Foundation.

de Knop, P. et al. (1994) *Youth-Friendly Sports Clubs,* Brussels: VUB (Free University of Brussels) Press.

de Knop, P., Engstrom L-M., Skirstad, B. and Weiss, M., (eds) (1996) *World-Wide Trends in Youth Sport,* Champaign, IL: Human Kinetics.

Kremer, J., Ogle, S. and Trew, K. (eds) (1997) *Young People's Involvement in Sport,* London: Routledge.

Lyle, J. (2002) *Sports Coaching Concepts: A Framework for Coaches' Behaviour,* London: Routledge.

Lyle, J., Allinson, M. and Taylor, J. (1997) *Factors Influencing the Motivations of Sports Coaches,* Research Report 49, Edinburgh: Scottish Sports Council.

MORI (2004) *Sports Coaching in the UK: Final Report,* London: MORI.

National Coaching Foundation (1992) *After-School Sport: 24 Recipes for Action,* Leeds: NCF.

National Coaching Foundation (1993) *Champion Coaching 1993: More Recipes For Success,* Leeds: NCF.

National Coaching Foundation (1996) *Champion Coaching: The Guide,* Leeds: NCF.

National Coaching Foundation (1997) *Champion Coaching Summary Report 1996/97,* Leeds: NCF.

National Coaching Foundation (1998) *Annual Report,* Leeds: NCF.

Pawson, R. and Tilley, N. (1997) *Realistic Evaluation,* London: Sage.

Obare, R. and Nichols, G. (2001) The full sporty: the impact of a sports training programme for unemployed steelworkers, *World Leisure,* 43(2): 49–57.

Rossi, P.H., Freeman, H.E. and Lipsey, M.W. (1999) *Evaluation: A Systematic Approach* (6th edn), Thousand Oaks, CA: Sage.

Sanderson, I. (1998) Beyond performance measurement? Assessing value in local government, *Local Government Studies,* 24(4):1–25.

Sports Council (1991) *Coaching Matters: A Review of Coaching and Coach Education in the UK,* London: Sports Council.

Sport England (2004) *A Framework for Sport in England: Making England an Active and Successful Sporting Nation – A Vision for 2020,* London: Sport England.

Sport England (2008) Sport revealed as priority for local authorities, http://www.sportengland.org/index/news_and_media/news_pr/sport_a_priority_for_local_authorities.htm, accessed 20 August 2008.

Sport England/MORI (2000) *Young People and Sport in England,* London: Sport England.

UK Sport (2001) *The UK Vision for Coaching,* London: UK Sport.

UK Sports Council (1999) *The Development of Coaching in the United Kingdom: A Consultative Document,* London: UK Sports Council.

Weiss, M. (1998) *Evaluation: Methods for Studying Programs and Policies,* Upper Saddle River, NJ: Prentice Hall.

Youth Sport Trust/Sport England (2008) *PE and School Sport: Information Bulletin for School Sport Partnerships and County Sports Partnerships,* No. 1, London: YST/Sport England.

CHAPTER 9

MANAGING DEVELOPMENT IN CLUB SPORT

The Amateur Swimming Association and Swim 21

Mike Collins and David Sparkes

INTRODUCTION

The sports club is repeatedly referred to as 'the grassroots', 'the bedrock' or 'the foundation' of British sport. The British tradition has been of small, single-sport clubs, mostly geographically parochial, which are socially strong but financially and numerically weak. The total numbers for England are estimated at around 105,000 for those affiliated to NGBs, but with perhaps another 50,000 that play regularly but less formally. The small size is affected by the fact that almost 40% of the total is found in association football, many of them single-team clubs. Clubs that own their own grounds are often larger – running three or four teams in sports like rugby and hockey – and with a strong social life backed by a clubhouse with a bar and, increasingly, fitness facilities, whereas players in clubs renting public or non-profit facilities would either resort to a local pub or sports centre bar, or disperse to home or work at the end of a match.

Club membership took a knock in the 1980s as the number of young people fell by 25% (or up to 40% in inner cities) and in traditional team games in particular as a world-wide trend towards small-side or individualistic sports strengthened in Britain (Kamphorst and Roberts, 1981; Cushman et al.,1996). At the same time a host of other sport, leisure and consumer opportunities vied for people's attention, and more individuals sought to become consumers of public or commercial pay-as-you-play venues serviced by professional staff, rather than club members expected to put time and effort back into the organisation. The problem of an aging and static volunteer workforce and ever-larger demand from both members and agents of the state (see pp. 182, 185–6) made NGBs aware that they must manage and reward volunteers better, and the state recognised that efforts to 'modernise' and rationalise NGBs' central offices were not enough, and that attention had to be paid to the branches/roots (e.g. DCMS (2002) in *Game Plan* and Sport England (1997) in *The Sporting Nation*).

For swimming (as with other NGBs) prioritising the allocation of resources results in tension because of the competing objectives in the Amateur Swimming Association's mission. The ASA's core objectives are to ensure that:

- everyone has an opportunity to learn to swim;
- everyone can achieve his or her personal goals;
- everyone has the opportunity to enjoy swimming as part of a healthy lifestyle;
- Great Britain can achieve gold medal success (ASA, 2004: 4).

In 2004 the ASA recorded 1,569 clubs in Britain with 95,000 registered members (ASA 2004a: 1). With an average of 120 members, swimming clubs are at the top end of 'middle-sized clubs'. But swimming is unusual in how far it requires a working countrywide partnership with local authorities and schools/colleges, because the basic swimming pool infrastructure is too complex and expensive for clubs, and increasingly schools, to build and run. Swimming pools were the first major form of public indoor sports provision, extending in the 1890s onwards from washhouses to keep industrial workers clean, to the second partnership function – teaching people to swim so that they might be safe in water and to minimise accidents and deaths by drowning. In recent times, swimming and diving medals have become more salient as a symbol of national success and prestige. Swim 21 is the ASA's programme for getting its clubs into better shape managerially and developmentally; but before we examine this process, some context on swimming in the late twentieth century is necessary, in terms of participation, pool infrastructure and management issues.

SWIMMING POOLS

In a cold, wet climate, swimming pools are more expensive structures to build and run (with heating of air and water) than in warmer climates where outdoor pools are the norm, though all settings share similar costs of staff to clean the water, maintain the plant, coach and lifeguard, and manage the visitors. The Edwardian pools came in a great variety of shapes and sizes, and by the time of plans to provide every community with a pool in the 1960s (Sports Council, 1971) many were time-expired and were replaced with fairly standard 25m pools, and open air lidos, a great fashion in the 1930s, also virtually disappeared. In the 1970s, some 40% of all current pools were built (Sports Council, 1992: 23). But in the 1980s along came a new type of fun facility – the leisure pool –

mainly free-form, with more shallow water, ending in a beach, and features like labyrinthine water slides, flumes, water cannons. Their lighting and planting were more like those in restaurants and nightclubs, than the traditional tiled wet box of competitive pools. These were for fun, for splashing, and for a while there were fears that they would displace teaching and training facilities. But design compromises, like having a single straight side and deep area partly met this issue, and in any case leisure pools need a larger catchment to generate enough customers to meet their running costs.

In 2007, Sport England's Active Places database showed 4,606 pools in England (including about 1,600 in schools). Of these, 61% were main pools (with conventional rectangular tanks), 23% were for teaching, 9% were in lidos, 6% leisure pools (often non-linear with beaches and wave machines) and 1% for diving. The South East and South West have disproportionately high numbers of lidos and leisure pools, whereas in the North East a third of pools are teaching pools compared with the national average of 23%. Between 2004 and 2008, 69 pools were closed and 74 opened (Hansard, Commons, 17 June 2008, 858W), though many new pools replaced smaller, more local old ones, with increased travelling required.

Table 9.1 sets out pool provision in relation to population. The East, SE and SW regions have more pools in relation to population and a higher partici-pation rate than the other six; the two measures have a strong correlation of 0.77, the value of which assumes that all local authorities have provided accu-rate and up-to-date data to the database. In the same three regions it can be seen that there is more pool water per population. Almost half of this water, however, is in commercial and hotel pools with very limited community access, in many pools with dimensions unsuitable for swimming, or in lidos open only 12 to 16 weeks a year. So the ASA argues for a standard, based on 13m^2 of 'fit-for-purpose' water per thousand people. The final column shows shortfalls of 25% in London, 20% in the West Midlands, and 14% in the North East and East Midlands. A strong correlation of participation and pool water area means that extra water would enable more adult swimming participation.

For schools, the House of Commons Culture Media and Sport Select Committee (2001) reported a total of 2,300 pools, among which 1,600 were heated. Nonetheless this meant that only 13% of schools had a swimming pool on site (HNI International, 2001), and for the remainder the journeys off campus to swim averaged 24 minutes. The ASA asserted that school pools were being closed at the rate of 10% a year, and if Private Finance Initiatives were involved, could not be included in Building Schools for the Future projects (*Daily Telegraph*, 29 February 2008).

Table 9.1 Provision of pools and water area

Region	Pools	Population per pool 2001 (000s)	Participa- tion rate 2005/6 (%)	Pool water per 000 people (m²)	Pool water (000m²) compared with ASA standard
East	558	9.7	14.1	18.77	+4.2 (+6%)
East Midlands	368	11.3	13.4	16.58	−7.6 (−14%)
London	546	13.1	13.2	16.66	−23.1 (−25%)
North East	231	10.9	12.5	15.10	−12.0 (−14%)
Yorkshire & Humber	395	12.6	13.4	15.42	+11.0 (+11%)
North West	597	11.3	13.4	16.63	
South East	917	8.7	14.9	21.27	+6.7 (+10%)
South West	548	9.0	14.8	21.08	+8.1 (+8%)
West Midlands	446	11.8	12.8	14.85	−13.5 (−20%)
England	4,606	10.7	13.8	17.67	+86.2 (+14%)

Source www.swimmingstrategy.org/ASA/files/GSE1-facilities.doc.

The 1990s saw two trends that demanded more space in conventional pools: the fitness boom which generated demands for water-based exercise – aquarobics and lane swimming for fitness – and the development of more structured programmes to support the training and competition of promising and elite competitors. In the latter case, there was a need for more 50m pools, said to be costly to run because it is difficult to use all the water area efficiently. However, this argument was proved fallacious with a new generation of 50m pools, such as Grand Central Pools in Stockport, opened in 1992, with a moveable bulkhead and floor, an element of leisure water and a fitness suite generating high attendances, and operating costs similar to that of a 6-lane 25m pool. Britain had few 50m pools compared to its competitors for medals (see below, p. 180).

To overcome the backlog of refurbishment, Sport England reckoned that £2bn would be needed over a decade, while the Local Government Association more conservatively reckoned the figure at £1.8bn over fifteen years (SCCMS, 2001), to remedy a situation it had described as a 'time bomb' a decade earlier (Sports Council, 1992). But at 13% of respondents, swimming topped the list of sports that people would like to do (Fox and Rickards, 2004) and almost a third of local authorities thought their citizens would like new pools. There was an increasing shift into pools in the independent (university) and private (hotels and fitness clubs) sectors, and to techniques for marketing small-group and one-to-one tuition, analogous to that of commercial fitness clubs.

PARTICIPATION AND USE OF POOLS

First, let us examine current facts and recent trends about children's and adults' swimming. Concerning children, since 1994 the National Curriculum required that by the end of Key Stage 2, pupils aged 10–11 should be able to swim at least 25 metres. Ofsted (2001) found that four out of five pupils could do this, but only two-thirds in inner cities and deprived areas. In 2006, £5.5m extra was provided by the DfES to help pupils who failed to reach this target. Yet in 1995 the Department for Education and Employment reported that 15% of primary and 40% of secondary schools did not provide swimming, and in 2006 a *Times Educational Supplement* survey found that the proportion unable to master survival skills like floating had risen to 35% from 30% in 2003 (J. Salter, *Times Educational Supplement* 12, September 2006). In Key Stages 3 and 4 swimming was an option until, without consultation, the DfES removed it from the curriculum in 2006.

Table 9.2 clearly shows that:

▪ Secondary school participation fell to a third of that by primary children.
▪ Swimming was the most popular school sport for about one in five children.
▪ Over twice as many children (and slightly more girls) swam frequently out of school than in school.
▪ A quarter of regular swimmers aged 11–16 were club members, again with slightly more girls.

Closure of small, old expensive-to-run school pools (at some 10% a year, according to the second author), pressure on the school curriculum, and the costs of taking pupils off campuses led to declines in time devoted to swimming in primary (HNI International, 2001) and secondary schools (King *et al.*, 1997), leading to expressions of concern from teachers and the public about competence in the water and hence safety (ASA *et al.*, 1998). Money was put into school swimming in 1997, and at the same time there were new government programmes concentrating on school sport and offering Lottery money for school facilities (e.g. Space for Sport and the Arts), especially if they were open to the community and for an extended school day. The major programme Building Schools for the Future, however, relegated swimming pools to being part of the 'supplementary net area' and guided LEAs to seek non-educational funding like the National Lottery and, curiously, the DCMS which had no such budget line.

Regarding adults, the massive Active People survey with a sample of 364,000 (Sport England, 2006) confirmed the figures in Tables 9.3, 9.4 and 9.5 that:

Table 9.2 Children's participation in swimming, 1994 and 2002

	All schools		Primary		Secondary	
	1994	2002	1994	2002	1994	2002
% 6–16s swimming frequently* in school	32	32	47	48	15	13
% for whom swimming was the most enjoyed school sport	25	21				
% 6–16s swimming frequently* out of school	50	51	60	63	39	37
boys	49	48				
girls	51	55				
% members in swimming clubs	10	10	12	12	7	7
boys	9	8				
girls	11	12				

Source MORI, 2003.
Note * frequently = at least ten times in the last year.

- The static state of swimming over the previous fifteen years had continued, with 13.8% of adults swimming at least once a month (5.6 million people).
- But the proportion of women continued to rise – in 2006 to 17.1% compared to 10.3% among men.
- Two in five regular swimmers were in sport or fitness clubs.
- There had been a sizeable recent increase in competitive swimming and a somewhat smaller rise in tuition, facts that should please the ASA, though the demand probably substantially outstrips the supplies of pools and qualified coaches.
- Unlike most sports, swimming peaked in the 30–44 age group.
- Reflecting sport in general, there was a strong social gradient (perhaps reflecting disposable income), but apart from those not in work, this was much narrower in club membership.

Swimming participation overall provided 12% of all sport's contributions to physical activity (Rowe *et al.*, 2004).

After the 1970s injection of pools, participation in swimming doubled between 1977 and 1986, with growth especially among women, older people and people in semi-skilled occupations. Swimming had traditionally been kept cheap by pricing that involved a subsidy of at least half and in some cases up to four-fifths of the cost. The Conservative governments of the 1980s thought that for

172

Table 9.3 Adults' participation in swimming, 1987–2002

	1987	1990	1993	1996	2002
% participating in last 4 weeks	13	13	15	15	14
men indoors	10	11	12	11	10
women indoors	11	13	14	15	14
% participating in last year	35	42	43	40	35
% members of a club in last 4 weeks					
men				41	44
women				25	32
% competing in last 12 months					
men				32	39
women				10	14
% receiving tuition in last 12 months					
men				19	30
women				27	45

Source Fox and Rickards, 2004.

Table 9.4 Age of adult swimmers, 2002

Age	%
16–19	19
20–24	18
25–29	17
30–44	20
45–59	13
60–69	7
Over 70	3

Source Fox and Rickards, 2004.

Table 9.5 Socio-economic group of swimmers, 2002

Socio-economic group	Any swimming in last 4 weeks	Club members
Large employer/higher manager	24	46
Higher professional	20	42
Lower manager/professional	17	43
Intermediate	13	39
Small employer/own account	12	40
Lower supervisory/technical	11	32
Semi-routine	9	30
Routine	8	31
Never worked/unemployed	8	19

Source Fox and Rickards, 2004..

efficiency reasons, the consumers should bear more of this cost and non-user taxpayers less, and under policy pressure and guidance from the public finance watchdog, the Audit Commission (1989), prices rose continuously above inflation. In 2007/8 prices for adults were 171% above the Retail Price Index for leisure compared to ten years earlier and for children 180% above – not an effective way, argued the Chartered Institute of Public Finance and Accountancy of combating obesity, especially in children (CIPFA, 2007).

Nonetheless, by 1994 there were concerns that swimming was in decline. In two-thirds of authorities there was an estimated loss totalling some 7 million visits over the previous year, perhaps with some being diverted to commercial fitness clubs. Losses of users in both conventional and leisure pools in 1992–1994 averaged 7% for adults and juveniles (Taylor and Kearney, 1995). Two-thirds of local authorities attributed this to competition from commercial health and fitness suites, and other indoor leisure provision (cinemas, ten-pin bowls, games centres, etc.), a third attributed it to deteriorating pools, and a quarter to entry prices and reductions in school PE. The only sub-market to increase was in lower-cost swimming, using discount cards (Collins, 2003). More strategically, the ratio of juvenile to adult swims had declined to 1:1, from 3:1 in the 1960s and 2:1 in the 1980s.

Early results from Sport England's benchmarking service (2000) showed that 84% of pool time was given over to casual swimming and lessons, and 4% to lane swimming, 3% to fun sessions, 2% to aquarobics, and only 2% to sub-aqua, polo, synchro, lifesaving and other activities; 4% of time was unused.

The results also showed that 59% of the space was for casual use, 29% for lessons, 9% for clubs, and 3% for other purposes. The general public accounted for 66% of the use, schools/colleges for 15%, adult sessions 6%, junior sessions 5%, women-only sessions 2%, and others 6%. Concessions operated in 9% of pools, 30% for deprived/low-income groups and 35% for all residents.

Lessons for children showed an 8% growth, but school lessons a 9% decline. Both family and discounted attendances declined, the latter by 15%, which Collins and Taylor surmised might be the results of price increases by contractors or by Direct Service Organisations under Compulsory Competitive Tendering. Junior swimming prices in public pools rose by 38% between 1998 and 2001. The provision of new pools, or trends in dry-side use showed no correlation, with equal numbers of cases showing increases and decreases. Collins and Taylor (1997: 149) opined that there was a battle to retain customers. New pools appeared to attract new swimmers, but quality is a real issue if latent demand is to be tapped in existing pools.

174

MANAGEMENT ISSUES

Three issues are relevant to this piece: the inclusion of ethnic minorities, free swimming for children and older people to improve their health, and the provision of 50m pools for elite training.

1. Swimming is popular but not adequately inclusive

In schools, ethnic minorities have the same curriculum as the indigenous majority – and few opt out. Collins (2002) studied eight primary schools in inner city Nottingham and Leicester, and found that three-quarters of the children enjoyed swimming, both in and out of school, and participated more than the national average in public pools: 72% of the boys and 65% of the girls swam in their leisure time with family or friends (80% white, 76% Asian, 61% black). But this translated to very low participation in clubs (6% of boys and 7% of girls) and galas (only 1% and 2%) compared to the figures in Figure 9.1.

Table 9.6 shows three sets of reasons why children said they did not swim in their free time. It is clear that having no one to go with was important for girls,

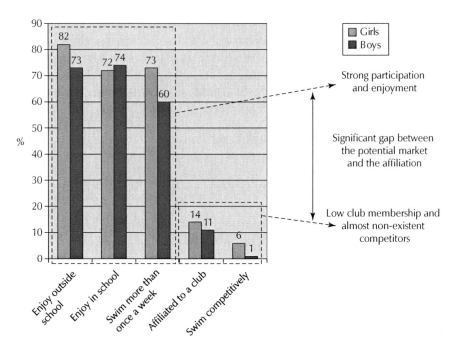

Figure 9.1 Swimming from popular pastime to invisible sport (Collins, 2002)

Table 9.6 Reasons for not swimming in leisure time (% citing)

	Boys	Girls
Pool-related reasons		
Session times inconvenient	14	12
Distance to pool	34	16
No car	21	9
Personal reasons		
No one to go with	24	44
No time to go	14	12
Can't swim well enough	30	23
Parental reasons		
Parents not wish (culture)	10	14
Parents not wish (other)	10	4

while travel arrangements for boys and being self-conscious about not being able to swim well enough were important for both sexes. But as far as the children were concerned, parental prohibitions, perhaps surprisingly in such communities, were said to be issues for a tiny minority. The study did not record the parents' perspective on this; some teachers and club officials clearly felt this was a bigger issue than the children did, and it certainly was both for parents and children in adolescence and puberty in secondary schools. Regarding the small number at this tender age who said they had no time, two teachers also said that the requirements of Islamic teaching and prayer often took one to two hours a day.

Only three local swimming clubs had regular and productive links with schools, one claiming a quarter of its members from ethnic groups, and with an Asian girl in the national squad, who 'encouraged and inspired others'. Another, however, said that the low priority accorded to swimming discouraged it from bothering with local schools. Neither city had a Sports Development Officer dedicated to swimming. But none of the reasons account for the precipitous drop in participation, and Collins (2002) could not help but believe that some cultural influences were operating in homes beyond what the children mentioned or perceived.

Nationally, 2.8% of adult swimming pool users were from ethnic minorities, who make up 5.2% of the population – under-representation by half that was even more marked in national squads. The ASA (2001) adopted a Racial Equality Strategy (Sport England intermediate level), but an ASA witness to the Select

Committee, Kelvin Juba, said 'probably less than 2% of people who are swimming are from ethnic minority groups . . . this is a real problem that swimming and swimming pool operators are going to have to address' (SCCMS, 2001, para 43). David Sparkes, ASA's CEO, added 'what we have not yet done is to get them to connect with the elite end of the sport' (ibid., Question 41).

All of this confirms what HNI International (2001: 53) reported to the ASA:

> The small number who swim . . . clearly gives rise to the notion that not enough is being done, nor is sufficient known about how each regards swimming. Consequently no solutions have been offered to help some of these groups take part in swimming. All too often, it is easier to disregard their interests on the basis that they are just too difficult to include. The competitive outlet through swimming clubs in England merely serves to reinforce the perception of swimming as very much a sport for those families who can afford it or are willing to make financial sacrifices for it.

Despite a stubbornly static level of swimming participation, the 2006 Active People survey showed 13% of adults cited swimming as the activity they would like to take up, the highest for any sport, especially for women and those in their 60s. So the ASA launched eight Everyday Swim projects in 2005, with the aim of increasing participation by 2% a year, and to involve various groups, chosen by the host authorities (see Table 9.7).

Table 9.7 'Everyday Swim' pilot schemes

Area/Focus groups	Comm'y	Older people	Youth	Disabil./ Health needs	Disadv.	Black/ Ethnic	Participa- tion rate
Wirral		X					12.3%
Easington			X	X			11.8%
Kirklees	X			X			13.3%
Telford/ Wrekin			X	X	X		13.8%
Suffolk			X		X		12.9%
Islington	X						12.3%
Lewisham		X	X			X	13.7%
Woking	X						15.8%

Source Shibli et al., 2008.

Monitoring of early results showed:

- some success in gaining new partners, especially PCTs;
- risk aversion, inertia and concerns with day-to-day procedures and red tape;
- a conflict between local needs to meet 'bottom line' targets versus the longer time needed to develop new markets, and hence increasing 'swims' rather than 'swimmers';
- lack of buy-in by some partners and middle managers, needing senior support.

There was no overall strategy, but some strategic actions (e.g. the social marketing campaign planned in Telford), so a larger-scale and more focused operation was needed to achieve market development rather than narrow, but increased penetration (Shibli et al., 2008).

2. Free swimming for inclusion and health

A further step from concessions is to offer swimming for free. Concerns for declining attendances and even more for child health led Glasgow to offer this in 2001/2, and led to a 123% increase in attendances, after a fall of 15% in the previous four years, after which use settled at a lower level, but still above earlier figures (Table 9.8).

After an Easter 2003 pilot, the Welsh Assembly tried a countrywide scheme in summer 2003, involving 86 pools where 70% of swims were free, and 803,000 children attended, compared to 387,000 the year before (+107%); 30% of sessions included structured activity, and two in five parents thought that their children's ability in the water had improved (Sports Council for Wales, 2004). In 2004 the Welsh Assembly decided to extend the scheme to the over-60s and to run a nationwide pilot. (There are more details in Bolton, Chapter 13.)

At Easter 2004 similar schemes were run in five London boroughs, more than doubling attendances, but at a cost of £1.28 per swim (Parsons, 2004). Other schemes included Birmingham, Nuneaton, Blackburn, and Plymouth. Only in Plymouth, as part of a Local Exercise Action Pilot, was the health effect being

Table 9.8 Swimming attendances in Glasgow

Year	1997/8	1998/9	1999/00	2000/1	2001/2	2002/3	2003/4
Attendance (000)	282	269	258	239	532	370	321

measured (Barker, 2004). Nonetheless, in Wales and Glasgow the schemes were continued, and extended to people aged over 60 in 2004/5, at a cost in Wales of £1.3m which the First Minister of the Assembly compared to the £500m annual cost of inactivity and unhealthy lifestyles. Glasgow officers believed their scheme removed price as a barrier, provided a beneficial activity in safe, supervised settings, and increased participation among children in some of the city's and country's most deprived areas. But monitoring showed that while attendances were up 72% (with their attendant costs), only 2% were new swimmers and few from priority groups (Shibli, 2008).

There are costs in promotion, card administration, extra lifeguarding and reception staff, water cleansing, and some queuing and displacement of other users. The evaluation issue is whether to go with an open access scheme with those effects, or a lower-cost one, more closely targeted at particular groups – but such a scheme is more difficult to explain and market to the public.

In 2008, Sport England (2008) launched a new strategy, focused on increasing participation. As part of the promotion the new Minister for Sport, Gerry Sutcliffe, gathered £80m from the Departments of Culture Media and Sport; Children, Schools and Families; Communities and Local Government; and Health. This was to be used to fund free swimming in 2009–2011 for over-60s, to increase participation by under 18s, and fund local swimming coordinators. In addition £60m capital was to be provided for which LAs can bid for renovation and maintenance. DCMS (2008) described it as 'a key component of our physical activity plans and . . . a signal of the raised level of our ambitions'. Critics asked how this would be sustained. HMG aspired to offer free swimming to all by 2012 (*Hansard Commons*, 17 June 2008, 858W and 861W), while Sparkes opined that this could cost £1.5bn a year. The experiences of 60+ swimming schemes in Glasgow and Wales was that a substantial proportion of swimmers were people who could already swim, either swimming more often, or substituting free swims for paid ones. For young people many providers would like to concentrate on formal lessons, but the scheme did not allow this. The government's aspiration is for all to swim for free by 2012, but Ralph Riley, Chief Executive of the ISRM, argues that this will require many more new, accessible well-managed pools (*Leisure Opportunities* 479(2), 24 June 2008). One big challenge is that two in five of over-65s in England cannot swim (Shibli, 2008).

3. Provision of 50m pools for training elite swimmers

50m pools are essential for training for long-course competitions, yet in 2001 the only English pool capable of holding international competitions was

Sheffield's Ponds Forge, yet even this did not have a 50m warm up/swim down pool expected for such events. Indeed, England had only fourteen pools, a number equalled by Berlin and Paris alone; Germany counted ninety-two, Holland twelve (SCCMS, 2001). The ASA developed a strategy for thirty-four 50m pools, including pools at branches of the English Institute of Sport on several university campuses, but this needed exchequer or Lottery funding.

SWIM 21 CLUB PROJECT

The ASA numbers 1,569 clubs in Britain with 45,000 registered swimmers and 196,000 members (ASA Integra database 2007). It also has some 6,000 officials and 30,000 volunteers who offer 2.75 million hours a year, valued at £30m (British Swimming, 2007). As we shall see in the conclusions, the ASA national organisation is in a phase of major change – but the clubs have to change too. In 1999 it was decided that there should be a structured development programme enabled by a newly expanded regional Development Officers team led by the second author, and for a time advised by the first (Collins, 2001). Swim 21 required officers and members to work in three stages:

1. First, each club was to undertake an extensive *audit* of its financial, skills, human and organisational resources, including its links with other clubs and partner bodies (involving a questionnaire of almost 100 items which would tell the ASA far more about its affiliates than it ever knew before).
2. Then, to consider and agree an *action/improvement plan* on whether to consolidate activities at the current level, or to seek to develop to the next level.
3. Finally, a club could, with the support of the Regional DO, be passed or referred for modification by a national committee, and then accredited as a club competent to entrust one's children or oneself to.

The ASA listed the benefits/outcomes of the process as:

1. Enabling swimmers to achieve their full potential in a safe, quality-assured system.
2. Recognition by Sport England as a safe, effective, child-friendly environment.
3. Offering support systems and resources for club staff.
4. Enhanced access to funding through the DES's *Physical Education, School Sport and Club Links* programme and County Sports Partnerships (see Chapter 5).

5. Providing ways of spreading the load for support staff, and attractions for members and volunteers to join clubs (all ASA regions had support programmes and forty-four Volunteer Coordinators were in post in 2005).

(www.britishswimming.org, accessed 20 August 2006)

Depending on the quality of the club's record and the skills of its officers, the audit could take from a few weeks to several months. But the action plan stage was difficult, often contentious, and made volunteers' heads hurt to work through, because moving up a level often meant wholesale organisational change for everyone from helpers though coaches and officials, and moving out of a comfort zone.

The four levels were (1) teaching, (2) skill development, (3) competitive development and (4) performance. Major 'step changes' occur from the second to third and from the third to fourth levels, as can be appreciated from greater expected pool times for each squad, and the paramedic/sports science support expected. The stages in the accreditation process are shown below. In forming their Action Plan clubs had to decide whether to consolidate and improve their services at the current level, or seek to move up or down a level. Even in the two lower levels rising expectations could mean a higher turnover of youngsters and their parents, often core volunteers.

THE STAGES IN THE SWIM 21 ACCREDITATION PROCESS

Phase 1: Develop understanding and commitment

Application form and Regional Development Officer advice.

Phase 2: Assess current situation

Complete audit of:

(A) Compliance – as a well-managed, safe, child-friendly club (31 questions)
(B) Workforce development –recruiting, training, rewarding volunteers (24 questions)
(C) Athlete development – coaching and specialist support (23 questions).

Phase 3: Identify Swim 21 level

With RDO's help.

> **Phase 4: Action planning and implementation**
>
> Plan submitted to RDO, implementation begins; Regional Panel scores submission and issues silver or gold certificate for four years; any discrepancy referred to National Panel.
>
> **Phase 5: Annual validation of maintained standards and improvements**
>
> Annual reports to RDO with plan for following year; at the end of the fourth year, club submits another audit, provides new evidence action file and seeks re-accreditation.

By February 2004 the ASA (2004a) reported that four out of five affiliated clubs had registered for the process, half had completed an audit and a quarter an action plan, but only one in eight (103 clubs) were accredited at one or more levels: 37 for teaching, 67 for skill development, 11 for competitive development and 10 for performance. So there was still a long way to go. To ease things for large clubs that operated at two or all three levels 2–4, a simplified process was introduced in early 2006 (ASA, 2006), and modifications made to link up with the 'long-term development of (elite) athletes' process outlined by Sport England. By January 2009 there were 497 accreditations from 399 clubs for all four disciplines – 36% for teaching, 49% for skill development, 9% for competitive development and 6% for performance. The 2009 strategy sought to raise this to 726 (ASA, 2009: 3).

In 2008, nine out of ten parents said it was important for their child to be involved in an accredited club, and two-thirds said that this affected the club they chose, and that their club had improved since accreditation. One said:

> I know staff are child-protection aware, they are qualified, there is structure to the club for movement/development, and I get what I pay for!
> (www.britishswimming.org, accessed 29 November 2008)

The long-term implications of not being accredited must be to lose credibility in the eyes of parents and potential members, and eventually even to wither away. Also, being accredited automatically gives a club Sport England's Clubmark status, rendering it more eligible for grants. But this rigorous process, which several major NGBs, like rugby union, are pursuing in analogous forms, is demanding of volunteers who find their roles changing, their responsibilities growing (or even disappearing in their old guise), and more training being demanded of them, with no or only partial financial recompense.

Nevertheless, club officers recorded substantial support for seeing the outcomes as worth undertaking the process:

> Swim 21 has given us the confidence to carry on doing the right things for our members and ensured that we have access to the training we need to do the right job.
>
> (Ian Moore, Secretary, Selby Tiger Sharks SC)

> Swim 21 has created a stronger bond and a willingness to share resources between clubs.
>
> (John Moore, Sedgefield 75 SC)

> Swim 21 has given us the incentive to continuously reassess our club and make it more attractive to swimmers and parents.
>
> (Joyce Chadwick, Halifax SC)

> Swim 21 has empowered us to become more structured and focused, using action plans, job descriptions and finely tuned CPDs for all our volunteers, teachers and coaches, based on the needs of the athletes.
>
> (Kim Edwards, President, Bromsgrove SC)

> Swim 21 helped us to formalise our administration and identified areas where we needed to improve our policy. Members have commented on the good organisation within the club, so it was very worthwhile.
>
> (Lesley Houlston, Droitwich Dolphins SC).

Having discovered great variations in the scope and quality of teaching in different settings and localities, the ASA also launched a National Plan for Teaching Swimming, which its development officers are marketing to public leisure centre managers and schools (Anon., 2004).

The DES/DCMS (2003) launched the *Physical Education, School Sport and Club Links* scheme in 2003 as part of a £459m strategy for youth sport, and swimming was one of the first seven sports involved. The programme tried to link clubs to schools in 250 clusters of primary and secondary schools over five years to 2008, and to increase the 5–16 year old club members from 14% to 20%.

In June 2004, as part of its modernisation programme, Sport England granted money to the ASA to set up regional structures for swimming in the NE, SW, and West Midlands.

CONCLUSIONS

The Select Committee (SCCMS, 2001) concluded that 'swimming is recognised as beneficial to the nation's wellbeing and health. Swimming is uniquely beneficial across the whole of society, and as the country's most popular sporting activity it merits appropriate investment.' The government responded to the strongly worded report by referring to its current sport and community policies, arguing that dedicated funding for pools might put an 'undue burden' on local authorities relative to 'more essential services'. In any case, the government claimed, the NOF Lottery funds were available (soon thereafter rolled into a more generic Big Lottery Fund), and equivocated about the 50m pool issue. It acknowledged the transport problem for schoolchildren, especially in urban areas (DCMS, 2002b). Such Lottery grants as are available for pools, however, are much reduced in scale, and contributions have to be sought from public–private partnership moneys or the Public–Private Finance Initiative.

In current circumstances an NGB is not a free-standing, autonomous agency that can act regardless of public policy or commercial actions. Swimming, because of its tie to the (mainly public) real estate of pools, is less free than some others; but grant aid for medal hopefuls and coaches on the one hand and capital grants for pools and support for local swimming development on the other gives an accountability issue to politicians and auditors. Success brings opportunities for new sponsorships and the responsibility of helping them meet their commercial objectives. Likewise the business of training tens of thousands of youngsters with the badges, kit, certificates and fees involved is a major revenue earner.

While the bulk of the ASA's five-year corporate plan from 2005 (ASA, 2004b) focused on extending or completing current lines of development, it envisaged major developments in linking swimming with personal and community health (Table 9.9). These are on a scale that would transform the budget and operations, as selected financial items in Table 9.10 show:

In 2007/8 the ASA had to prepare a new strategy and a whole sport plan submission to Sport England for the pre-London quadrennial, proposing by 2013, among many other things (ASA, 2009):

- For learning to swim – moving from 78% to 85% of primary school meeting Key Stage 2 targets, and every one offering curricular swimming.
- For participation – increasing participation by 1% a year – to 2 million people swimming once a month or more often, 600,000 new adult swimmers, which would be one-third of all new participants sought by Sport England.

184

Table 9.9 Major items in the ASA's Corporate Plan, 2005–2009

Section/item	Target by 2009
Starting – learn to swim, 'the magic moment'	Reduce non-swimmers to 5%; additional 48,000 qualified teachers; 240 accredited teaching clubs.
Lifelong – staying in the water	Support swimming in 524 Surestart programmes for under 5s; incorporate it into 45 local physical activity programmes; link 400 School Partnerships to 800 clubs – total 1,480; 400 new swimming activity and health coaches.
Stay and succeed – individual athlete development	100 qualified coaches; a single competition framework; 2,400 team managers.
Excellence – swimming to win	400 swimmers supported by World Class programmes each year; 160 involved in TAS Scholarship programmes; 8 regional coach development centres.
Volunteering – self-fulfilment	8,000 extra volunteers and 2,000 officials (10 per club); 1,700 volunteers recognised by national awards framework.
Facilities – access to all	26 50m pools; 53 8-lane and 3 10-lane 25m pools; 8 regional diving centres; 72 accredited Performance clubs (50 to World Class).
International influence	35 officials/administrators on special courses each year; 10 more technical officials for 2006 Melbourne Games, and 12 on international exchanges.
Equity and ethics – a level playing field for all	Achieve Intermediate level of Sport England Equality standards and Child Protection Charters.
Governance and partnerships – delivery with integrity	8 regions with elected Boards and paid managers; increase membership by 2%.
Monitoring and evaluation	Centralised tracking and monitoring/evaluation systems.

Source ASA, 2004b.

Table 9.10 Selected items from the ASA financial summary (£m)

	2005/6	2008/9
Total expenditure	12.0	23.7
of which:		
Learn to swim	1.2	4.4
Lifelong participation	0.9	8.5
Athlete development	1.2	2.2
Excellence	4.5	4.8
Governance/partnerships	3.1	3.2
Income from:		
The sport	3.2	3.7
DfES school swimming	0.1	3.0
DoH Healthy Living	0.2	8.0
Other external grants	0.6	0.1
Sport England grants	7.9	8.9

Source ASA, 2009.

- For facilities – 22 more 50m, 29 new 25m 8-lane and one 10-lane, and 4 international-standard diving pools. It would not be realistic to seek by 2013 all the 86,000m² of extra water space indicated in Table 9.1 (equivalent to 405 4-lane 25m pools) so the ASA proposed a gentler progression: if all plans for new or replacements come to fruition by 2013 this would produce sixteen 50m pools (an increase of 206%) and thirty-four 8-lane 25m pools (an increase of 57%). This would still leave the two Midland regions and the NE with a deficit.
- For athlete development – moving to a talent pool of 4,600 athletes (including 3,465 speed swimmers), and increasing world-ranked swimmers by 10%.
- For workforce development – training 4,300 volunteers in 2009/10.
- For club development – moving from 192,000 to 206,000 registered members, and from 3,500 to 4,700 accredited club administrators, and from 42% to 65% of schools linked to swimming clubs.
- For governance – moving from 32% to 45% of Swim 21-accredited clubs; developing 209 local aquatic strategies (from 36).

By this plan, the ASA aimed to become 'the best governing body in England'. CEO David Sparkes described Swim 21 as 'driving quality into the voluntary sector . . . to strengthen the talent pathway' (ASA, 2009: 2). In March 2009 the ASA agreed a new six-year, £15m sponsorship deal with British Gas, with the money divided equally between elite and grassroots activity.

Sport England awarded swimming sports £20.9m for 2009–2013, and UK Sport £37.25m (£25.7m for swimming); Paralympic swimming was awarded £10.1m (Sport England, press release, 4 February 2009; UK Sport press release, 3 December 2008).

The government is looking for more effective action from NGBs – and that means, first, more swimmers, starting at school; so the DfES introduced the Swimming Charter for Schools in 2004, supporting the compulsory curriculum for 5–11s but encouraging provision for older children through high-quality cost-effective swimming lessons they can choose to deliver. To assure the government that this can be delivered, the ASA, the Royal Life Saving Society and the Institute of Sport and Recreation Management formed the Strategic Alliance for Swimming to coordinate their respective resources and effort (ASA, 2004b). This argued for moving closer to the health agenda in helping to activate obese children and sedentary adults, a policy agenda running alongside that for 50m pools, gold medals and a legacy from the 2012 Olympics. In 2004, 395 local accredited Swimfit programmes were running.

REFERENCES

Amateur Swimming Association et al. (1998) Swim for Your Life: The Teaching of Swimming in Schools, Loughborough: ASA.

Amateur Swimming Association (2004a) Annual Report and Accounts 2004, Loughborough: ASA.

Amateur Swimming Association (2004b) Building on Change: Executive Summary of ASA Corporate Plans for GB and England 2005–2009, Loughborough: ASA.

Amateur Swimming Association/ISRM/RLSS UK (2004) Swimming: Making the Difference, Loughborough: ASA/ISRM.

Amateur Swimming Association (2006) Following the Swim 21 Accreditation Process, Loughborough: ASA.

Amateur Swimming Association (2009) The ASA – the Essential Element: More than a Governing Body Draft Strategy 2009–2013, Loughborough: ASA.

Anon. (2004) Growing the grassroots: the ASA, Sport Management, 8(3): 52–5.

Audit Commission (1989) Sport for Whom?, London: Audit Commission.

Barker, Y. (2004) Free swimming consultation event: summary report, www.culture.gov.uk, accessed 9 September 2005.

Bolton, N. et al. (2008) Free Swim: An Evaluation of the Welsh Assembly Government's Initiative, Cardiff: Sports Council for Wales.

British Swimming (2007) A Vision for Swimming, Loughborough: Amateur Swimming Association.

Chartered Institute of Public Finance and Accountancy (2007) *Charges for Leisure Services Statistics 2007/8,* London: CIPFA.

Chartered Institute of Public Finance and Accountancy (2008) *Culture Sport and Recreation Statistics 2007/8,* London: CIPFA.

Collins, M.F. (ed.) (2001) *Evaluating the Swim21 Amateur Swimming Association Project,* Loughborough: Loughborough University.

Collins, M.F. (ed.) (2002*) Swimming for Children from Ethnic Minorities in Nottingham and Leicester,* Loughborough: Loughborough University.

Collins, M. (2003) *Sport and Social Exclusion,* London: Routledge.

Collins, P. and Taylor, P. (1997) Swimming participation – down and out or on the up?, in *Proceedings Taking Sport to Heart,* ISRM conference, Glasgow 14–16 October, Melton Mowbray: Institute of Sport and Recreation Management.

Culture Media and Sport Committee (2001) *Testing the Waters: The Sport of Swimming,* London: Second Report Session 2001/2, HCP 418 18 December.

Cushman, G., Veal, A.J. and Zuzanek, J. (1996) *World Leisure Participation: Free Time in the Global Village,* Wallingford: CAB International.

Department for Culture Media and Sport (2002a) *Game Plan*, London: DCMS.

Department for Culture Media and Sport (2002b) *Testing the Waters: The Sport of Swimming: Government Response to the Second Report,* CM 5480, London: HMSO.

Department for Culture Media and Sport (2008) *Playing to Win: A New Era for Sport*, London: DCMS.

Department for Education and Skills/DCMS (2003) *Physical Education, School Sport and Club Links Strategy,* London: DES.

Fox, K. and Rickards, L. (2004) *Sport and Leisure: Results from the 2002 General Household Survey,* London: Stationery Office.

HNI International (2001) *Swimming for Life,* Swindon: HNI.

Kamphorst, T.J. and Roberts, K. (1981) *Trends in Sport: A Multinational Perspective,* Culembourg, NL: Giordano Bruno.

King, L., Smithson, C. and Taylor, P. (1997) *Swimming and the National Curriculum,* Melton Mowbray: Institute of Sport and Recreation Management.

Local Government Data Unit et al. (2008) *Welsh Assembly Government Free Swimming Initiative: Data Summary Report April 2004–Sept 2007,* Cardiff: LGDU.

MORI (2003) *Young people and Sport in England: Trends in Participation 1994–2002,* London: Sport England.

Office for Standards in Education (2001) *Swimming at Key Stage 2,* London: Ofsted.

Parsons, T. (2004) London's Kids Swim Free, Easter 2004, evaluation report, Institute of Child Health, UCL.

Rowe, N., Beasley, N. and Adams, N. (2004) Sport, physical activity and health:

future prospects for improving the health of the nation, in *Driving up Participation: The Challenge for Sport,* London: Sport England.

Select Committee on Culture Media and Sport (2001) *2nd Report Session 2001/2: The Sport of Swimming,* London: SCCMS.

Shibli, S. (2008) Free swimming – will it work? Paper to ISRM conference Alton Towers, November, available from www.isrm.co.uk.

Shibli, S. *et al.* (2008) *Everyday Swim, Making Waves in Participation?* Sheffield: Sports Industry Research Centre.

Sports Council (1971) *Sport in the Seventies: Making Good the Deficiencies,* London: Sports Council.

Sports Council (1992) *Provision for Swimming: Main and Technical Reports,* London: Sports Council.

Sport England (1997) *The Sporting Nation,* London: Sport England.

Sport England (2000) *Best Value through Sport: Survey of Sports Halls and Swimming Pools in England,* London: Sport England.

Sport England (2006) Active People survey 2005/6, factsheets on www.sport england.org, accessed 12 December 2006.

Sport England (2008) *Grow, Sustain, Excel: Strategy 2008–2011,* London: Sport England.

Sports Council for Wales (2004) *Report to the Welsh Assembly Government on the Free Swimming Pilot – Summer Holidays 2003,* Cardiff: SCW.

Taylor, P. *et al.* (2004) *Widening Access through Facilities,* Sheffield: Leisure Industries Research Centre for Sport England.

Taylor, P. and Kearney, J. (1995) *Swimming in Decline?,* Melton Mowbray: Institute of Sport and Recreation Management.

CHAPTER 10

SPORTS DEVELOPMENT IN MICROCOSM

Braunstone Sport Action Zone

Caron Walpole and Mike Collins

BACKGROUND AND CONTEXT TO THE SAZ

Braunstone, an estate in west Leicester, was designated in 1999 as a New Deal for Communities Pathfinder project by the government, on the grounds that it was the most deprived ward in the East Midlands. £49.5m was allocated to regenerate the estate over seven years, and Braunstone Community Association (BCA) was set up to deliver the programme. Braunstone was then designated as a Sport Action Zone (SAZ) in 2001 by Sport England – the smallest in England, by area and population.

The estate has a population of over 13,000 people, and is divided north and south by Braunstone Park (see Figure 10.1). It is a white, outer suburban estate in a city with the largest proportion in Britain of citizens of Indian origin. The estate has a strong sense of community and many strong, longstanding family ties, partly as a result of a relatively stable population, many residents having lived there all their lives, or having returned 'home' at a later stage of life.

Braunstone remained an area of social and economic deprivation, but had received little regeneration funding as an 'outer' rather than an 'inner' city estate. Key indicators of this situation were typical of the socially excluded states in *Bringing Britain Together* (SEU, 1998):

- the highest mortality rates in the city;
- poor housing;
- the second highest level of unemployment in the city;
- low levels of educational achievement;
- high crime rates;
- low pay;
- lack of community and shopping facilities.

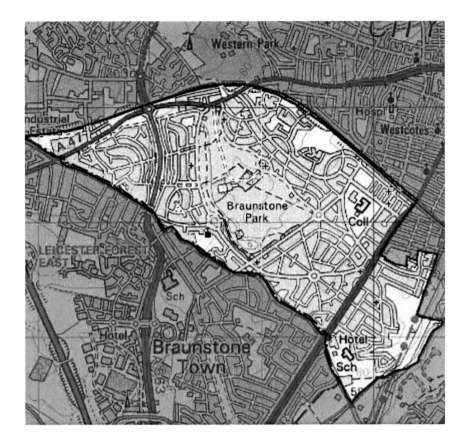

Figure 10.1 Braunstone Sport Action Zone

Source Hall Aitken, 2008, with permission of Braunstone Community Association

Sport is an important part of the culture of this estate, but clearly suffered as a result of its deprivation. The SAZ team carried out a comprehensive needs assessment in 2001/2 and was given a detailed picture of local sport by residents, with the main conclusion that facilities were in a very poor condition, and opportunities to play sport outside school were very limited for both children and adults.

The SAZ was hosted by Braunstone Community Association which also employed a Manager and Assistant Manager in July 2001, the latter being put in place so that a local resident could be appointed and mentored by the Manager, with resulting credibility among residents. The appointee had been following a personal development plan, including a secondment to manage the 'Reducing Youth Crime through Sport' project.

By 2004, BCA had more than sixty members of staff, including secondees from statutory agencies. Its working structure was resident-led, comprising a Board of Directors, mostly elected residents, but also strategic directors from key agencies like Leicester City Council (LCC), Leicester City West Primary Care Trust (PCT) and the local Learning and Skills Council. It also had theme groups, each taking responsibility for a main aspect of its delivery plan. The work of the SAZ was integrated into the Board primarily through a Health and Wellbeing group, and others like those for Environment and Economy.

The SAZ also had its own steering group (SAZSG), with representatives from the BCA as host, Sport England as the main funder, and LCC as the most important partner for sport and PA, though it is clear that the SAZ's credibility was enhanced by being under the BCA's aegis rather than of the City Council, which was blamed by residents for chronic neglect. The commonality of themes is clear in Table 10.1. The SAZSG helped to push forward the recommendations in the Needs Assessment and Action Plan, and kept a focus on the team's advocacy work, trying to ensure that it didn't get submerged in day-to-day project management.

The BCA derived benefits from hosting the SAZ, with two additional members of staff during structural changes in 2003, and significant input in consulting residents on and drawing up revisions to the delivery plan. The one contentious issue arising from being hosted by the BCA was that the Association instituted a freeze on spending for six months in 2003 so that it could concentrate on its reorganisation and plan revision. While this was important for the BCA's future, it meant the SAZ losing a tenth of its delivery time because new projects could not be progressed, and job security was questioned, despite staff's commitment to improving residents' quality of life in a way rarely seen in national sports

Table 10.1 The commonality of BCA and Sport England themes

BCA delivery plan themes	Sport England themes
1. Making Braunstone safe	Sport and community safety
2. Making Braunstone work	
3. Improving the living environment	
4. Making Braunstone fit and healthy	Sport and health
5. Raising educational attainment	Sport, education and lifelong learning
6. Making Braunstone united and confident	Sport and social inclusion
All the delivery themes identified above combine to deliver regeneration to Braunstone.	Sport and regeneration

192

development programmes where SD Officers (SDOs) working at district or citywide scales can become detached from small local communities.

STRUCTURES AND PROCESSES OF DELIVERY

Sport England required each SAZ to complete a Needs Assessment and Action Plan (NAAP) in its first twelve months. The aim of the NA was to paint a picture of sport in Braunstone and identify issues that needed addressing. The AP aimed to identify priorities for achieving the vision for SD in Braunstone over five years. The small scale of BCA allowed a community-level focus; it became clear that this was very successful, as it had significant impacts on working with individuals and clubs, and provided evidence of how sport can help to regenerate a small community.

The first step in the NA was to decide how to undertake the work, while ensuring that it was community-driven. After discussion with BCA colleagues, it was decided to use the same robust, participatory consultation technique that had proved successful in exploring food poverty in Braunstone for a project called 'Nosh and Dosh'. The team formed to carry out this work consisted of the SAZ Manager and AM, the BCA's Inclusion Officer and Assistant, and for the first three months the senior LCC Sports Regeneration Officer.

The important contribution of the BCA Inclusion team was to question and challenge traditional SD ways of thinking and working, keeping the focus on the needs of individuals, and not just on the needs of sports. They already had experience of talking to residents on the streets and doorsteps of Braunstone, but welcomed the opportunity to develop their skills and thinking in a new area of work.

The team considered the following points:

- They didn't know what residents wanted, and so needed to ask.
- Formal surveys and questionnaires were not appropriate for this work.
- They needed to ensure that residents were active in the process.
- They needed to ensure that the schemes developed were needed and actively used.
- They wanted to identify different involvements by both residents and professionals in projects.
- Participation and involvement was the keynote.

So, the aim of the needs assessment was 'to find out how to get more residents involved in sport'. To achieve this, the SAZ team needed to:

193

- Talk to people *not* involved in sport and find out why.
- Find out what sports *were* going on in Braunstone.
- Find out what Braunstone residents wanted from sport.
- Identify and develop new sports projects to help residents experience and enjoy sport.
- Work with individuals and groups to achieve common goals.
- Use sport as a way of improving the quality of their lives, especially in the spheres of health, education, environment, crime, and employment.

The team spoke to over 700 individuals (about 5% of the population) during its consultations, marking on a large-scale map where each lived. This helped to ensure that the team spoke to enough people in different parts of the estate, especially the most deprived areas. They also visited schools and a wide range of sporting and non-sporting groups. Halfway through the process, they reviewed the profile of respondents, and recognised they hadn't reached the most excluded people. One of the strengths of this participatory appraisal was that it enabled the team to adapt their techniques to fit individuals and locations. So, they decided to work on pavements, in front of shops and to knock on doors to reach residents not involved in groups and clubs. This was an important part of the work, because such residents gave them significant information about sport and the factors affecting their lives, like trying to pay the bills while on benefit or low pay, suffering ill-health, being bullied, not going to school, or living in poor housing. This period of the NA work was a defining moment for the team, as it influenced how to work in the future, and created personal commitment to carrying out the recommendations.

The team held three 'reference' group meetings during this process so as to involve other partners in the work. The first was in December 2002, aiming to explain the techniques the team was using and give an update on the work; the second was in February 2003 to share results with statutory partners, and the third in March 2003 for sports governing bodies. Each gave potential partners an opportunity to identify and sign up to the project areas that interested them, and more than sixty did so. The team was unsure about how partners would react to results from such non-traditional work, but feedback was really positive, and showed that they found the process informative, interesting and challenging. Further, it provided the team with an excellent foundation for future cooperation.

caron walpole and mike collins

THE RESULTS OF THE NEEDS ASSESSMENT: A PICTURE OF SPORT IN BRAUNSTONE

Participation

The Needs Assessment and Action Plan highlighted:

- that the majority of residents played some sport;
- participation in more than 60 sports;
- but residents wanted more choice – making a list of over 80 sports, with swimming at the top;
- a need for more coaches and volunteers to increase local choice and availability;
- a need for a greater range of local sports clubs and support to ensure sustainability;
- positive attitudes around sports' contribution to wider social objectives;
- enjoyment and health as the main reasons for playing sport;
- a need for improvements to local sports facilities.

Often it was residents who didn't play sport who desired to go swimming. This is an important message for policy makers, as swimming appeals to all ages and both genders (see Chapter 9). Most people who played lots of sport were young – aged 6–15; as expected, among older people participation decreased, and by the time they reached age 66 very few took part in sport at all.

A few partners were developing sport for the community in Braunstone, again focused mainly on young people. Leicester City Council, mainly through its Sports Regeneration Unit, ran a 3-year SD project in primary schools, funded by the Council, and BCA trained local coaches so they could run lunchtime and after-school clubs. A School Sports Coordinator and Specialist Sports College project covered most schools in Braunstone, bringing some extra time and resources. Very few SDOs from county governing bodies worked on the estate, nor had the city's major professional clubs much involvement, except for tag rugby through Leicester Tigers, and some youth basketball work by Leicester Riders. It was clear that the main reasons for this were poor or missing facilities, residents presenting numerous barriers to playing sport, and the estate's negative image.

Barriers to participation

Numerous barriers to playing sport were identified by citizens, as summarised in Table 10.2. These were common to non-participants generally, but exacerbated by poverty or disability (Collins, 2003).

Many mentioned more than one barrier; for example, a single parent on benefit with children and no transport will face barriers of cost, no transport, and childcare, making trying to play even more off-putting. It also meant that policy by the different Departments of LCC or different agencies had to be 'joined up' if interventions were to be effective (Collins, 2003).

The participatory process emphasised how important it is to see sport in the context of everything else in someone's life. If a resident hasn't enough money to pay their bills, has to walk to shops to buy food (there were no supermarkets on the estate), has children who don't want to go to school because they are being bullied, sport is not a priority for them, especially if they have their own personal barriers as well. The key to regeneration is about seeing a person as a whole, and not just the part that concerns sports providers. Most people had been failed by a wide range of service providers over many years, and this had built up the social exclusion and low expectations, and it would take more than a year or two to regenerate it. It was crucial for the SAZ to link closely to the other agencies trying to combat these other factors. This meant a new approach was needed in how sports providers worked with residents, on a much more sustained and individual basis. Current national SD approaches were of

Table 10.2 Barriers to playing sport in Braunstone

Barrier	Examples/details
1. 'I can't . . . because of children and families'	Many female respondents had to care for several children of and below school age, and for them it was difficult to find time to play sport. Very often they had no transport, meaning that shopping, walking to the doctors, to school, etc., took up significant time in their days. They also needed good childcare while they played, and often crèches in leisure centres operated only between 9 a.m. and 3 p.m. on weekdays. Parents said there were few opportunities to do activities together as a family.
2. 'Health problems' – arthritis, asthma, multiple	Some residents reported (sometimes multiple) health problems that stopped them walking long distances or playing sport. They also said that some sports sessions were too demanding for them. Most residents thought that sport could benefit them, but felt that they had no opportunity to take part.

3. 'Too old'	Some residents had played sport in the past but that it was no longer for them because they were too old – for some, this meant before the age of 50. Very often these residents were thinking about sports they used to play, such as football.
4. 'Girls can't . . .'	Some girls at primary and secondary schools felt sport was only for boys, demonstrating a lack of role models. Some girls in primary school Year 6 didn't like PE because they were embarrassed at having to get changed in front of the boys; others said that boys 'hogged' sport in school, and didn't let them play.
5. 'Too big'	Some women said that they were 'too big' to play sport, unable to find track/swimsuits to fit them or would feel embarrassed. Most would like to do sport as they knew it would help them lose weight; some said they had put on weight after their children left primary school when they did less walking.
6. 'North vs. South' – territory	Residents of all ages said that they thought the south (or north) of the estate had the better facilities. They also said they wouldn't go to the other part to play sport.
7. 'Costs too much'	Many residents thought it was too expensive to play sport (buying kit, bus fares, paying for activities, joining a club or a gym). This was particularly important for residents, especially those on state benefits with several children. It was very difficult to pay for the whole family to do sport together, or even for all the children.
8. 'No transport'	Car ownership is low in Braunstone, so more people rely on walking or buses. It is therefore very difficult/costly for families with young children, older or disabled people to get to sports activities outside Braunstone that are not on a bus route.
9. 'No facilities, activities'	Residents said there were very few facilities for playing sport or activities, especially local to them.
10. 'Poor information'	Residents said they were not aware of what was going on in Braunstone, including local clubs, activities, facilities, opportunities to qualify as a coach – probably lower-than-average computer ownership.
11. 'I work, unsociable hours, shifts'	Some, especially women, residents reported it was difficult to find time to play sport because they had one or more part-time jobs and had to look after families. Some also worked in the evenings and at weekends.
12. 'Disabilities'	Some respondents were disabled (including wheelchair users, people with walking problems and with learning difficulties) who said there were very few opportunities to play sport locally.

Source Needs Assessment, 2003.

197

working with target sports and target age groups (most usually young people – see Chapter 2) and for providers to decide when, where, and what type of activity is supplied, and how much it should cost. The work of Braunstone SAZ shows that this approach is not appropriate in a deprived community: sports providers need to work much more closely with residents and to change their service delivery mode.

While most facilities were poor, during 2003/4 a new 'state-of-the-art' sports hall was built on the estate by LCC Education Department at Fullhurst Community College, with funding from the New Opportunities Lottery Fund. Although the College was keen to encourage local residents and clubs to use the facilities, there was no subsidy available for those unable to meet the prices, which was proving a major barrier to residents and local clubs. The City Council's Cultural Services and Neighbourhood Renewal Departments also built a new £9m Braunstone Leisure Centre (BLC) with money from the Sport England Lottery Fund and BCA. Opened in December 2004, it is located in the 27th most deprived ward in England, and has two swimming pools, a sports hall, gym, crèche and café. It became the more crucial as the small, older Braunstone Recreation Centre on the northern part of the estate was damaged by arson in 2003 and then further vandalised, leading to closure and demolition.

Braunstone Park is another important part of the estate's outdoor formal and informal sport and recreation. It was home to several local football clubs, and important for walking and fishing. It had a 'caged' hard play area which, although the only one of its kind on the estate, was disused because of vandalism and lack of maintenance. The main priorities identified for sport in the park were improving the football pitches, providing good changing facilities and improving the 'cage'. To be successful, this needed to be done as an integral part of the regeneration programme. The SAZ team was closely involved in overall plans to regenerate the park, and led consultations with over 350 local residents preparatory to submitting an outline planning application in December 2003, which made it clear that many residents saw the park as 'the jewel in the crown' of the estate, knew it better than the professionals, and had a valuable contribution to make in improving it.

In 2007/8 Hall Aitken (2008) undertook another survey with the help of Sally Davis, now SAZ manager, this time of 460 under-16s and 404 adults, using some questions from the 2006 Active People survey, plus on-street surveys about Braunstone Park (102 interviews) and volunteering (96), focus groups in primary schools (98 children), and face-to-face questions with stakeholders, project providers, local sports clubs and grant recipients (312).

198

Some main findings were:

- 86% doing some sort of PA, an increase of 17%.
- Those doing five sessions of 30 minutes of vigorous activity were slightly above the national average at 34%.
- Relatively few children – 17% – did five sessions of an hour's activity a week.
- 51 sports were mentioned, with five of the top ten the same (cycling, badminton, aerobics, dance and multi-sports coming in – the last two influenced by the offers of the ER Crew and Score4Sport and teenage lifestyle clubs respectively).
- Of sports people wanted to do, swimming came first, and six of the top ten were the same, with cricket, ice-skating ,dancing, and gymnastics entering the list.
- The use of SAZ-funded facilities was high (see Table 10.3), especially of BLC, where nearly three out of five went for some purpose.
- At 22% for men and 11% for women, competitive sports participation was above the national and Leicester averages.
- Barriers of cost, availability of clubs and facilities, and transport no longer seem significant, but lack of time and interest were still major barriers.
- Four out of five residents agreed that sport can aid health, three-fifths likewise crime and social inclusion, and over half employment prospects.
- 77% thought sport had improved the area, with 69% of youth and 84% of adults thinking provision was adequate.

THE ACTION PLAN AND EARLY PROJECTS

The vision for Braunstone SAZ was 'to use sport as a way of improving the quality of life for residents living in Braunstone now and in the future', with four strategic aims. The first aim was to get more residents involved in sport, and the other three focused on influencing and changing how sport is provided – at policy

Table10.3 Use of SAZ-funded facilities, (self-reported) %

	Adults	Young people (aged 8–24)	Total
Braunstone Leisure Centre	58	67	63
The Cage/multi-use games area	10	34	24
Braunstone Park football pitches	11	22	17
Braunstone Park/green space	24	51	38

Source Hall Aitken, 2008.

level, by sports providers, and by cross-cutting agencies like police authorities and Primary Health Care teams. The Action Plan ran four projects that would get different partners involved, and collect monitoring and evaluation information to demonstrate the need for change and to influence policies and how partners work in deprived areas. But it also had to respond proactively to new initiatives and new sources of funding in years two to four, while using results to provide and influence advocacy work for years four and five.

FAB (Fit and active buddies)

FAB emerged as the SAZ's top priority. It sought to work on a one-to-one basis to break down the multiple barriers facing residents who did not currently play sport but wished to. Its origins can be traced to the first of many doorstep conversations, with a woman who said she would like to go swimming but couldn't find a swimsuit big enough, whose daughter had been absent from school for ages because of bullying, who was worried about how overgrown her back garden had become, and whose dog had fallen down the stairs. The team knew that, with the requisite time and resources, they could have conveyed her to the shops to buy a swimsuit and then to the swimming pool. FAB began in November 2003 as a 2-year project hosted by Leicester West Primary PCT, and funded by BCA and Sport England and later by the PCT and European Social Fund. It used female and sessional mentors. Having identified a resident's barriers to participation, they devised solutions, mobilised resources, and if company was needed, went with him/her to play, like Solent and West Yorks sports counselling schemes for 'youth at risk'. The main tool was a personal sports plan worked up by the resident and the mentor together, which was used to monitor and evaluate involvement. There were also group sessions (Calorie Killers, Fit Chicks and a Teenage Lifestyle Club) run jointly with the Community Food Project.

FAB's first two years were resoundingly successful. After 130 participants, it still had a waiting list, and became recognised as one of the most attractive projects on the estate. Staff used the project to get people involved in several activities – swimming, walking, aerobics, line dancing, climbing and going to the gym. This project was also linked to other health projects in Braunstone, particularly where such links were powerful, as with 'Nosh and Dosh' nutrition, and a smoking-cessation scheme.

The most impressive part of FAB was the benefits to individuals and families, including significant weight losses, increased self-confidence, reduced stress and depression, reduced medication, and newly formed friendships. Every participant had their own story, and this project changed the lives of most. An unforeseen benefit was where involved individuals 'cascaded' FAB through their families, and it changed how they behaved as a family – like father and son playing badminton together, or husband and wife cooking healthy meals together. Governments have rarely succeeded with attempts at such 'trickle-down' effects. It was clear that FAB worked successfully and had its intended impact. Other schemes in Braunstone are 'Get active 5–13s', using a British Heart Foundation model (two workers), and Ilesmere College running MEND nutrition and PA for 7–13 year olds attending with a member of their family.

Although FAB seems an expensive project at first sight, the success of increasing participation rates and improving both physical and mental health so significantly among some of the most excluded residents in Leicester and the East Midlands must cause policy makers to consider whether this is a more effective way of delivering than by traditional means of SD. It also raises the question of how cost-effective is the substantial funding to encourage schoolchildren to play more sport when so little funding is given to encourage their families to get involved and provide a supportive and potentially sustaining context. But support periods have been longer than expected, and exit routes are still being developed.

Score4Sport (reducing youth crime through sport)

The Score4Sport (S4S) project is hosted by the National Association for the Care and Resettlement of Offenders (NACRO), funded by Positive Futures, Connexions, the Football Foundation and V-point. The aim was to work with young people already involved in, or at risk of, crime, vandalism or antisocial/ nuisance behaviour and was extended to training for employment. The project team comprised a coordinator, four coaches and volunteers, who worked with targeted groups and individuals on an outreach basis. The team organised activities like football and basketball, while working with the young people to address other aspects of their behaviour. 'Mini moto', for example, is a scheme teaching youngsters road safety.

The project ran sessions on at least three evenings a week during school terms, and in the mornings, afternoons and evenings of every weekday in school holidays. A number of partners were involved – the police and fire services, the Youth Offending Team, the local LCC housing office, and a local young offenders' institution. A number of these agencies and some parents referred young people to S4S.

Besides the regular sports activities, S4S ran a junior football organisers (JFOs) course in summer 2004. For some of these young people, it was their first time in a 'classroom' for a long time, and the first 'qualification' some had ever achieved. All the JFOs became involved in organising tournaments/events to give them practical experience, and some older ones proceeded to Level 1 football coaching certificates, and then got practical experience volunteering as coaches for local amateur clubs.

The project worked with the fire service, completing in 2005 a project called 'Fireball' (Braunstone had the highest incidence of arson in Leicester, and was a priority for fire-prevention work). It involved firefighters working as volunteer coaches/team managers with youth teams, coaching and getting them ready for a major 5-a-side tournament. As part of this process, the young people were taken to the local fire station to learn about the personal and social consequences of arson.

S4S soon demonstrated benefits: the housing office and the police saw falls of 23% in local antisocial behaviour and vandalism. Agencies were referring their clients to the project, and individuals started to change their lifestyles, especially older teenagers. It met all its targets for numbers of youth.

Braunstone Sports Grants scheme

This project sought to support local sports clubs, the SAZ team working with BCA to operate a local grants scheme, with a fund totalling £15,000 a year and a maximum grant of £1,000. Its key features were an easy-to-complete application process, a maximum time of four weeks for decision, and clubs being able to apply for funding both for existing and new teams – a conscious decision, the priority being to support clubs to strengthen themselves and not to encourage them to do development work they could not sustain.

The scheme funded any sports recognised by Sport England, including dance, and, amongst other things, equipment purchases, training for coaches, support for volunteers, transport, and facility hire. Ninety-six grants totalling £68,000 were disbursed in 2001–2006, mainly for equipment and one-off events. This project was commended for its simplicity and ability to respond flexibly to needs, but its criteria may have been too loose (Hall Aitken, 2008). It is about to be relaunched, with a focus on club infrastructure (coaching and volunteer development).

Facility development

The new Braunstone Leisure Centre soon had a very positive effect on the estate. Not only was it well used by residents, especially children and young people, but it also helped make Braunstone a 'destination' – somewhere in Leicester to visit. The SAZ team worked closely with LCC to help embed it into the community, and give people more confidence in the City Council, notably in association with 'Braunstone Working' to recruit, train and give work experience in existing sports centres to twenty-five local residents so that they developed the competencies to fill jobs in the new Leisure Centre, as receptionists, duty managers and assistants. The outcome was that over half of the staff were local residents.

The SAZ team continued to work with the Leisure Centre staff to develop the programme. LCC provided a 25% discount for all residents and an additional 50% discount for residents on benefit for the next sixteen years, to enable real access to the Centre. This was part of a funding deal with BCA, where the Centre was being used by local clubs like Braunstone Boxing Club, Braunstone Swimming Club, and some local youth projects. Residents welcomed the Centre. Accessibility was improved by diverting a bus route into BLC and providing a nursery as part of a Surestart programme. Other accessibility projects were:

- a women's sport conference and international women's week at the Centre with the City's Education Department, emphasising football, cycling, street dance and trampolining;
- Street Sports for 8–15 year olds, offering five months of free coaching for 1,655 youths in football, hockey, skateboarding and basketball, each one averaging 4.4 attendances.

One litmus test is how much vandalism occurred – little or none. Other important outcomes have been:

- The forecast of 400,000 users annually was achieved with 51% female, a subsidy of £1.25 per user (which helped lower the City's overall city subsidy for sports users from £3.10 to £1.78 each, and met CPA indicators).
- 68% of users were from the estate, and 54% from C2, DE groups.
- BEM customers increased from 24% to 35%, disabled from 1.7% to 3%.
- Using FAB's 70% discount, monitored participants have often lost 10% of body weight, lowered blood pressure and diabetes, and reduced cholesterol and use of medication/anti-depressants and painkillers.

A challenge that emerged was that only 8% of visitors were aged over 60, against a City average of 17% and its CPA upper threshold of 14%. So management introduced a free swim initiative with a 2006 target of 11% from this age group (LCC, 2006). By 2005/6 usage was 400,000 a year, but local residents' share had fallen from 69% to 43% of the total; whether this was the end of a 'honeymoon' or the effect of BLC becoming a city-wide venue is not clear (Hall Aitken, 2008: 43). Its annual subsidy is £550,000, an indication of the City Council's commitment.

Improving Braunstone Park was a major plank in the BCA's Development Plan for 2008–2011 (BCA, 2007), spending £680,000 to make it a 'community sports park', involving replacing the worn-out paddling pool with a street sport area, and developing paths and other areas in consultation. The New Opportunities Fund and Single Regeneration Budget 5 had already awarded £191,000 to improve the four turf football pitches to senior Combination League standard, and the Active England Fund and BCA had awarded over £700,000 to replace 'the cage' with a new floodlit multi-use games and training area, with two staff for its first three years; 34% of youth and 10% of adults reported using it weekly. Adjacent, a new Youth House was built by LCC with funding from BCA, as the focal point for all youth services in Braunstone, and with shared management. At the rear of this building were new changing rooms for six teams, built with £375,000 from the BCA and £250,000 from the Football Foundation. All teams and clubs booking are required to show 70% residing in the NDC area. A female resident said 'different sports on the park would improve the area'.

These facilities contributed to improving Braunstone's environment, and they provided jobs, offered training and learning opportunities for residents, improved health, and helped to prevent antisocial behaviour. An important consideration was sustainability, and these facilities should be maintained for future generations, and be looked after. Pride on the estate has grown.

Hall Aitken (2008: 56) summed up their review thus:

> Although the evaluation results are overwhelmingly positive, the 'job' is not yet done. Some residents are still not engaged in any sport and physical activity, barriers to sport still exist and some planned delivery is still in its infancy (for example Braunstone Park improvements). There is a danger the portfolio of projects and initiatives will disband or weaken. Already, some projects face issues of mission drift, and others have a range of other objectives to meet (i.e. not necessarily solely focused on Braunstone).

So, the SAZ has been relaunched as 'Sporting Braunstone', a local Sports Alliance involving as partners:

- Braunstone Sport Action Zone
- LCC Sports Regeneration Unit

caron walpole and mike collins

- Braunstone Community Association
- Braunstone Leisure Centre
- Sport England/Lottery fund
- Ellesmere Sports College 11–19
- City Council
- Score4Sport
- Braunstone Grove youth sports facility
- Special Olympics Leicester July 09
- NACRO mini moto
- Leicester City PCT
- SI Sports (multi-sport coaching)
- Braunstone Working
- StreetVibe (youth work)
- Get Active (sports and PA for 5–13s).

It will work through a Strategic and an Operational group, with four aims, to

- increase participation;
- improve infrastructure, organisation and management of sport and PA;
- yield high quality and performance at all levels;
- produce benefits from increased activity relating to social welfare, education, the local economy and health.

Its course leaflet (Sporting Braunstone, 2009) offered training in minimum operating standards for facilities, over forty opportunities for Level 1 and 2 NGB sports coaching (including for disabled performers), leadership, employment and volunteering opportunities, including in the Special Olympics and Braunstone Sports Festival, training being offered free or cheap to local residents.

The BCA has spent £25m of its initial capital and levered in another £18m; it has renovated over 200 homes and, amongst 60 projects for training, crime reduction and culture, has a new library, a new health centre, a Surestart centre, and the Youth House (BCA, 2005). The sport element is over £12m of this – a high level of leverage against £50,000 p.a. core funding. The Braunstone project became quite widely known. In 2005 it was awarded a Good Practice prize by the Institute of Sport and Recreation Management (Edwards and Mills, 2006), and more significantly was a major plank in the successful application (LCC, 2005) to the Office of the Deputy Prime Minister for Beacon Status as an authority succeeding in providing culture and sport (including arts, museums, libraries and festivals) for hard-to-reach groups; and subsequently in its being awarded European City of Sport in 2008.

CONCLUSIONS: LESSONS AND CHALLENGES TO CONVENTIONAL SPORTS DEVELOPMENT

Over the last ten years SD has become almost 'clinical' – it is about target sports and target groups. Much of it doesn't look at the individuals involved, and it is rarely in a position to respond to their needs on this scale. It is all about formula-based working as passed on from one SDO to another: set up a sports coaching course for young people at a certain time at a certain price at a certain venue, do some publicity, and they will turn up. Yes, 'they'' will turn up, but 'they' are usually the well-organised, middle-class young people already involved in sport. They are often seen as customers, not as clients. What difference has the work of the SDO really made? The motivations of SDOs often come from a personal interest in playing sport, but is their work thought-provoking, and challenging for themselves or their clients/customers?

What happens to the child who comes from a single-parent family with four other children, on benefit and without a car? What about the overweight mum who would love to go swimming to lose weight but doesn't think they make swimsuits in her size (and which she probably couldn't afford to buy anyway)? What about the retired man with a heart problem, who finds it difficult to walk, has fond memories of playing football, but doesn't think sport could involve him again? Who is thinking or caring about such people?

The experience in the Braunstone SAZ and some other projects working in deprived communities shows that conventional SD will not work for the majority, and certainly not effectively. It is time for SD to move on from sports organisation to genuine development work which sees people as individuals and active citizens, gives them the chance to get involved and have a say. Braunstone SAZ team's experience shows that such work can make a significant difference with so-called hard-to-reach groups, and identifies seven keys to success:

1. SD work in any community should be built on a thorough needs assessment based on ongoing consultation and involvement with residents. This will give the solid grounding for work in the future and open up partnership working and external funding opportunities.
2. The development of projects from the needs assessment material should involve residents in identifying what a project should deliver, for whom, how, where, when, at what price, and how to judge success.
3. SD work in deprived communities should happen in partnership with regeneration agencies, because clearly sport can make positive contributions to improving the quality of life there. This recognises that individuals have

caron walpole and mike collins

multiple issues and constraints in their lives which must be addressed by various agencies in 'joined-up' projects, and sport is an excellent tool to support this.

4. Each current/potential sports participant should be seen, consulted and treated as a whole individual. They need to be asked about the best solutions for themselves; this needs to be built into the planning process, and when they own the solutions, most will work.

5. Visible 'passion' and personal commitment from staff working in SD is the only thing that will get results; leaving the job after two/three years is not good enough evidence in tackling tough issues in such communities – it is the 'carrier pigeon' approach they are all too used to and sceptical about.

6. Patience – this community development approach to SD involving residents often takes longer than anticipated, and than driving, managerialist approaches, but it is far more successful (Tungatt and MacDonald, 1992).

7. SD work in a community must not be 'hijacked' by funding sources or partners, particularly national agencies, for their publicity needs – it needs to remain true to its local vision.

Reviewing outcomes of the BLC/SAZ programmes, partners commented very favourably:

> Sport is having . . . an impact out of all proportion to its size . . . in Braunstone, more than any other theme.
>
> (Keith Beaumont, CEO,
> Braunstone Community Association)

> BLC is making a significant contribution to tackling health inequalities . . . and is an excellent example of creative, innovative and successful partnership work.
>
> (Deb Watson, Assistant Director,
> Western and Eastern Leicester PCT)

> Our leisure centre is the best thing that has ever happened to the estate.
> (Braunstone resident (LCC, 2006))

Subsequently Sport England published Ipsos/MORI's (2006) findings on the impact of four SAZs – Barrow-in-Furness, Liverpool, Bradford and Luton, and revealed statistically significant increases in participation in the first two, both deprived areas, especially among the over-50s, white people and C2DE (semi-skilled and unskilled groups) but not in the last two, for reasons that could not be diagnosed (Table 10.4).

Table 10.4 Increases in participation in Barrow and Liverpool SAZs

Category	Barrow		Liverpool	
	2001/2	*2005/6*	*2001/2*	*2005/6*
All	66	**72**	60	**65**
Aged over 50	53	**60**	36	**48**
Men	72	75	66	**72**
Women	61	**69**	54	59
White	66	**72**	60	**66**
Black/Ethnic minority	n/a	n/a	56	59
C2DE social group	61	**67**	43	**53**

Source Ipos/MORI, 2006.
Note Participation = taking part at least four times in an average 4-week period, including walking; statistically significant figures at 95% interval in bold.

A year later these results were combined with Sport England's (2008) monitoring of grants via the Active Communities Development Fund, and shared common conclusions about thirteen critical success factors in driving up participation locally:

1. Appoint a highly motivated charismatic leader who can quickly establish credibility.
2. Establish clear strategic direction supported by a systematic needs assessment.
3. Create a focused paid delivery team, engaged with the local community.
4. Build strong partnerships in and beyond sport.
5. Empower local people through a listening, bottom-up approach.
6. Promote local volunteering capacity, while expecting turnover of individuals.
7. Invest in facilities but focus on people as keys to success.
8. Provide small grants to engender goodwill and trust.
9. Ensure communications and marketing are tailored to local groups.
10. Run low-cost taster sessions, and ensure progression routes.
11. Offer a wide diversity of activities tailored to what works for different groups.
12. Make local identity/community work for you – be part of 'us', not 'them'.
13. Make it last – build a culture of sustainability and self-help.

In the foreword to his 2005 report, Lord Carter wrote about these factors:

> Arguably the most important thing . . . is that there is nothing actually remarkable. In effect there are no real surprises. They all represent good

community sports development principles and practices. However, what is highly significant is: firstly how these factors have been strategically applied together in a concerted and focused way over a five-year period; and secondly because of our focused and continued research we can say with confidence that this way of working has led to real participation increases amongst some of our most hard to reach priority groups.

Clearly Braunstone SAZ incorporated all thirteen of these; signs are hopeful, but in all the SAZs more time is needed to say whether the results are sustainable. The work in Braunstone SAZ has already been under way for seven years, and has brought more successes than ever imagined at the beginning. But it becomes part of the team's life, more than a job. It is harder and slower work than expected, and this made the team worry that they won't be able to do everything that they wished and planned. Their expectations are high; this isn't just about running a series of coaching courses or events; it's about trying to improve people's lives, however, modest a difference it may be.

The experience described in this case study is all about working locally, at the heart of a small community. The lessons learned could be used in any small community, whether deprived or middle-class, rural or urban, white or ethnic minority. They have been known for over half a century to the Community Development movement (Taylor et al., 2000) and workers in that movement. The keynote is the personal contact made by SD professionals with citizens, and the latter getting to know, trust and have confidence in their skills and ability to help deliver. It is all about professionals building their knowledge, layer by layer, changing it to reflect happenings in the community, and involving the local people at every stage of project development and management. It is all about professionals and residents understanding that they are each experts in their own sphere who need each other and must talk and listen together frequently. Only then can a difference be made in people's lives – it starts at the bottom and works its way up.

There is an important role for a strategic SD level, influencing, giving messages, changing policy. But it should not be forgotten that the point of this is to help change locally in communities, to help get more citizens into more enjoyable sport, more often. The two levels of SD need to mesh better to the same ends. One issue that governments and agencies fail to see is the time that effective change takes; another is how large schemes, including the large SAZs like West Cumbria, Cornwall or North Notts/North Derby can work – mostly by developing a series of local 'oases' of development not unlike Braunstone. Clearly there is so much left to do and to learn.

ACKNOWLEDGEMENT

We are grateful for the help of Sally Davis of Sporting Braunstone for the Hall Aitken (2008) review and other update material for this chapter.

REFERENCES

Braunstone Community Association (2005) *Changing Lives – 5 years of a New Deal for Braunstone,* Leicester: BCA.

Braunstone Community Association (2007) *Annual Report 2006/7,* Leicester: BCA.

Carter, Lord (2005) *Review of National Sport Effort and Resources,* London: DCMS.

Collins, M.F. (2003*) Sport and Social Exclusion,* London: Routledge.

Edwards, P. and Mills, C. (2006) Everybody matters, *Recreation,*10: 22–4.

Ipsos/MORI (2006) *Understanding the Success Factors in Sport Action Zones: Final Report,* London: Sport England.

Hall Aitken (2008) *Sport Action Zone Evaluation, Final Report,* Manchester: Hall Aitken.

Leicester City Council (2005) Application for Beacon Status, downloaded 10 August 2008 from www.leicester.gov.uk.

Leicester City Council (2006) *Braunstone Leisure Centre Case Study,* Leicester: LCC.

Social Exclusion Unit (1998) *Bringing Britain Together,* London: Cabinet Office.

Sport England (2008) Impact: Innovation working in communities, increased participation, Sport Action Zones, ACDF, Magnet Fund, in *3D: Driving Change, Developing Partnerships, Delivering Outcomes,* London: www.sport england.org, downloaded 10 August 2008.

Sporting Braunstone (2009) *Course Brochure,* Leicester: Sporting Braunstone.

Taylor, M., Barr, A. and West, A. (2000) *Signposts to Community Development* (2nd edn), London: Community Development Foundation.

Tungatt, M. and MacDonald, D. (1992) *National Demonstration Projects: Major Lessons and Issues for Sports Development,* London: Sports Council.

caron walpole and mike collins

CHAPTER 11

'SPORT FOR GOOD'?

Streetsport in Stoke-on-Trent

Fiona McCormack

INTRODUCTION

The long-standing belief that sport and leisure opportunities bring benefits for individuals and communities has dominated the provision of leisure services throughout the later twentieth century. However, policy concerns in the 1990s focused on social exclusion, and funding was allocated from sources like City Challenge and the Single Regeneration Budget, and there was a growing concern 'to assess whether there is any evidence of the social benefits that accrue from sport and leisure initiatives in pursuit of community development' (Long and Sanderson, 2001).

The context for the development of initiatives to prevent/avoid youth crime can be traced to growing pressures in the 1980s to extend non-custodial sentences, and a consequent search for solutions to combat juvenile delinquency/disorder. They generally sought to provide activity programmes for inner city youth, sometimes as part of wider inner city regeneration (e.g. in Glasgow, see Suzuki, 2007). The work of such projects and their value to the youth involved has become the focus of much public debate.

Rationales for such work can be traced to a range of theories in sociology, criminology and leisure studies (see McCormack, 2000; Coalter, 2007) seeking to explain why young people offend. These identify factors embedded in the fabric of society and its power structures, mediating factors like the actions of managers and gatekeepers, and factors of self-perception and behaviour of individuals (see pp. 214–15). It has often been suggested that, unless guided to positive, 'pro-social' activities in their leisure time, humans can naturally be drawn to antisocial acts, and that this has been the case ever since the work ethic and 'rational recreation' were introduced in the Industrial Revolution. This belief, that 'the devil makes work for idle hands' was basic to Cyril Burt's (1925: 29) study *The Young Delinquent*: 'so long as there is neither work nor school, mischief fills the empty hours'.

The Scarman Report (1982) into the causes of the inner city riots centred around Brixton in south London, identified a need for constructive leisure opportunities to be provided. Cantle's (2001) report nineteen years later, after riots in Bradford and Oldham, made the same diagnosis and recommendation. But in a previous study of another group with substantial free time, unemployed people, Glyptis (1989) concluded that constructive recreational programmes could not replace the role of work in filling free time, or offering as much structure and meaning, producing income and sustained challenges and achievements as work. Linking delinquency to factors like a need to achieve status questions the validity of sport and recreation in preventing delinquency.

The boredom theory, however, should not be viewed in isolation: boredom alone cannot be used to explain the complex motives behind delinquency. This study examines the main theories before establishing a relationship for such theories with intervention methods which include active leisure. It will also address the question about factors that contribute to effective interventions by drawing on the experiences of one well-established project, Streetsport in Stoke-on-Trent.

STREETSPORT

Streetsport is an example of an outreach sports intervention operating in Stoke-on-Trent at primary level (i.e. one which seeks to alter the milieu and avoid youth falling into crime) in estates with high levels of deprivation, unemployment and little recreation provision. It sought to increase their welfare rather than diverting them from crime (secondary intervention), or rehabilitating them after offending (tertiary intervention). For examples of tertiary intervention, see McCormack (2000) on Solent Sports Counselling, and Nichols and Taylor (1996) on its West Yorkshire equivalent.

Streetsport provided 2-hour sports sessions across the city, in places where young people were known to gather. The sessions were held each week, and youth could attend free of charge for as long as they wished or needed. They were part of a wider service to local communities demonstrated through a City Council Community Service Department (CSD) programme which was the brainchild of a dedicated manager with a vision for community services:

212

I fought hard to achieve the style of community recreation that I believe communities want and value. I am prepared to stand against policy which may threaten this, even if this makes me unpopular.

(Kevin Sauntry, interview, June 1997)

Streetsport was the result of a successful funding application to the Sports Council, West Midlands. In April 1994 outreach services were launched with a 3-year start-up grant. However, its roots lay in a 1970s detached youth work project in Hanley. Three years later the Manager of Community Recreation summarised its philosophy thus:

There is a negative lagoon of drugs, crime, prostitution and victimisation. Youth work must be preventative and work upstream of this lagoon, with the objective of getting inter-generational talking going, and a network of community support.

(Kevin Sauntry, interview, June 1997)

The response to this need was a mixture of community development and recreation services which he described as 'a programme of activities including play schemes, play training, community events, establishing residents' associations, and formal community networks'.

Although Streetsport did not provide regular headcounts, youths' diary entries and observations suggested that average sessional attendance was around twelve youngsters. There were seven sessions a week, and some daytime ones in school holidays (weather permitting), implying an average of 84 youngsters a week, and an attendance for fifty weeks a year of 4,200.

Unlike Action Sport (Rigg, 1980) and other programmes, Streetsport was not actively marketed, and did not aim to bring more youth out on the street; it aimed to contact and provide for those already on the street. In this way it directly addressed a significant cause of nuisance and community friction, especially to older people – youth 'hanging about' (Audit Commission, 2009). Such youngsters are often seen as 'hooligans' and the cause of crime, but they are more often victims, especially young men.

As an outreach initiative, Streetsport used mobile sports equipment carried in a van, such as temporary football goals, to facilitate sessions on sites, often just open grass; in the evenings sessions were supported by gas-powered telescopic floodlights. The CSD was also responsible for parks and playgrounds and this led to the concept of 'Sports Courts' – multi-purpose hard courts developed from kickabout areas piloted by the Sports Council and taken on by Bolton City Council with 'Reczones' (Morgan, 1998). The court design had a hard area marked out for various sports, including football and basketball, plus fixed goals, basketball posts and timed lighting for evening use, and a seating area for youth. The originals were funded by SRB and Lottery grants, and once open freed the van for other sites.

To analyse key aspects of this scheme, and to devise an evaluation methodology, a framework was applied which had been successfully used for secondary and tertiary interventions (Brantingham and Faust, 1976: 284–96; McCormack, 2000). As Figure 11.1 shows, this related level of intervention and philosophy (right-hand side) to the causes of risk of committing crime identified from multiple literatures (left-hand side). The data was gathered over two years from on-site interviews and group discussions with youth (mainly aged under 16) over

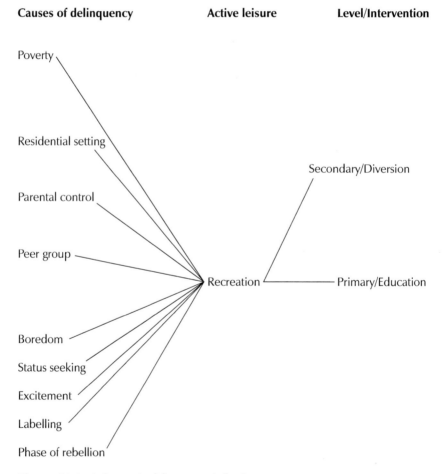

Figure 11.1 A theoretical framework for Streetsport

fiona mccormack

pop and crisps, and with the leaders and policy makers, and other local interests – youth workers, a head teacher, police and local residents.

Streetsport sessions had outcomes for both young people and their deprived communities. First, it and the Sports Courts diverted youth from hanging around on street corners into positive activity. It removed them from peer pressure and other delinquent influences. It offered them a new perspective on leisure opportunities and offered fun and entertainment. For residents, it reduced the perceived threat posed by youth, and reduced nuisance and hence inter-generational friction. The sessions offered education and skills development through a mentor or interested adult, which many of the youngsters lacked. For the youth themselves, the sessions provided improved confidence, awareness and communication skills. The positioning of this intervention as part of community development gave the young people a chance to change their views of their communities and to increase their involvement as citizens.

Risk factors related to delinquency in youth have been defined in terms of personal, social, and environmental factors (Huskins, 1998; Witt and Crompton, 1996). Many of these factors are linked to social exclusion (Collins, 2003); the case study estates of Bentilee, Cobridge and Stanfields in Stoke-on-Trent demonstrated this.

On Bentilee a detached youth worker suggested that the key issues for youth were drugs, unemployment and a lack of leisure opportunities. Bentilee was the largest housing estate in Europe when it was built after the Second World War. It is still a large and sprawling development of mainly terraced and semi-detached houses, built into 'villages' (but with none of the social coherence implied by the name). Recent initiatives had attempted to encourage a greater sense of identity and community spirit. Most youth had experienced short- or long-term unemployment, either personally or in their families. It had a large proportion of single parents, which may explain the lack of young women at the sessions. Those who had children had their leisure time drastically reduced. During one sports session, two young women with children under five watched their partners play; though they expressed no wish to play, they admitted their childcare made their free time almost non-existent. In recent years, housing associations which had come to dominate dwellings management had invested to improve the houses, and sought to address the problems of drug abuse and burglary, so prevalent that some parts were considered 'no-go areas' for families.

There were some playschemes and youth clubs which addressed the needs of younger children, but as they grew out of these activities, there was no acceptable alternative. Hendry (1993: 56) showed for his sample of Scottish youth that the transition from structured leisure activity at age 13 or 14 presented similar problems:

'sport for good'?

This seems like the classic no-win situation. A number of respondents claim that the rules at leisure clubs, youth clubs and sports clubs were too strict. On the other hand, lack of supervision was clearly not appreciated.

This resulted in young people hanging around places like the shops, causing disturbance to other residents. This situation was confirmed by the manager of the Youth Action Project in the local high school:

> Young people in this area suffer from the effects of poor housing, low parental support, poor leisure opportunity, drugs and unemployment [which led to a] culture of low aspirations and poor expectations.
>
> (Interview, May 1999)

There was a similar situation in Cobridge, which was further strengthened by negative press coverage of young people: 'young criminals are making life misery for families on the Grange estate in Cobridge' (*The Sentinel*, 7 September 1999). This was further complicated by the multicultural nature of the Cobridge community. The ethnic minority youth were seen to be breaking away from the strict family control that had been especially associated with these communities and were now 'involved in petty crime and drug dealing, as well as some cross-cultural conflict '(Manager, Cobridge Community Centre, interview, May 1999).

In Stanfields young people also faced high unemployment and little economic prosperity, and the poorest level of facilities of the three estates. Stanfields was the only area to receive two Streetsport sessions a week, the second achieved through external funding. Stanfields was a small, low-rise council housing estate to the north of Burslem; it was on the edge of its electoral ward, which had problems of urban deprivation, crime and unemployment, exacerbated by a lack of local government funding. The 1991 census provided up-to-date population data: unemployment was 10.9%, with lone-parent families accounting for 3.9% of the inhabitants. There was a significant youth population (aged under 30) of 59% of residents. Observation showed pockets of run-down housing and few leisure resources for youth. There was a large open space next to Port Vale (professional) Football Club which Streetsport used in the summer. The high school provided some community activities after hours, but had little to offer in terms of a drop-in centre for adolescents; it did allow Streetsport to use an all-weather pitch in the winter, which had the advantages of basketball posts and a surface hard enough for roller blades.

The success of Streetsport in providing sustainable leisure for socially excluded youth was closely linked to effective leisure education. The outreach workers took time out of the sports sessions to mingle with spectators and those not

fiona mccormack

currently involved in playing. This was demonstrated to be effective in building a positive relationship with all attenders, and in providing ongoing support.

Streetsport exercised no limits of age of attenders, or the length of time people could attend. This continued support produced examples of education that met the changing needs and abilities of groups and individuals. At Stanfields, players wanted to set up an association football team in a junior league, and the Streetsport workers enabled them to establish a team and win a set of kit in a local competition.

Streetsport's role, however, was not just one of leisure education, but also covered social education, best demonstrated by an individual case study. This participant, then in his early twenties, had attended regularly for more than four years; he had had various problems in his adolescence, including drug abuse, unemployment and crime. He was making an effort to revise his lifestyle, and attributed this in part to the continued support of the Streetsport team. He identified the importance of regular sessions where he was accepted as an individual, was not excluded if he failed to meet the general standards of play, but was pointed to a certain standard of behaviour in such ordered activity. This gentle approach to youth work and counselling helped him to survive difficult years, and had given him space to develop a perspective on his lifestyle options.

In a wider analysis of reported leisure for participants and non-participants in Streetsport, the data revealed some significant differences in behaviour. Its sessions targeted young people on the street and the interviews sought to establish how common this was, as shown in Table 11.1.

Table 11.1 Reported leisure venues for young people in Stanfields

Activity	Participants (14)	Non-participants (11)
At home	3	3
Hanging around	8	10
Pubs	4	4
Leisure centres	1	0
Parks/sports courts	7	3

Young people who spend their time hanging around are at greater risk of offending for various reasons. Residents and the police said that youth congregating resulted in telephone calls to the police about nuisance, whether justified or not. The presence of these youth was synonymous for older residents with the threat of crime, as an interview with one local showed:

'sport for good'?

The problem of petty crime and vandalism must come from the groups of youngsters who are always on the streets. When they are there in big groups at night, older residents are frightened to go out.

(Resident A, Stanfields, interview, September 1999)

As Burslem, the Local Police Unit reported the fear that translated to nuisance calls:

We get quite a lot of petty nuisance calls regarding young people causing a disturbance. We have to address this and respond to the residents, but this creates friction between us and the young people as we are always moving them on. From this situation there is a risk that problems can escalate.

(Interview, September 1999)

Young people gathering on the streets are also vulnerable to negative influences from their peer groups and others. Therefore, if Streetsport altered leisure behaviour and moved youth off the street, this had a positive outcome, and the evidence the author gathered demonstrated this was so (McCormack, 2000): only 57 per cent reported this as a significant feature of their leisure, whereas ten out of eleven non-participants did so. It would be naive to suggest that there is a simple and direct link between Streetsport and reduced hanging around. But since Streetsport operated through outreach work, all its young people had been hanging around before joining, as confirmed by a female participant from Stanfields:

I found out about Streetsport through my friends when we were just hanging around . . . I don't hang around on the streets as much any more, in summer I prefer to play sport in the parks, in winter I only go out now if my friends are there.

(Female participant aged 16, interview, September 1999)

The evidence from interviews with participants who had been involved with Streetsport for more than six months indicated that the project had changed leisure behaviour. As demonstrated in Table 11.1, there was greater use of parks for informal sports, and this was confirmed by established players in both Stanfields and Bentilee:

Before Streetsport we might kick a ball around in the streets but we rarely met at the park and organised a kick around. Now we have the team and meet to practise regularly, there is less time to hang around.

(Male aged 18, interview, Stanfields, July 1999)

218

fiona mccormack

The sports area is open all the time and we sometimes play outside the sessions.

(Male aged 16, interview, Bentilee, July 1999)

Reported leisure patterns for this group were varied, including football, tennis, snooker, golf, rounders, cinema, pubs and play schemes; for one in three these activities were done in family groups, the remainder with peers. They wanted to participate primarily to socialise and for enjoyment. Competition and exercise, as for the population at large, were secondary motivations.

It would seem therefore, that for Streetsport to be effective in changing leisure patterns, participants had to take part for more than six months: all of this group reported playing some sport outside the sessions and hanging about less. There was a City Council discount card scheme called Recreation Key, which gave reduced price entry to people, among other things, on low income. But only one Streetsport participant had heard of this, so there was little evidence of Streetsport improving knowledge of opportunities. (It also has to be said that many listed facilities were some distance away, incurring bus fares.)

Two aspects were key to achieving a positive outcome in terms of community development and reducing problems associated with poor leisure facilities – the nature of the service organisation, and the process of implementation.

The organisation

The Community Service Department evolved from an independent community-based detached youth service initiative, the Hanley Youth project, whose work and ideals were incorporated into the CSD. The CSD team was able to provide non-facility-based services in local communities, drawing on a range of funding including the SRB and a successful Lottery bid. Several different functional areas came together to form the CSD – parks, greenspace, special needs, children's play, community art, events, outreach services and environmental conservation. They were combined with an emphasis on involving communities in planning and enabling individuals, via providing training opportunities, focused on using local parks and open spaces.

The implementation process

Streetsport's criterion was simple: The outreach workers were there to meet the young people's needs. This was pursued with a full-time worker – 'the initial

'sport for good'?

outreach process identifies the community resources available and the interests of the young people' (interview, July 1988). This was seen as a continuum of provision from childhood, through adolescence to adulthood. Initially, community recreation reached residents through play services, and comprehensive delivery of holiday play schemes aimed at children aged up to twelve. Then the recreation team sought to offer a transition from play schemes to community involvements. The approach to delivery was conducted in three ways –'outreach workers, hangout shelters alongside sports areas, the Sports Court network' (CSD internal document, 1995). This ensured that delivery was not seen merely as another football session, simply providing a few hours' diversion, but part of a planned process to meet youths' needs in their communities. The process engaged youth in visible positive activities, often in the form of soccer sessions. It sought to encourage a positive dialogue with the community, and increased recognition that these needs of young people must be addressed.

Delivery relied on consultation with youth and their communities at every stage; CSD's documentation pointed out that:

> An important factor in the initial development work was to utilise and strengthen existing links within the community . . . the first contact with young people was able to take place only after contacts with core groups of teenagers in each location, establishing ground rules that ensured minimal conflict and ascertaining from teenagers what their recreational needs are.
>
> (*Annual Report*, 1994: 2)

The results demonstrated the importance of local solutions involving the community, feedback about citizens and youth, and observation suggested that, despite the recommendation by Cooper (1989), there was little evidence of multi-agency provision. Despite claims about such, there were problems in establishing links with other providers; despite the potential for close connection with youth work, differences in working practice had led to friction rather than cooperation. Streetsport dedicated considerable resources to community liaison and consultations, which were observed to form more than half of the daytime work of the two full-time members of staff.

CONCLUSION AND POSTSCRIPT

Leisure has shown to be a part, but unlikely to be all of the solution to juvenile delinquency and social exclusion; in Coalter's (2001) words, it is a 'necessary

but not sufficient condition'. Therefore, better links and 'joined-up' provision are proposed by the Social Exclusion Unit's (1998) and DCMS's (1999) reports. In Streetsport this was shown to require significant allocation of resources, in terms of staff workload and hence continuing cost implications (see below) – but still less than the costs involved in policing nuisance behaviour and delinquency and the on-cost of justice services.

Studies and reports in this area have continued to pour out, and we review only a few significant ones here. Positive Futures (PF) was a 5-year (2000–2005) programme funded by the Drug Strategy Directorate of the Home Office, providing £5m a year to 123 local projects, and a programme of monitoring, with another 24 projects funded with £3m from the Football Foundation over two years. In 2007 this,

- involved 29,600 young people over 517,000 contact hours, with three-quarters of youth attending for over twelve weeks;
- delivered 19,800 activity sessions.

Crabbe suggested that by moving from diversion to medium-term development (Crabbe, 2006), PF 'protects them against risk factors other programmes have failed to tackle' (Home Office, media release, 20 November 2007). PF frontline staff also had a degree of autonomy from managers, and sustained effort, rather than short-term hits.

Crabbe (2006: Executive summary) argued that 'rather than reflecting a dichotomy with structural responses to the "causes" of crime on the one hand and a focus on the individual on the other, Positive Futures appears to represent a key element in a "layered" response that embraces both'. Further, he characterised most projects with at-risk youth as a sports development 'residual' from the Victorian Rational Recreation and Muscular Christianity driven by activities and focused on mass participation, and contrasted PF as an emergent approach to social inclusion, focused on personal and social development of youth, using flexible outreach approaches, community-based and led. We comment that this seems unfair to sustained programmes like Streetsport, the two Sports Counselling schemes, and some Fairbridge projects which learned the same lessons and do the same things PF claims. In 2005 PF was handed over to Crime Concern to manage (Home Office, media release, 24 November 2005); its budget was sustained to 2008/9 (and indicatively for two more years) when a review was due.

Nichols (2007) drew together eight case studies of sports programmes in which he used a wide range of research methods and Pawson and Tilley's (1997) critical realism approach to evaluate their outcomes and impacts. He classified them according to their mechanisms – in diverting or deterring youngsters from crime and whether they were serving youth through primary interventions (low risk of offending), secondary interventions (medium risk) or tertiary (high risk/already offending) (Nichols 2007: 181). He concluded:

1. Regarding diversion, sport is a hook for getting involved those attracted to it, but can have limitations among, for example, girls and obese youth.
2. Regarding pro-social development, it also acts as a medium for personal achievement and developing self-esteem, for coping with fears and managing risk (in outdoor challenges), for developing responsibilities and relationships with others, and even developing work-related skills in sport.

Sport did not seem to develop new friendships (as also found by Andrew, 2002 (in Collins, 2007)) but did develop relationships with mentors/leaders that were very formative. Most of these schemes were small and relatively short-term, but Nichols thought it could offer long-term diversion:

> In the long run, good practice in crime prevention through sport as a diversion becomes the same as in sports development work – enthusing participants, identifying barriers, overcoming them and providing viable 'exit routes' for independent participation . . . [Relative to arts, conservation, religion and other alternatives] . . . an advantage of sport is that it offers a wide range of viable exit routes, through many sports and many different providers. It also contributes to a public health policy agenda (2007: 199) . . . [And as a tool, sport's] value depends very much on the ability of programme staff to use it that way.
>
> (in Collins, 2007: 204)

Using a survey of 56 local projects, 17 focus groups and a review of funding, HMG's financial watchdog, the Audit Commission (2009) opined strongly that 'sport and leisure have major roles in preventing antisocial behaviour'. It also concluded:

- Preventive projects are cost effective: a youth in the criminal justice system costs the taxpayer over £200,000 by age 16, compared to one given support to stay out of under £50,000.
- Projects must be accessible (in every sense), reliable, and tailored to individuals' needs.

222

- Young people value those mentors who take an interest in them and offer support.
- Most Local Area Agreements (two-thirds of the 150 signed in 2008) have targets for reducing/avoiding youth involvement in the justice system, *but*
  - most are isolated, and not linked into comprehensive area-based schemes;
  - most funding is short-term with limited impact, ignoring the accumulated evidence that sustained effort is needed (as in Positive Futures);
  - few involve the youth themselves in planning or delivery;
  - half of schemes had no evidence on their impacts, and only 27% of their value for money.
- Half of all funding comes form HMG but through complex and unco-ordinated arrangements, and a project leader can spend a third of his/her time chasing funds. One said 'I have 19 cost centres . . . I'm required to respond to a range of different funders with budget material, and I have the day job'.

The Chairman of the Commission called the grants system 'a dog's breakfast', and went on 'it's ludicrous that funding schemes for young people in trouble with the law should be so complicated. . . . Project leaders are thwarted in their attempts to keep young people out of trouble by wasteful, inefficient and bureaucratic funding arrangement for diversionary projects' (Audit Commission, press release, 28 January 2009).

All these reports do little more than confirm what has been said numerous times, including in the author's experience, but having the weight and independence of the Audit Commission may improve matters.

REFERENCES

Audit Commission (2009) *Tired of Hanging Around; Using Sport and Leisure Activities to Prevent Antisocial Behaviour by Young People,* London: Audit Commission.

Brantingham, P. and Faust, F. (1976) A conceptual model of crime prevention, *Crime and Delinquency,* 22(3): 284–96.

Burt, C. (1925) *The Young Delinquent,* London: University of London Press.

Cantle, T. (2001) *Community Cohesion: A Report of the Independent Review Team,* London: Home Office.

Coalter, F. (2001) *Realising the Potential of Cultural Services: The Case for Sport,* London: Local Government Association.

Coalter, F. (2007) *A Wider Social Role for Sport: Who's Keeping the Score?* London: Routledge.

Collins, M. F. (2003) *Sport and Social Exclusion,* London: Routledge.

Collins, M.F. (2007) Leisure studies and the social capital discourse, in Collins, M., Holmes, K. and Slater, A. (eds) *Sport Leisure Culture and Social Capital: Discourse and Practice,* Leisure Studies Association publication 100, Eastbourne: University of Brighton.

Community Services Department (1994) *Annual Report 1994,* Stoke on Trent: City Council.

Cooper, B. (1989) *The Management and Prevention of Juvenile Crime Problems,* London: Home Office.

Crabbe, T. (2006) *Going the Distance,* Manchester: Substance Consultants.

Department for Culture Media and Sport (1999) *Sport and the Arts Policy Action Team 10 Report,* London: DCMS.

Glyptis, S. (1989) *Leisure and Unemployment,* Milton Keynes: Open University Press.

Hendry, L. (1993) *Young People's Leisure and Lifestyles,* London: Routledge.

Huskins, J. (1998) *From Disaffection to Social Inclusion: A Social Skills Preparation for Active Citizenship and Employment,* Kingsdown: Huskins.

Long, J. and Sanderson, I. (2001) The social benefits of sport: Where's the proof?, in I. Henry and C. Gratton (eds) *Sport in the City,* London: Routledge.

McCormack, F. (2000) Leisure exclusion? Analysing interventions using active leisure with young people offending or at risk, unpublished Ph.D., Loughborough: Loughborough University.

Morgan, D. (1998) Sport off the streets: A preliminary analysis of the need for 'Reczones, in 'The 3Ds area of Bolton' paper to Sport vs Youth Crime Conference, Reebok Stadium, Bolton.

Nichols, G. (2007) *Sport and Crime Reduction: The Role of Sports in Tackling Youth Crime,* London: Routledge.

Nichols, G. and Taylor, P. (1996) *West Yorkshire Sports Counselling: Final Evaluation Report,* Halifax: WYSC Association.

Pawson, R. and Tilley, N. (1997) *Realistic Evaluation,* London: Sage.

Rigg, M. (1980) *Action Sport,* London: Sports Council.

Scarman, Lord (1982) *The Scarman Report,* London: Penguin Books.

Social Exclusion Unit (1998) *Bringing Britain Together,* London: Cabinet Office.

Substance (2007) *Putting the Pieces Together? 2007 Annual Monitoring and Evaluation Report,* Manchester: Substance Consultants.

Suzuki, N. (2007) Sport and neighbourhood regeneration: Exploring the mechanisms of social inclusion through sport, unpublished Ph.D. Glasgow: Glasgow University.

Witt, P. and Crompton, J. (1996) *Recreation Programs that Work for At-Risk Youth: The Challenge of Shaping the Future,* College Station, PA: Venture Publishing.

CHAPTER 12

PHYSICAL ACTIVITY PROMOTING HEALTH

What should we do?

Len Almond

INTRODUCTION

I attempt in the first section of this case study to lay the foundations for promoting all forms of physical activity (PA), particularly sport, for their health benefits. Sport has often claimed that health is one of its main benefits but this has never been spelled out in detail. In the second section I set out a menu of ideas to illustrate how sport and all forms of PA can be used to promote health. It is by no means exhaustive, but outlines where organisations need to address their time and energies and demonstrate a significant role to play in health promotion. Initially, let me outline what I mean by PA: it refers to a wide range of activities encompassing sports, dance, activities in a fitness suite, exercise classes, walking, cycling and swimming as well as domestic activities like gardening, yoga and tai chi, where regular participation has the power to improve body systems, energise the body and mind, and enhance health and well-being.

THE VALUE OF PURPOSEFUL PHYSICAL ACTIVITY TO HEALTH

The Chief Medical Officer's report, *At Least Five a Week: Evidence of the Impact of Physical Activity and its Relationship to Health* (CMO, 2004) recognised the significant impact physical activity can have on public health through reducing the risks of chronic disease and disability, which can cause serious and unnecessary suffering and a seriously impaired quality of life. The estimated costs of inactivity in England were highlighted because they represent a significant burden of direct costs to the NHS and indirect costs to society relating to absence from work, loss of productivity, and premature death, totalling £8.2 billion each year (excluding obesity costs of £2.5 billion). That report went on to suggest that encouraging active lifestyles for all ages must be an important element of any future public health strategy.

Regular PA is important for all body systems, but it also enables people to widen their views about what they can do in their lives so that they can extend their capabilities. This statement is relevant to all age groups, from children in early years settings to older adults. In the case of older adults, widening their perspectives about what they can do is a realistic expectation if they view daily PA as an essential part of feeling well.

The CMO's report made a significant statement, that:

> Smoking cigarettes and an unhealthy diet have long been established as major causal factors for chronic disease. This report establishes that physical inactivity is equally important.
>
> (CMO, 2004: 1)

This is important, because allocating funding for smoking cessation and promoting healthy eating had long been a more urgent and higher priority in health development. This recognition and endorsement provides the starting point for revisiting what kinds of PA can be promoted to contribute to well-being and health. One objective in a concern for the nation's health, is to encourage more active lifestyles and ensuring that people with particular medical conditions understand that regular PA can significantly and positively affect their condition.

Sport, dance and all forms of exercise and purposeful physical activity can be used for a multitude of positive community objectives, as previous chapters show, including health. Health is dealt with locally through Primary Care Trusts (PCTs) but it needs to be recognised that their agenda deals with long-term medical conditions. The role of purposeful PA in health care needs to be better understood and recognised.

In our communities and local neighbourhoods PA can be used to address both prevention and treatment health agendas. In the prevention agenda, PA can:

- reduce the risk of people developing health problems;
- ensure that people do not gain excessive weight;
- delay functional decline and onset of dependency in older adults;
- reduce the risk of developing complications and poor quality of life from immobility.

PA, however, also can play a very important role in reducing the risk, delaying or slowing down the progress of Dementia, Parkinson's and Alzheimer's diseases.

226

len almond

In therapy and treatment, PA can be used for:

- treating chronic conditions, having a beneficial effect on many chronic diseases or disorders;
- treating mild depression;
- helping obese and overweight adults to lose weight;
- avoiding and rehabilitating after falls;
- restoring physical capacity and maintaining independence, helping coping with life's demands.

In addition it can be used as a social tool to combat loneliness and isolation for older adults, but also as a means of bringing communities together to enhance their well-being.

All of these factors mean that PA is a resource we need to cherish because it energises daily living, enhances the quality of living and improves our well-being. Organisations can promote health without any reference to PCTs or GP practices. Simply getting more people to commit to doing something physical regularly can promote their health and daily well-being, but this requires committing time and energy, if not money.

The diversity of local projects is very clear from the catalogue of 88 schemes run by the BHF National Centre for Activity and Health (2008) providing for women and girls (10), older people (19), those disabled (9), sufferers from mental illness (10), and people in economically depressed (21) and Black and Ethnic Minority communities (11). These usually operate in isolation, and without the benefit of collaboration. Nevertheless, there are some very good illustrations of partnership working. However, it is very clear that if Britain is to achieve a substantial rise in activity rates throughout the life course, it needs to work in partnerships to deliver shared agendas. The choice of form of activity promotion is often left to individual preference (as in DoH, 2009), and so media-publicised flavours of the month dominate thinking, and available uncoordinated funding streams dictate the choice of activity. This is particularly important for priority groups who are easily overlooked – disabled people, older adults and ethnic groups, some of whom are under-represented or not represented because for them PA has been neglected.

If the roles of purposeful PA are to be addressed, there is a clear priority: Britain needs an infrastructure of people working in partnership who recognise and consider national, regional and local priorities and have access to base-line information and health impact assessments (Regional Public Health Observatories are often the best source). This needs to be supplemented by local community views being incorporated, especially from groups who do not find it easy to organise and articulate their needs (those mentioned in the last paragraph).

Existing structures of Local Strategic Partnerships, Community Strategies, Local Neighbourhood Renewal Strategies and PCT Local Development Delivery Plans, together with parallel strategies from planning and transport, environment, open space, and culture including sport can provide drivers for action, assuming that PA has been adequately represented to these interests (see below on DoH's 2005 and 2009 Plans). Here Regional Physical Activity Forums together with County Sport Partnerships have a role to play; the earliest PA Forum formed in 1996 in the NW represents 70 different organisations.

To illustrate this, I draw on experience of chairing a community partnership in a local authority eighteen years ago and more recently in a city borough, with the same problem of how to get organisations from diverse cultures, different age groups and representing different forms of PA to work together. The first task was to generate partnerships which created communication channels. As funding was a priority, this provided the motivation to come together, and work towards shared agendas of increasing participation, avoiding duplication, and using a united voice. This last point is important because PA is a low priority for many decision-makers. As seven in ten of the population are inactive, it is likely that most people making decisions also fall into this category and many will view PA negatively. In this scenario, a local authority alliance was needed to produce evidence-based reviews to support the cause, crucially backed by a champion. School Sport Partnerships can do these things, and so can CSPs (Pro-Active regions in London) and district/local Community Sports Networks (CSNs). Their early domination by sport is changing, and now DoH expects all to take on PA; PCTs are recognising the value of such partnerships, and to provide funds. Yet there is still no body for the diverse organisations interested in PA; maybe the new Activity Alliance will play this role.

Objectives for promoting purposeful physical activity and health

I see these as to:

- Raise public awareness and understanding of the role of regular PA in their health and well-being.
- Educate and motivate all ages and abilities to participate in regular, sustainable and achievable PA programmes that can be built into daily routines to enhance their well-being.
- Ensure that appropriate and consistent advice for encouraging PA is available

and tailored to meet the needs of different groups, especially those most in need.

- Work towards ensuring that the physical environment and local culture promotes and enables an active lifestyle at home, at work, and for recreation and transport.
- Ensure that a full range of acceptable and accessible opportunities in a variety of settings for PA and sport are available which welcome all members of the population to participate regardless of their current levels of activity or ability.
- Target specific groups whose participation and achievement base is low.
- Link a PA and health strategy with sport and emerging strategic policy directions across government.
- Develop cohesive local partnerships to offer direction for local implementation of strategies to enhance health and well-being through the promotion of physical activity and active recreation.

It is arguable that the DoH plan for 2009–2013 articulates this and its complexity for the first time (see Conclusions, p. 239).

A MENU OF INITIATIVES

In recent years, some key national initiatives have influenced the direction of health promotion and PA in particular. The White Paper *Choosing Health: Making Healthy Choices Easier* (DoH, 2004) set out a programme of action to support people in making healthy choices and thereby turn the tide of public health in England. Subsequently DoH (2005a) also published a delivery plan *Delivering Choosing Health: Making Healthier Choices*, listing forty-five 'big wins', key interventions which evidence and expert advice suggested would make the greatest impact on health in the shortest time, and describing how government would drive delivery through targets to improve health, new partnerships between industry, the voluntary sector and professional groups, and new services delivered by local authorities and the NHS. This was in turn followed by two action plans, one for choosing a healthy diet and one (DoH, 2005b) specifically on PA – *Choosing Activity: A Physical Activity Action Plan* (PAAP). This aimed to 'promote activity for all', centred on five themes for 2005–2008:

1. Choosing activity in a consumer society.
2. Starting on an active path (children and young people).
3. Active communities.
4. An active healthcare system.
5. Choosing activity in the workplace.

Within the second theme, about children and young people, there was a strong commitment to encourage all schools to become Healthy Schools by 2009 (half by 2006). The National Healthy Schools Standard was supported by a *Healthy Living Blueprint for Schools* (DES, 2004) to improve whole curricular and school organisation, nutrition, and PA, through the already launched *Physical Education, School Sport and Club Links* programme (*PESSCL*) (see pp. 79–81). But the complexity of what was expected and of how many agencies is shown in Table 12.1. The other feature common to New Labour's policies was the speed expected of implementation: of the 124 actions in the 2005 Plan, 4 had been achieved and 11 were ongoing, 76 (61%) were expected to be implemented by the end of that year, and a further 27 (22%) by 2007.

Table 12.1 The Physical Activity Action Plan's (2005) schedule of actions

Leaders for actions	Promoting PA	PA and children	Active communities	Active healthcare	Workplace PA
DoH	6	4	6	6	8
DCMS	1	2	7		
DfT	7	1	12		2
Defra			4		
DES		12			
HO			3		
ODPM			8	1	1
Sport England	2	1	4		2
Reg Sp Bs			1		
PCTs			3		
NHS					2
Reg PHGs					2
Skills PH				2	2
Countryside Alliance					
Busin ITC			2		
LAs		Youth ST	SCUK	SHAs	Big Lottery
			NICE		Br. Heart
			ASA		Found.
			Br Waterways		
			Eng. Nature		
			For. Comm.		
			Sustrans		
			Ass NPAs		
			Health Com		
			Highway Agency		

Targets for physical activity

Government documents such as *Choosing Activity* (DoH, 2005b: 7) stated:

> Based upon a baseline of 32% of adults currently meeting the Chief Medical Officer's minimum recommendation, the 70% target would necessitate a year-on-year increase of 2%, converting approximately 21 million people to active living. Such an increase has eluded other Western countries. The most successful 'top three' countries – Finland, Canada and New Zealand – have only achieved around a 1% increase in participation per annum.

> In his final report, *Securing Good Health for the Whole Population*, Derek Wanless [2004] recommended delivery of the lower, 'medium term' *Game Plan* target by 2020, i.e. 50% participation, with short- and medium-term objectives fixed for 2007 and 2011. This would aim for a prevalence of physical activity in England that is similar to the levels found in Canada and Australia, and a 1% per annum trajectory. Such a target would be both stretching and would require strategies to help individuals to build activity into their daily lives. Responses to the Choosing Activity consultation expressed overall agreement with this view . . . we acknowledge the 70% target as an aspirational goal.

Scotland and Northern Ireland have adopted a 1% target. 3% may be achievable if there is a concerted effort to target the irregularly active – those people insufficiently active for health benefits, but doing something (this suggestion does not exclude the inequalities agenda which has to receive high priority). In the conclusions, the editor raises doubts about the feasibility of this because of structural differences between England and places like Finland. Targeting the sedentary and hard-to-reach groups may be counter-productive in the first instance.

After Britain's CMO (2004) report, the US Department of Health and Human Services (US DHHS, 2008) produced detailed guidelines for PA at different ages endorsed by the American College of Sports Medicine and the American Health Association. Drawing on both these sources, I outline in Table 12.2 what consensus would suggest is best for different ages.

Among the many PSA targets for ages 0–5 (DoH, 2008) there is nothing for physical activity, nor (as I had hoped) does the new plan (2009: 34), though it says it covers all ages; it is to be hoped that a forthcoming Child Health strategy will do so.

Table 12.2 Recommendations for physical activity

Group	'Dosage'	Moderate exercise	Vigorous exercise
Children and youth	At least 1hr a day moderate or vigorous (latter on 3 days), plus Muscle strengthening x 2 days Bone strengthening x 2 days	Hiking, skateboarding, cycling, brisk walking Rope climbing, sit-ups, tug-of-war Jumping rope, running and skipping	Cycling, skipping, soccer, running, ice/field hockey, basketball
Adults	At least 30 minutes x 5 days moderate, plus muscle/bone strengthening x 2 days	Same as above	Same as above
Pregnant women	30 minutes x 5 days moderate, after seeing doctor		
Disabled adults	30 minutes moderate x 5 days, plus 30 minutes x 3 days vigorous		
Older adults	Same as above, or cumulative 10-minute sessions	Especially cycling, walking, stretching, balance	
People with medical conditions	Within limits of their condition – see doctor	See doctor	

Sources CMO, 2004; US DHHS, 2008.

The accumulated evidence for inactivity in children, young people, adults and older adults enables us to identify clear priority groups for promoting active living and encouraging more people to be more active more often, namely:

- children in early years;
- women of all ages;
- older adults, especially those vulnerable and frail;
- groups identified in other ways as socially excluded (Collins, 2003) – people who are disabled, in ethnic minorities, or poor, disadvantaged or vulnerable groups.

A MENU OF ACTIONS FOR ACTIVE LIVING

In most cases I suggest that activities like walking are particularly valuable for people new to PA. However, there is clear evidence that many people would like to play sport and acquire the skills needed, but not as it is currently organised, where an over-emphasis on competition and training (for both children and adults) and an expectation of commitment for a playing season for much of the year can create barriers. Neither may sports clubs be the right venue if they expect 'the right kit' and act like cliques. The sporting world needs to reflect carefully on this.

Active information and campaigns

There is a need to promote PA opportunities through easily accessible local information and community-wide campaigns. In addition, a wider range of leisure and active venues than on Sport England's Active Places database within a mile of any postcode need to be mapped and publicised widely, in GP surgeries, schools, community centres and libraries. *Change4Life* is a new £75m social marketing campaign from the Department of Health aimed initially at children and their parents (http://www.nhs.uk/Change4Life/Pages/default.aspx), and is linked to children's play (and can build on existing holiday play schemes), swimming and biking. At the same time, promoting health-enhancing PA in all its forms will need many volunteers to work with the dedicated professionals already in post.

A comprehensive directory of delivery agents with local knowledge and proven track record needs to be compiled and apprised of promotion plans. Extended schools can make facilities for PA available during evenings, weekends and

233

school holidays. Religious organisations and leaders in churches, temples, mosques and other sites of worship for recognised religious groups need to be considered as potential deliverers.

Activity-friendly environments

Many organisations can play a significant role in promoting more regular activity. Planning is essential to support being more active in town and country through home zones, use of open spaces, green space development, safe play areas, and safe multi-activity areas. Walking and cycling are seen as government priorities for the Department for Transport, local authorities and National Parks to promote (DoH, 2009). Major new residential developments – including proposed eco-towns and the redeveloped East London in the wake of the 2012 Olympics – provide opportunities for such 'Active Places' (Sport England, 2008a). However, to instigate such a scheme and build on existing practice, and publicise it widely, would require a coordinator together with trained volunteers. Such projects have the potential to reach numbers of people exceeding those going to fitness classes, for example.

Active travel

Initiatives include safe routes to schools and active recreational spaces, and active travel plans for schools, workplaces and shopping facilities; there is a target for all schools to have fully endorsed Travel Plans by 2010. There is strong evidence that children and young people who walk frequently to school, play more and engage in more PA. Active travel plans for worksites are largely underused and should be considered.

Early years

PCTs need to work closely with children's services and SureStart projects to ensure that purposeful PA for children's health is fully recognised in policy and practice, which will involve:

- promoting the value of physical play in all early years settings and providing daily opportunities for frequent aerobic activity;
- working towards providing safe, attractive and challenging services and programmes for pre-fives;

234

- working towards providing a safe, attractive network of indoor and outdoor play facilities for pre-fives.

School-aged children and young people

LAs and PCTs need to work closely with School Sport Partnerships to encourage:

- All head teachers, especially in primary schools, to provide two hours of high-quality PE each week (only one-third achieve this currently). In addition, the SSPs need to lead a campaign to make sure that all schools accept that the public health message for PA is an hour of at least moderate activity daily.
- An inclusive policy to raise participation levels of boys and girls with disabilities, all ethnic groups and those in vulnerable communities, from their current low levels.
- Girls to be given special priority because of their consistently lower levels of engagement from primary school until late adulthood.
- All schools to become fully aware of active travel plans and support those available locally.
- Making playground activities a significant contributor to 60 minutes of daily PA; there is new funding for playground activities.
- All schools to recognise the part schoolday activities can play in reaching 60 minutes of moderate PA daily activity; and to encourage all schools to increase the activities they provide; resources and training for Active Clubs and the Make Space project are available from the 4Children programme.
- All schools to support the Healthy School Programme and work towards achieving Healthy School status by 2009 (in fact 76% had done so, and Healthy Schools were being attended by 4 million children. Covering healthy eating, physical activity, personal social health and economic education (including drug abuse and sexual relationships) and emotional health and well-being (including dealing with bullying)). With one in seven schoolchildren obese and three out of ten boys and four out of ten girls insufficiently active for their health, there is public concern, and a PSA target for under-11s. PCTs and SSPs need support to developing an integrated obesity strategy for children and their families, integrating healthy eating and ways of reducing sedentary behaviour, especially out of school hours, and providing a support network and ways of rewarding weight-loss behaviours.

Adults in later life

This is an important section of the population, because more than 85 per cent of them are not active enough to benefit their health and well-being. All can benefit substantially from becoming more active more often, but here are three specific groups to consider:

1. Older adults with choices – to be treated as other able adults, except it would be useful to promote the idea that some may like to become *peer mentors* to encourage their neighbours and friends to become more active. If tackled properly, this would delay by at least five years the numbers who enter the second group.
2. Older adults who are moving towards dependency – here LAs need to consider with their PCT and Social Services if they can develop, in addition to the new free swimming, a coordinated programme of walking, and dance/movement classes. This would reduce the need for falls-prevention courses; among the over-70s, people tend to fall because of lack of strength, mobility and coordination brought on by years of inactivity.
3. The frail elderly – here chair-based and other coordinated programmes need to be made relevant for people in all care settings.

The BHF National Centre *Moving More Often* programme should be looked at closely, to provide practical suggestions and training for how this can be achieved.

DoH's (2005c: 26) Green Paper *Independence, Well-being and Choice* is an important document because it makes clear that independence and well-being cannot be achieved without promoting better PA services.

Healthy Further Education colleges

FE Colleges have been neglected, in PA and sport. Indeed, unlike HEIs (see Chapter 6) only half of them have sports facilities. Like schools, they now have sports coordinators (FESCOs), and local CS/PA networks need to work with them to be part of the Healthy Colleges movement.

Primary care: GP practices

At least three-quarters of patients at all GP surgeries will be in need of advice on PA, and so information and such advice must be readily available for all age

len almond

groups, and those with medical conditions who can benefit from regular physical activity, and awareness-raising clinics/sessions need to be planned. The BHF's PA toolkit should be a regular source.

Where PA can benefit a specific medical condition, it needs to be recognised in each care pathway and protocol. Likewise, GP staff need to recognise that each clinic could be enhanced by using the opportunity to promote more regular PA; the Healthy Walking movement began in the 1970s in a New Forest General Practice.

Therapeutic services

These services include cardiac rehabilitation and falls prevention, a difficult area for two major reasons: one, there are many conditions that could benefit from therapeutic PA; and second, so as to reach as many people as possible on Practice registers, local community sites need to be made available. Thus, it may be appropriate to explore in a 'long-term conditions' strategy how an integrated approach can best serve most patients, with implications for support staff and their training.

The obesity agenda for adults needs to be addressed in a more targeted way, i.e., focusing on people with a Body Mass Index of 30–32 who are doing some PA, because those who are irregularly active but doing something, only need to add more activity into their lives to meet the public health recommendations. This group are more likely to succeed than a group of wholly sedentary obese patients; and once again a food-reduction programme, combined with specific advice on daily PA throughout the day, together with reducing sedentary behaviour is likely to lead to weight loss, and health gains independent of that. A pedometer programme will provide motivation and evidence of improvement; one target could be an extra 1,000 steps each day, or another 10% of the normal step pattern. Indicators of the success of PA can simply be a reduction in waist size and weekly pedometer scores (BMI is not sensitive enough).

One of the problems of providing pedometers is that some participants are reluctant to return them, which means that many Practices cannot afford frequent use; one way to avoid this is to use libraries as a lending source. There is ample evidence to show this tactic is very successful, and also it promotes access to information on healthy lifestyles. Another tactic may be relevant here, for a group of GP Practices to invite all their patients with a BMI of 30–32 to attend a meeting where personal action plans can be explained and a combined programme launched, instead of working separately.

GP referral schemes

Hundreds of these schemes have arisen, but they can only cope with those who have serious conditions; the BHF National Centre produced a toolkit in 2009, and DoH (2009: 44) is undertaking research on which programmes work. In addition to LA leisure services, there are local walking and cycling programmes, 'green' exercise spaces (Green Gyms), tending allotments and active environmental conservation, as well as home-based self-managed programmes (which tend to have a high drop-out because there are no leaders/friends/companions to encourage adherence).

Workplace schemes

The workplace as a setting for promoting the well-being of employees is neglected compared to other countries – in Scandinavia, Germany, or Japan, for example. Currently, half of adults are in some sort of work, spending a considerable proportion of their day there. A local health promotion, SD or active recreation team can play a significant role with employers, workers and Trades Unions, and workplaces are a suitable locale for a holistic health strategy (incorporating cycling to work, health checks, healthy eating, smoking cessation, moderate drinking and stress reduction as well as PA).

This was a new area for Sport England which with BHF in 2004–2007 ran a series of nine Well@work pilots in 32 workplaces covering public, private and voluntary factories and offices, a hospital, a prison and a General Practice, and covering 10,000 workers (Bull et al., 2008). All reported better awareness of and motivation to eat healthily, four out of five losing weight, 70 per cent gaining more energy, and half increased confidence. The lessons will be rolled out by the promoters, and DoH (2009) wants to make the health service an examplar for all employers. But, in the first instance any workplace promotions need to start with the local authority, the LEA and the SSP, and the PCT, as identified in the Delivery Plan (DoH, 2005a).

The voluntary sector

No opportunity has been taken to explore this area in any depth, but many areas of social care, including promoting PA for well-being and health cannot be fully achieved without the commitment and efforts of organised as well as informal volunteering. Via Capacity Builders, Volunteering England has a special programme encouraging volunteering by individuals, and in various organisations (local clubs, NGBs and local volunteer centres), see www.volunteering.org.uk/WhatWeDo/Projects+and+initiatives/volunteeringinsport/.

CONCLUSIONS

Evaluation and capturing learning

There are many small and diverse projects in any area, as well as larger PA initiatives that do not appear to have any evaluation or record of their achievements. This is a major omission, because the impact of these schemes and their achievements cannot be shared nor can other groups learn from their experiences. Simple evaluation protocols are available to enable scheme organisers to record their achievements and provide evidence of their effectiveness and impact.

Infrastructure

Sport has had an infrastructure since the 1960s, but those involved in promoting all forms of PA have been frustrated by having nothing equivalent. DoH's new plan, published as we go to press, said 'Sport England's new role is to focus exclusively on developing and investing in sport' (2009: 30) but gave equal weight to PA. It set up a new structure with:

- a cabinet committee and a Health Improvement Board, chaired jointly by DoH and DCMS;
- a new Physical Activity Alliance of public and commercial interests with which to work, and to use the Regional PA coordinators appointed after the 2005 *Action Plan*;
- CSPs to become CS and AP partnerships (CSCAPs) and be given £1m to develop local delivery plans for PA (£3m in 2009–2020);
- much action taking place through the 370 Local Strategies and Local Area Agreements.

It estimated the costs of inactivity as £8.3bn (NHS costs £1bn–1.8bn, £5.5bn from absence from work, and £1bn from premature death). Cycling England's modelling suggested a 20% increase in cycling by 2015 could save £52m, £87m and £107m on these respective costs, and even a 1% reduction in broken hips would save the NHS £200m a year.

It would be guided by four principles:

1. informing choice for individuals, and promoting activity;
2. creating an 'active' environment (with Departments for Transport, Children, Schools and Families, and Department of Communities and Local Government – see Sport England, 2008b);
3. supporting those most at risk (people with chronic physical and mental illness, disabled people, the aged);
4. strengthening delivery.

It will use the £75m Change4life movement with play, swimming, and biking, and GP referral schemes. A sizeable component is to promote active transport (walking and cycling) with the Department for Transport taking the lead.

REFERENCES

British Heart Foundation National Centre (2008) *Opening Doors to an Active Life: How to Engage Inactive Communities*, Loughborough: BHFNC.

British Heart Foundation National Centre (2009) *A Toolkit for the Design, Implementation and Evaluation of GP Referral Schemes*, Loughborough: BHFNC.

Bull, F.C., Allen, E.J., Hooper, P.L. and Jones, C.A. (2008) *Well@work Evaluation of Pilot Projects*, London: British Heart Foundation/Sport England.

Chief Medical Officer (2004) *At Least Five A Week: Evidence of the Impact of Physical Activity and its Relationship to Health*, London: Department of Health.

Collins, M.F. (2003) *Sport and Social Exclusion,* London: Routledge.

Department for Education and Schools (2004) *Healthy Living Blueprint for Schools,* London: DES.

Department of Health (2004) *Choosing Health: Making Healthy Choices Easier,* London: Department of Health.

Department of Health (2005a) *Delivering Choosing Health: Making Healthier Choices Easier*, London: Department of Health.

Department of Health (2005b) *Choosing Activity: A Physical Activity Action Plan,* London: Department of Health.

Department of Health (2005c) *Independence, Well-being and Health*, Green Paper CM 6499, London: Department of Health.

Department of Health (2008) *Child Health Promotion Programme: Pregnancy and the First Five Years of Life*, London: Department of Health.

Department of Health (2009) *Be Active, Be Healthy: A Plan for Getting the Nation Moving*, London: Department of Health.

National Institute for Clinical Excellence (2006) *Four Commonly Used Methods to Increase Physical Activity*, London: NICE.

Sport England (2008a) *Planning for Sport in Growth and Regeneration Areas*, Planning Bulletin 20, London: Sport England.

Sport England (2008b) *Active Design: Promoting Opportunities for Sport and Physical Activity through Good Design*, London: Sport England.

US Department of Health and Human Services (2008) *2008 Physical Activity Guidelines for Americans*, Washington, DC: HHS.

Health Select Committee (2004) *Third Report of Session 2003/4, Obesity HC23–1*, London: Stationery Office.

Wanless, D. (2004) *Securing Good Health for the Whole Population: Final Report*, London: HMSO.

CHAPTER 13

PROMOTING PARTICIPATION AND INCLUSION?

The free swimming initiative in Wales

Nicola Bolton

INTRODUCTION

As the second most popular activity for participation among adults in Wales (Sports Council for Wales, 2005) swimming has considerable potential to raise overall participation levels. It has the added advantage of being weightless and therefore appropriate for everyone, regardless of age or disability (Lawton et al., 1995). In 2005 the population of adults aged 15 and over living in Wales was 2.49 million (Office for National Statistics, 2005). Of these, 299,000 people had been swimming in the previous month. Participation data reveal the importance of swimming also for children and young people, among the top six curricular activities for 7–11 year olds and as an extra-curricular and club activity (Sports Council for Wales, 2006a). Among 11–16 year olds, swimming remained popular as an extra-curricular and club activity but was less important in terms of the PE curriculum (Sports Council for Wales, 2006b).

This chapter considers the unique example of a continuing national intervention to raise physical activity levels in Wales through swimming and other water-based activities. Free swimming in Wales is a Welsh Assembly Government initiative comprising two separate, but related schemes. Free entitlement was offered, on a pilot basis, from the summer of 2003 to 2007 to people aged 16 and under during school holidays. A second pilot scheme operated from November 2004 to 2007, offering free swimming to the over-60 age group outside school holidays.

There are three aims for this chapter which should interest policy makers and practitioners involved in sports development. First, the implementation of the Free Swimming Initiative (FSI) is briefly outlined. Secondly, the policy framework is analysed regarding its impact on implementation. This analysis reveals tensions between mass participation and free entitlement on the one hand, and sustainable sports development through structured participation on the other. Thirdly, this experience demonstrates the need for policy makers and practitioners to prioritise explicitly between competing aims and objectives. An understanding of the policy context for this initiative is examined both in terms of how it was established and how it progressed over time. The impact of constitutional devolution provides an important context for this. The fact that in 2007 the Minister for Sport in England announced a similar national intervention provides further interest.

THE FREE SWIMMING INITIATIVE

Following Welsh Assembly elections in 2002, the government committed itself through its overarching strategy, 'Wales a Better Country', to provide 'free access to local authority swimming pools for children in the school holidays and older people' (Welsh Assembly Government, 2003: 10). As part of this process, civil servants and local authority chief officers were aware of existing schemes including those in Glasgow City and Torfaen Borough, South Wales. These experiences were used in developing a national initiative for Wales. It was initially piloted in ten local authorities during the 2003 Easter school holidays. Some small-scale research was undertaken on the pilot, and the positive feedback provided momentum for launching free swimming in all twenty-two Welsh local authorities in time for the summer holidays. Research and evaluation undertaken in the summer of 2003 provided further positive evidence that there were significant increases in the number of swims, especially among disadvantaged communities (Sports Council for Wales, 2004).

Based on this success, free swimming for the 16 and unders was established as a national pilot, and in November 2004 it was extended to include free swimming for the over-60s. Together, these two schemes became known as the Free Swimming Initiative, with some 120 pools being typically involved at any one time. Amounting to £15m of public investment between 2004 and 2007, the pilot was the single biggest intervention to raise physical activity levels in Wales.

Operational guidelines established minimum requirements for both schemes and these were agreed annually by the Chief Officers for Recreation and Leisure. Between November 2004 and September 2007 a further evaluation of the FSI was undertaken. Details of the evaluation evidence gathered are given in five interim reports to be found on the Sports Council for Wales' website (Bolton

243

et al., 2005a, 2005b, 2006, 2007a–c), together with a final evaluation report (Bolton *et al.*, 2008).

Since the introduction of free swimming, there has been an increase in the numbers of summer holiday swims taken by both the target age groups. In 2002, the year before the introduction of FSI, 387,000 swims were taken by the 16 and unders during the summer holidays (Sports Council for Wales, 2004) which rose to 560,000 in 2003. There was a decline over the following two years, but in 2006/7 participation remained greater than in 2002.

The total annual number of free swims (both casual and structured) peaked in 2004/5 at 830,000 – an average of 75,000 a week, from which figure the number declined to 69,000 in 2005/6 and 64,000 in 2006/7 (Table 13.1), shared by equal numbers of boys and girls. Since time restrictions were applied to free swimming, it is worth noting that taking free and paid swims together, there has been a notable increase in swimming during summer holidays: in the summer of 2006 there were 400,000 free swims and 165,000 paid swims, representing a 46% increase on 2002.

The over-60s took just over 1.5 million swims under the Initiative between November 2004 and July 2007, evenly divided between men and women. At the national level, there was a pattern of gradual and sustained growth. In November 2004 the number of free swims was 42,000, while the peak months were September 2006, October 2006 and January 2007, when there were 58,000 swims (Figure 13.1).

Table 13.2 shows the range of activities offered to the over-60s. What is notable is the popularity of Aquafit sessions, often a response to specific marketing, and which pool managers and Sports Development Officers (SDOs) thought was one of the successes of the scheme, especially amongst women.

Table 13.1 Total number of free swims by holiday period and year (000s, unstructured and structured swims combined)

	2003	2004/5	2005/6	2006/7
Easter	–	130,000	130,000	120,000
May Half-term	–	55,000	65,000	50,000
Summer	560,000	500,000	425,000	400,000
October Half-term	–	60,000	60,000	50,000
Christmas	–	15,000	10,000	17,000
February Half-term	–	70,000	70,000	65,000
Total	560,000	830,000	760,000	702,000

Source Local authority data returns.

nicola bolton

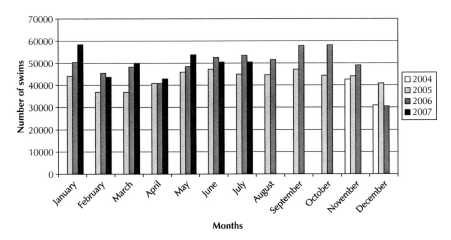

Figure 13.1 Over-60s Wales Free Swimming participation (unstructured and structured swims combined) (Bolton et al., 2008)

However, it was also obvious in the evaluation that there were barriers to participation: for the youth it was not knowing about the scheme locally (56%), or a poor second, not having anyone to go with (19%). For the over-60s it was not being fit enough (23%) and not having enough time (many retired people will say 'I don't know how I found time to go to work'). In addition there were other factors such as the location of the pool; the times when free swimming was available; the desire to avoid noisy over-crowded pools; and a dislike of swimming were all significant deterrents to participation. Simply providing free sessions is not, therefore, enough to secure participation by the majority of the eligible population (Bolton et al., 2008: 4).

Table 13.2 Activities offered as part of the 60+ free swimming scheme (%)

Activity	2005 (n = 85)	2006 (n = 80)
Adult-only sessions	75	89
Aquafit	69	71
Free swimming lessons	58	65
Dedicated 60+ sessions	46	36
Dedicated 50+ sessions	38	36
Fitswim Wales	32	34
Aqua gym	11	13
Other	7	10
Partly subsidised swimming lessons	–	7

Source Centre managers' surveys, 2005, 2006 in Bolton et al., 2008.
Note Respondents were able to select more than one multiple choice answer, therefore the sum of percentages will not equal 100.

POLICY DILEMMAS FOR FREE SWIMMING

Free swimming in Wales was characterised by a policy framework that established broad guidelines for participating local authorities, which gave the FSI a national focus but at the same time allowed considerable flexibility and interpretation that could take account of local circumstances. The differing requirements of the 16-and-under and over-60 schemes, taken together with this individual interpretation meant that many policy makers and practitioners viewed the Initiative as forty-four separate schemes.

The speed at which officials moved from obtaining political agreement to implementation was particularly rapid. Senior civil servants recognised the need for a short lead-in time, and talked of FSI being developmental, with improvements to be made over time. But there was no doubt that this situation placed both policy makers and practitioners under pressure to deliver FSI's results against its aims and objectives. The lack of capacity and dedicated officer support added further pressure. These issues were identified in the early evaluation reports, and were highlighted again in that of the Wales Audit Office (2007). In spite of policy makers' good intentions, the absence of robust planning and coordination, together with a picture of static resources (a fixed revenue based on a formula for the entire period) suggested that free swimming was a classic example of Weiss's (1998), not 'aim, steady, fire' approach but 'fire, steady, aim'.

Quite apart from some implementation issues, the tension between establishing a policy framework at the same time as providing sufficient flexibility for local interpretation is a key issue for people working in sports development. Multi-faceted aims and objectives are commonplace in sports development interventions (Coalter, 2007) and this analysis looks at some of the consequences when embracing multiple agendas simultaneously. Three issues are selected that highlight the challenges that faced practitioners:

1. interpreting the policy aims and competing objectives;
2. structured vs. unstructured swimming;
3. the needs of particular target groups.

The aim of the Free Swimming Initiative

The overriding aim was to increase levels of physical activity among the two target groups. The considerable significance of this is that the FSI was linked directly to the wider Assembly Government agenda, 'Health Challenge Wales' and at that time the draft national strategy for sport, *Climbing Higher* (Welsh

246

nicola bolton

Assembly Government, 2005) and later on its companion document *Climbing Higher: Next Steps* (Welsh Assembly Government, 2006). Given this aim, the restriction of free swims to the thirteen weeks of the school holidays for the 16 and unders, and to outside the school holidays for the over-60s was an obvious policy dilemma. The episodic nature was identified by practitioners as a significant barrier to the FSI's success, and negated any research opportunities to evidence explicitly the link between increases in physical activity to potential health gains. Chief Officers of Recreation and Leisure, who have the difficult job of linking sport to wider corporate and political agendas (Bolton and Fleming, 2007) were all too aware of this shortcoming, and considered the extension of the 16-and-under scheme to cover school terms as a logical and necessary next step. One Chief Officer interviewed made a clear connection between wider strategic priorities and free swimming by commenting:

> I would like the wider debate around *Climbing Higher* – has it got the political clout it should have in the Assembly? Let's use that. Let's use London 2012 as a target and a lever for investment and let's take a fundamental view of its importance. Is recreation and leisure important in the whole political agenda and if it is, let's fund it properly? If it isn't, then let's say so.

The restriction on providing free swimming all year was resources, although it is noteworthy that the over-60s scheme expanded incrementally, so that in practice by July 2007, twenty of the twenty-two councils were offering free swimming all year round. Two reasons help explain this: first, from its inception free swimming for the over-60s had more explicit links to the health agenda, including working with organisations such as Help the Aged; secondly, the considerably smaller take-up (numerically) and restricted availability of free swims at many pools (owing to term-time school swimming lessons) made such a response viable.

Structured and unstructured swims

The second policy dilemma was the division between structured and unstructured swims, a distinction identified in the annual operating instructions. In order to measure take-up consistently between local authorities, the following working definition was established:

> Free structured activities include all free activities which are led by an instructor or member of staff, e.g. swimming lessons, Aquafit and

247

lifesaving. This does not include free splash or activities such as inflatable sessions or casual lane swimming sessions.

(Local Government Data Unit, 2006)

Data from the evaluation overwhelmingly supported the message that 'free splash' remained the major part of the Initiative for the 16 and unders, accounting for 97% and 93% in 2004/5 and 2005/6 respectively. This was also borne out by a survey of managers where nine out of ten stated they provided free splash opportunities for this age group. Turning to the over-60s scheme, a similar pattern emerged where 95% of free swims taken between November 2004 and September 2006 were unstructured, but like the youth scheme, the number of structured swims has risen consistently.

The policy and practice of structured and unstructured swims revealed some ambiguities. The annual operating guidance clearly favoured programming unstructured swims, and accepted that all local authorities would open their doors to ensure large numbers. The 2004 policy guidance also clearly stated, however, that 'the ambition is to make the free swimming entitlement the basis for a new and constructive relationship with children and young people in Wales that fails if it simply proceeds on the basis of a "free splash" in the local pool'. This position was strengthened further in the 2006/7 policy guidance which stated: 'following customer evaluation of the FSI all parties associated with the initiative wish *to encourage a greater proportion of structured activity*' (Bolton et al., 2008, author's emphasis). Interestingly, as attention focused on structured swims, there was a concomitant downturn in the number of 'free splash' sessions, especially among 16 and unders.

Senior policy makers were not satisfied with the notion of 'free splash'. Although there is no doubt that free splash sessions could contribute to increasing physical activity levels and to supporting the health target (the primary purpose), this was viewed as inadequate and as a missed opportunity, a position summed up by one senior civil servant, thus:

> We could have, probably very quickly and very easily, said we would have free swimming and that means we just open the doors to whatever population group come in and have a splash around. . . . We thought if we did that it would be a terrible wasted opportunity. We were sure we could do much more with this if we put some thought into structured activity.

By investing public money in this Initiative, sports policy makers perceived a need to add value. This is in contrast to other 'free' initiatives in Wales including

248

nicola bolton

free medical prescriptions and free bus passes (Clark, 2006). An early example of an attempt to develop mechanisms that would provide appropriate pathways and opportunities for sustainable participation was a link to the Welsh Amateur Swimming Association's self-improvement programme, but surveys of pool managers demonstrated its unpopularity and low take-up. This dilemma was articulated by one policy officer:

> How do you convert kids coming in the holidays – loads of them, free swimming – into something organised? It does not really go, children in holidays want to have a free splash, they don't want to be organised.

As a response, sports development practitioners have become increasingly involved and in most local authorities have developed a structured sport programme alongside continued opportunities for free splash. Besides 'learn to swim' programmes, there have been courses on lifesaving, canoeing, canoe polo, water polo, snorkelling, sub-aqua and octopush.

One main outcome of developing structured activities was the perception by local authorities that sports development benefited from employing specific officers. Although the FSI's funding package did not specifically provide for such posts, over time the majority of local authorities employed an officer who was expected to network, develop relationships with pool managers and manage other external partners. The importance of this role was identified by a Chief Officer who explained:

> I think the critical success factor if you like for us, is that we recognised that we needed a swimming development officer from the outset. I know that some authorities didn't, couldn't find the funding, but we basically robbed other areas to make sure we could get one. At first, it was a part-time Sports Development Officer (now full-time) that we put in place and that helped us plan and coordinate the whole thing across all the sites that we had – it has been invaluable.

In contrast, another Chief Officer identified the absence of a swimming Development Officer as a real shortcoming to his authority's progression with the Initiative:

> We took an approach whereby we tried to create a situation for sustainability purposes of ensuring that free swimming was built into the roles of the senior managers. I have to say, for the most part, this has not worked. In retrospect, I would have taken a decision to have

somebody dedicated for free swimming. What we are looking to do now is to share a post.

The data also revealed significant variations in take-up, both between local authorities and between pools inside individual local authorities. The highest ratio of swims per young person was in Blaenau Gwent and Gwynedd where there were more than two per person in 2006/7. Among local authorities with a low ratio of swims to population were Newport, Swansea, Carmarthenshire and Conwy, recording 0.5–0.6 swims for each young person aged 16 or under.

Target groups

The third dilemma that emerged from the policy framework was the need to target certain underrepresented groups, including: ethnic minority communities, people with disabilities, and disadvantaged communities (referred to in Wales as Communities First Areas). The need to make appropriate connections to the wider cross-cutting agenda was especially important to senior civil servants (Welsh Assembly Government, 2004). The policy guidance established the target groups as part of the FSI's minimum requirements. The dilemma and problem for practitioners was that the minimum guidance was exactly that – a minimum amount of provision, a blunt instrument that obscured the need to be context-specific and aware of geographical communities.

During the evaluation, many local authorities commented on the difficulties of addressing these target groups. Although important to the Assembly Government, it was difficult to interpret these targets, which led in most cases to an ad hoc rather opportunist approach. For example, the review undertaken on disability provision highlighted mixed practices across Wales, where a handful of authorities were achieving some proactive initiatives whilst some others were directing grants into the existing club infrastructure to support such work. In a few authorities this target group was overlooked at that time.

For disadvantaged communities a similar picture emerged; there were no authorities, with the possible exceptions of Bridgend and Cardiff, where developments were part of a planned, rational attempt to address these issues. It was possible, however, to identify anecdotally numerous proactive initiatives that contributed to a sense that provision for Community First Areas was especially important. One such positive action was the successful provision of transport for a group of over-60s from the Gurnos estate in Merthyr Tydfil:

> We put on transport. There was a group in the Gurnos area of Merthyr who wanted to come swimming, but transport was a barrier. So, we

nicola bolton

financed the transport for the best part of the year to enable them to access the pool. It started as a minibus but there is a full coach now. There are usually between thirty and forty swimming and they are talking about coming twice a week.

One local authority was able to use the FSI as a means to targeting disadvantaged wards. It had funding to support community workers, operating in specific wards, five of which were in Community First areas. The ability to use this local resource and develop collaborative arrangements was clearly important as summed up by this sports development officer:

I am lucky that I have a partnership with the Community Officers so that every school holiday each Community Officer will bring a group to the pool for a structured session every week. They did activities such as water polo and swimming and practised for the aquatics festival.

The final evaluation report (Bolton et al., 2008) highlighted several other case studies illustrating good sports development practice. The dilemma for practitioners was that given the picture of fixed resources and the low specification of minimum requirements, it was easy to overlook real community needs. Some mistakenly assumed that because free entitlement included everyone, there was no need to target specific groups or areas.

Attempting to make sense of dilemmas

In the UK, many sports development initiatives have struggled to make the necessary impacts, owing to limited resources available and the short lead-in times for implementation (Collins, 2008). In many respects the FSI was a quite typical intervention. First, it had multiple aims (as outlined above) and secondly, the arrangements between the Assembly Government, local authorities and other partners was challenging, and raised issues commonly experienced among sports development practitioners.

Whilst policy makers are tasked with identifying a 'joined-up' agenda and actively promoting it (Welsh Assembly Government, 2004), practitioners tend to be opportunist and seek to exploit the agendas as they suit their particular context. This is viewed as a means of maintaining sport's position and propelling it towards partnerships and wider collaborative arrangements. The FSI in Wales is but one example of this. Local authorities recognised the limitations of the Initiative in terms of its inability to address all the aims and objectives, but equally wanted to be seen to make a positive response. As part of this response, local

251

authorities realised the importance of employing an SDO, and by 2007 most had one to address specific issues.

At the heart of the three dilemmas outlined above was the interpretation of Sports Development and Physical Activity. A cornerstone for sports development was the notion of sustainability, as recognised by Girginov (2008: 278) who wrote:

> Sustainable sports development is an ideal and a moving target. The history of any sport organisation will testify to that as it represents an ongoing evolution of ideas and changing organisational forms and performances. Sports development visions, therefore, represent ideals which come from ethics and values we hold and are essentially a moral enterprise.

Collins (2008: 78) has written of the dilemma of balancing the needs of the large mass and the small elite: 'the scale of provision, the span of time needed and other favourable contextual policies to provoke major lifestyle and participation changes are huge, challenging, and beyond the sport policy community which is marginal'. This was further supported by Coalter (2007: 164) who noted the 'limitations in the research evidence about the broader impacts of sport (further limited by much research being related to the more diffuse category of physical activity)'. The FSI is an excellent example of these emerging tensions between sports development on the one hand, and physical activity on the other. The offer of a 'free swim' will not turn around people's behavioural patterns, and although this is acknowledged by practitioners, there is also a need to realise that many SDOs do not necessarily have the right skill sets (as yet) to deal with community development and physical activity promotion. In the words of Collins (2008: 81), 'promotion of sport for health requires more officers on the streets and in the lanes, like SDOs, but with better public health knowledge and training'.

CONCLUSION

The FSI has been shown as a multi-faceted national intervention that had various aims and objectives. Launched as a pilot, the 16-and-under and over-60 schemes did result in increased swimming. Whilst free swimming among the 16 and unders witnessed some decline, in part due to the growing emphasis on structured swimming, the over-60s scheme demonstrated gradual and sustained improvements over time.

The principal driver for free swimming was the Welsh Assembly Government's emphasis on improving the rates of physical activity among the Welsh population. Earlier sections have shown how free swimming shifted from a general physical activity intervention to a programme with greater emphasis on sports development. This leaves a number of challenging questions for those involved in the policy and practice of both physical activity and sports development.

1. How might the initiative have been established to raise physical activity levels in line with the overarching strategy of the Welsh Assembly Government?
2. If resources were restricted, would it have been more appropriate to focus on one age group and provide a comprehensive scheme rather than a partial one to two client groups?
3. How far are SDOs able to reconcile the competing agendas of developing sport, addressing health issues and/or developing communities?
4. How much money is needed to sustain the FSI and can it be guaranteed for at least three years ahead, for planning and staffing purposes? (The English scheme is no more secure – see Chapter 9.)
5. How can individual managers be incentivised to be proactive and rewarded on their performances?

At its core was an assumption that not only would people be more active, but that there would be genuine development of sport that was sustainable. This was a high expectation given the history of sports development projects over the past twenty-five years, and the earlier National Demonstration Projects (Tungatt and MacDonald, 1992) highlighted these problems. Given the Welsh Assembly Government's continued support for the *Climbing Higher* strategy, together with its response to ask the Chief Medical Officer for action after the critical report from the Wales Audit Office (2007), new skills and ways of working will be required from the sporting community if they wish to retain a stake in the future of this strategy.

ACKNOWLEDGEMENTS

The author would like to acknowledge the funding for FSI evaluation, which was made by the Welsh Assembly Government and managed on their behalf by the Sports Council for Wales. She would also like to thank the support of colleagues at UWIC involved in the evaluation, including Melissa Anderson, Bev Smith, and Chris Jennings, and Professor Steve Martin at Cardiff University. She is also grateful to Professor Scott Fleming and Dr Rachel Hughes for their observations on an earlier draft.

The contents of this paper reflect the author's views and are not attributed with the above mentioned people or organisations.

REFERENCES

Bolton, N. and Fleming, S. (2007) Modernising local government: the impact of new political arrangements on Chief Officers for Leisure and Recreation in Wales, *Local Government Studies*, 33(5): 723–42.

Bolton, N., Smith, B., Jennings, C. and Wall, M. (2005a) *Evaluation of WAG's Free Swim Initiative 2004–2007, First Interim Report,* available from http://www.sports-council-wales.org.uk/13625 (accessed 8 December 2008), Cardiff: InVEST, University of Wales Institute Cardiff.

Bolton, N., Smith, B., Jennings, C. and Anderson, M. (2005b) *Evaluation of WAG's Free Swim Initiative 2004–2007, Second Interim Report,* available from http://www.sports-council-wales.org.uk/13626 (accessed 8 December 2008), Cardiff: InVEST, University of Wales Institute Cardiff.

Bolton, N., Smith, B., Jennings, C. and Anderson, M. (2006) *Evaluation of WAG's Free Swim Initiative 2004–2007, Third Interim Report,* available from http://www.sports-council-wales.org.uk/13628 (accessed 8 December 2008), Cardiff: InVEST, University of Wales Institute Cardiff.

Bolton, N., Anderson, M., Smith, B. and Jennings, C. (2007a) *Evaluation of WAG's Free Swim Initiative 2004–2007, 60+ Case Study of Blaenau Gwent, Fourth Interim Report,* available from http://www.sports-council-wales. org.uk/15513 (accessed 8 December 2008), Cardiff: InVEST, University of Wales Institute Cardiff.

Bolton, N., Shami, R., Anderson, M., Smith, B. and Jennings, C. (2007b) *Evaluation of WAG's Free Swim Initiative 2004–2007, Free Swimming Initiative: Developing Disability Sport, Fourth Interim Report,* available from http://www.sports-council-wales.org.uk/15515 (accessed 8 December 2008), Cardiff: InVEST, University of Wales Institute Cardiff.

Bolton, N., Anderson, M., Smith, B. and Jennings, C. (2007c) *Evaluation of WAG's Free Swim Initiative 2004–2007, Fifth Interim Report,* available from http://www.sports-council-wales.org.uk/17235 (accessed 8 December 2008), Cardiff: InVEST, University of Wales Institute Cardiff.

Bolton, N., Martin, S., Anderson, M., Smith, M. and Jennings, C. (2008) *Free Swimming: An evaluation of The Welsh Assembly Government's Initiative,* available from: http://www.sports-council-wales.org.uk/19175 (accessed 8 December 2008), Cardiff: InVEST, University of Wales Institute Cardiff.

Clark, R. (2006) Bus passes improve the quality of life but are they also an operators' gravy train?, *Western Mail*, 1 April: 24.

Coalter, F. (2007) *A Wider Social Role for Sport: Who's Keeping the Score?* London: Routledge.

Collins, M. (2008) Public policies on sports development: Can mass and elite sport hold together?, in V. Girginov (ed.) *Management of Sports Development,* Oxford: Butterworth-Heinemann.

Girginov, V. (2008) Managing visions, changes and delivery in sports development: Summary and prospects, in V. Girginov (ed.) *Management of Sports Development,* Oxford: Butterworth-Heinemann.

Lawton, J., Smith, F.D. and Way, V. (eds) (1995) *Introduction to Swimming, Teaching and Coaching,* Loughborough: Swimming Times Ltd.

Local Government Data Unit (2006) *Welsh Assembly Government – Free Swimming Initiative Data Summary Report, April 2004–September 2007,* Cardiff: LGDU.

Office for National Statistics (2005) *Registrar General's Mid-year Estimates of Population,* Cardiff: Local Government Data Unit.

Sports Council for Wales (2004) *Report to the Welsh Assembly Government on the Free Swimming Pilot, Summer Holidays 2003,* Cardiff: SCW.

Sports Council for Wales (2005) *Adult Sports Participation and Club Membership in Wales 2002/3,* Cardiff: SCW.

Sports Council for Wales (2006a) *Children's Participation Survey 2006,* Cardiff: SCW.

Sports Council for Wales (2006b) *Active Young People in Wales,* Cardiff: SCW.

Tungatt, M. and MacDonald, D.(1992) *National Demonstration Projects: Major Lessons and Issues for Sports Development,* London: Sports Council.

Wales Audit Office (2007) *Increasing Physical Activity*, Cardiff: WAO.

Weiss, C.H. (1998) *Evaluation* (2nd edn), Upper Saddle River, NJ: Prentice Hall.

Welsh Assembly Government (2003) *Wales A Better Country: The Strategic Agendas of the Welsh Assembly Government*, Cardiff: WAG.

Welsh Assembly Government (2004) *Making the Connections: Delivering Better Services for Wales*, Cardiff: WAG.

Welsh Assembly Government (2005) *Climbing Higher: The Welsh Assembly Government Strategy for Sport and Physical Activity*, Cardiff: WAG.

Welsh Assembly Government (2006) *Climbing Higher: Next Steps,* Cardiff: WAG.

PART D

CONCLUSIONS

CHAPTER 14

SPORTS DEVELOPMENT AS A JOB, A CAREER AND TRAINING

Andy Pitchford and Mike Collins

INTRODUCTION

In 2005 SkillsActive, the successor body to SPRITO, charged with undertaking supply and demand-side labour market analyses, asked Pitchford to undertake a survey of the profile, employment status, working practices and perceived training needs of paid workers and volunteers in the sector, since Collins's (1995) work was more than a decade old.

To inform the work, first, he undertook a desk review of relevant research and documents, notably Boutall (2003), Collins with Kay (2003), Collins (1995), CDF (2004) and SPRITO (2001). Much of this literature suggested that sports development had suffered from a series of constraints in relation to training and learning for community-level interventions, including:

- poor cooperation between professional bodies and associations;
- fragmented training and learning opportunities;
- lack of coherent career structures and career development opportunities;
- tendencies towards 'model-driven', managerialist interventions;
- limited understanding of parallel, but converging welfare agendas.

Second, five regional workshops were held in Leeds, Birmingham, London, Ormskirk and Gloucester during November 2004, involving fifty-two workers from a range of agencies and backgrounds.

An internet questionnaire survey was hosted on the SkillsActive website during December 2004, having been promoted via various stakeholders (Sport England and the forty-five County Partnerships, NASD, Positive Futures network, CCPR and NGBs, and the London Community Sport network). In the four weeks, 899 respondents completed it, well exceeding the target set of 600 (for a summary see SkillsActive, n.d.). Of these, 9% were part-timers or self-employed, and 13% were unpaid volunteers. One in eight worked in a specific neighbourhood, and as many again across several, two in five across a whole district/borough/city, a quarter across a county or region, and one in twenty nationwide.

In order to account for the somewhat nebulous nature of the sector, the survey was premised on an inclusive definition of community sport development, allowing for responses from those operating with a 'sport-focused' agenda, in addition to those using sport as a social intervention.

Compared to 1995, when Collins estimated that there were between 2,500 and 3,000 jobs in SD, it was estimated by SkillsActive that there were 4,000 to 5,000 people in full-time or part-time employment in the sector. We therefore consider this sample to be broadly representative.

A CURRENT PROFILE OF SPORTS DEVELOPMENT WORKERS

Collins (2005) had stressed the higher proportion of women in sports development than in other branches of sport. Pitchford found 41% in his self-report sample compared to Collins's 47% from a structured sample of 659. He found 8% were from an ethnic minority, slightly more than in the national population, and 3.8% considered themselves to have an impairment or disability. As ten years before, the age profile still suggested a young, developing workforce, with over half aged under 35 (Figure 14.1).

Respondents were strikingly highly qualified: only 1% had no formal qualification, while 74% had a first degree, and 22.4% claimed a higher postgraduate qualification (including a PGCE for teaching professionals). Collins's (1995)

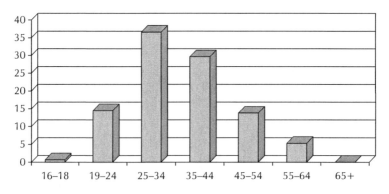

Figure 14.1 Age of sports development sample (%)

equivalent figures were 35% graduate and 8% postgraduate. This is partly a reflection of the government-backed growth of graduate study in the decade.

During the workshops, some thirty different job titles were identified by participants as relevant and current, and twenty-three were offered in the questionnaire. Table 14.1 shows the pattern of responses. There is a lower proportion of sports- specific officers than identified by Collins (2005) and fewer target group-focused other than for youth. Despite this wide range of choice, one in three were 'other', showing that the diversity of job descriptors (and implicitly of job focus) was if anything wider than in 1995.

In terms of job function, respondents identified the characteristics of their work and also their relationship to the end-users/participants, as follows:

- 22.6% – practical coaching, teaching, leadership, face-to-face outreach work
- 1.5% – adviser or counsellor

Table 14.1 Job titles in sports development

Title	%
Sports Development Manager (LA, NGB)	9.6
Sports Development Officer (including Youth, Community)	18.9
Sports-specific Development Officer (e.g. Netball)	9.7
Assistant Sports Development Officer	2.1
Sport or Leisure Officer	2.1
Community Sports Coach	1.8
Physical Activity Coordinator	1.2
Chief Leisure Officer	0.2
Programme Manager	3.1
Football in the Community Officer	0.4
School Sport Coordinator	0.9
Partnership Development Manager	2.0
Access Officer	2.2
Volunteer Development Officer/Coordinator	2.2
Health Promotion Officer/Worker	0.2
Youth Leader/Worker	1.3
Play Leader/Worker	0.1
Sports Coach/Leader	10.9
Outreach Worker	0.2
Helper/Assistant	0.8
Teacher/Tutor/Lecturer	2.5
Learning Support Worker	0.0
Other	31.2

Source Pitchford, 2005.

- 25.2% – facilitator or coordinator
- 26.0% – manager, strategist or planner
- 2.6% – senior or Chief Officer
- 19.5% – hybrid
- 6.4% – other.

Compared to 1995, this shows a higher proportion of managerial roles. It is a moot point as to whether this is a function of the survey or a development of the roles, or a move to 'more Chiefs and fewer Indians'. As Figure 14.2 shows, ethnic minority managers were notably lacking (ethnic minority staff were much more likely to be coaches/session leaders), and few women were senior managers.

More than forty types of agencies were cited by respondents as their employer (Table 14.2). Local authorities represented only 40%, a much lower proportion than ten years previously; but, of course, since then Leisure Trusts, Connexions, Sport Action Zones, Youth Offending Teams, Youth Inclusion Programmes, New Deals for Communities, County Sports Partnerships, and School Sport Coordinators have all appeared, many linked to local authorities and LEAs. More voluntary sectors posts also have appeared, so the job market is more fragmented. But many of these programmes and their posts are time-limited, commonly for three years only.

The work bases reflected this variety of employer:

- 42% – local authority/government agency
- 13% – from home

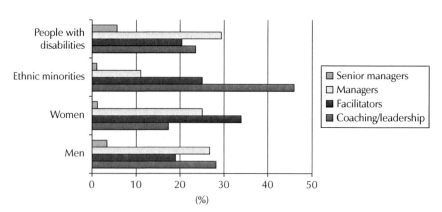

Figure 14.2 Sports development roles played by different people (Pitchford, 2005)

Table 14.2 Host organisations for professional and volunteer sports development workers

Type of organisation	%
Local authority	39.9
Voluntary/amateur sports club	11.2
Charity/Trust/Social enterprise	9.3
National Governing Body of sport, e.g. LTA	6.9
Education (school, college, university)	6.8
County Sports Partnership	5.1
Leisure Trust, e.g. Greenwich Leisure	2.1
Professional sports club, including *Playing for Success*	1.7
Voluntary youth club	1.1
Youth Service/Connexions	1.1
Youth Inclusion programme	1.1
Primary (health) Care Trust	0.9
Youth Offending Team	0.7
Community centre	0.7
Youth Sport Trust	0.4
Active Communities project	0.4
YMCA	0.4
New Deal for Communities project	0.3
Sport Action Zone	0.2
Other	12.6

Source Pitchford, 2005.

- 11% – school, college or university
- 8% – leisure centre
- 5% – neighbourhood office/community centre
- 4% – national governing body office
- 4% – sports club
- 3% – youth club
- 3% – sports stadium
- 0.2% – faith centre
- 8% – other.

Four out of five worked as part of a team (though this might not mean that there were other CSD workers), and only one in ten were lone workers, so isolation was much reduced from 1995, when it was a considerable problem. But CSD workers were away from base most of the time, often working long and antisocial hours, so they were not always in touch with colleagues on more conventional timetables. One in five had a mentor, and one in four were acting as a mentor for someone else.

The continuing immaturity of this field is shown. More than two decades after its initiation, 37.5% were in their first SD job, 29% had worked in one similar role, and the same proportion in more than one. Many – 56% overall – though especially junior staff, were not affiliated to the main professional body. This was more than Collins (1995) found (38%). Only 28% were affiliated to the National Association of Sports Development, 15% to the Institute of Leisure and Amenity Management, 1% to the Institute of Sport and Recreation Management, and 2% each to the National Association of Clubs for Young People, UK Youth and the Register for Exercise Professionals. Fewer than 1% were members of the Chief Leisure Officers Association.

Salaries reflected seniority:

£000 a year	%
Under 12	8.1
12–23.9	49.8
24–35.9	19.8
36–59.9	2.2
Over 60	4.8

As the occupation has developed, more people have worked for their employer for over five years (31%), but still 39% had been in post for less than 24 months. When asked how long they thought they would be staying with their present employer, the sample answered: 23% less than two years, 24% two to four years, 16% over five years, and 25% didn't know or were undecided.

THE FOCUS OF THE JOB AND THE WORKING OF COMMUNITY SPORTS DEVELOPMENT

Table 14.3 shows that most SD work is with multiple client groups, with less focus than in 1995 on any of the groups other than youth, with considerably less focus in the case of women and unemployed people.

The sports-specific focus was also dispersed:

- 12% soccer
- 14% other team sports
- 4% other individual sports
- 4% water sports
- 2% fitness activities in clubs

264

Table 14.3 Groups with whom Community SDOs work (%)

Group	Collins 1995	Pitchford 2005
Young people	52	41
Serving one or more specific sports	14	7
People with disabilities	42	4
Women and girls	49	3
Black/ethnic minorities	26	2
Older people	39	1
People unemployed	23	1
Other	n/a	6
Some/all of above	n/a	41

Source Pitchford ,2005.

- 2% outdoor pursuits
- 1% other community settings, e.g. walking
- 1% martial arts
- 13% other activities
- 54% some/all of the above.

Soccer was not only a sport-specific programme but, given its popularity, a major element in all youth-related programmes like those dealing with crime.

CSD has to balance working with small groups and knowing them well to undertake some delicate health/crime/drug-related work, and using larger groups as a way of raising participation, and maintaining a supportable unit cost/subsidy. The average size of groups that CSD staff worked with weekly were:

- 9% 15 or fewer
- 25% 16–50 people
- 15% 51–100 people
- 36% over 100 people.

More staff were working with large groups than in 1995 but, significantly, one in seven (15%) workers were unable to give a figure, an issue in basic measures of cost-effectiveness.

With CSD increasingly linked to wider cross-cutting outcomes of better health, economic and environmental regeneration, lifelong learning, community safety, social inclusion and community cohesion, originally Pitchford had hoped to distinguish respondents on the basis of such rationales for their work – as well as sport-based and social ones like success in sport, personal development, and empowerment – but when presented with a long list of these, workshop members suggested that this would be problematic for workers, since they would be involved in several or all of these themes. Some claimed that this was all underpinned by the concept of 'community development'. In part, this response was understandable, because SDOs or top managers were forced by the need to secure their work programmes and staffing by seeking a plethora of funding sources across social and welfare agendas, or chose to do so.

However, this flexibility and multi-skilling is also likely to lead to a lack of focus, and consequent difficulties in relation to goal-setting, and evaluating outcomes and overall effectiveness. Furthermore, at a macro level, it problematises attempts to identify a core body of knowledge for work in community sport development. Instead, a more sophisticated understanding of the various fields of knowledge which underpin work in this sector will be required if occupational standards and related training strategies are to be successfully implemented.

Among the respondents, and indeed the broader policy constituencies, there appears to be a consensus that a knowledge of sport, and a knowledge of the structures and systems of sports is inadequate for workers hoping to secure and maintain programmes in 'community' or 'inclusion' settings. This knowledge must be leavened or mediated by an understanding of the requirements of the setting, which broadly can be acquired in two ways: through (i) experience of the particular setting, and/or (ii) exposure to education and training grounded in the underpinning knowledge relating to that setting.

Despite the fragmented nature of the sector, it was suggested that job functions can be clustered into three main categories, remembering that these will be mediated by both the setting for the work and the mission of the employing organisation.

1. Coaching/leadership/face-to-face delivery

- Direct delivery to participants through coaching, teaching, leadership, outreach work.
- Likely to involve session planning, management and delivery.
- Some local financial control.
- Requiring an understanding of health and safety, child protection, equity, mentoring, progression/development guidance, management of challenging behaviour, referral or open access systems – depending on the nature of the intervention.

2. Facilitation or coordination

- Management or enabling activity removed from face-to face-delivery.
- Likely to involve partnership work, project planning and management, liaison and negotiation, in addition to monitoring and evaluation.
- Local financial and budgetary control.
- Requiring an understanding of inter-agency working, decision-making processes, governance at a 'micro' level, organisational change, consultation processes, monitoring and evaluation, in addition to managing casual staff and marketing – depending on the nature of the intervention or employing organisation.

3. Management

- Strategic, planning and resource management.
- Likely to involve responsibility for departmental human resource management, strategic planning, partnership development.
- Area/department financial and budgetary control.
- Requiring an understanding of strategic management, human resource management and planning, employment relations, financial planning, governance at organisational levels and contract management.

Short-term contracts and project insecurity are likely to be experienced in each functional area, so procurement and funding applications are common to all three.

While it is possible to propose some commonalities of experience for workers in these groups – at least in terms of their proximity to programme users or sports participants – it is unwise to assume that any of these categories will share an underpinning field of knowledge. This exchange, between two workshop participants, demonstrates that where workers appear to share similar job functions, their base assumptions and modus operandi can differ quite significantly. Both of these participants were confident that they were 'facilitators':

> 'I think a national certificate in sports development which provides entry level to the career ladder would be beneficial, but also additional management career development modules for managers – we are no different than any others in the industry. We *manage* people and contracts.'

> 'No, I'm not a manager. I facilitate. My job is about empowering communities. I don't manage, in the way you're describing – it wouldn't be appropriate.'

While the following figures should be viewed with this debate in mind, the ease with which survey respondents completed questions about their job functions suggests that these terms do indeed carry some currency in the sector. To these three main categories we added a 'hybrid' and 'senior management' option to questions, as well as a category for 'advisers or counsellors', intended to relate to the growth in referral systems in both physical activity and health promotion, and social inclusion projects. While the underpinning knowledge for some segments of this sector is relatively uncontested, for example the reliance of youth inclusion programmes on youth and community practice, in other settings relationships are less clear. For example, would an after-school sports club be best informed by Physical Education, health promotion, playwork or youthwork? The following profiles emerged when the survey data were interrogated about these functional groups.

1. Coaching/leadership/face-to-face work (23% of the sample):

- 70% male, perhaps about average for overall sports participation and employment
- 16% from ethnic minorities, above average as already said
- 4% had a disability or impairment
- 44% employed full-time; 8% part-time; 6% self-employed; 40% volunteers
- 45% in their first role in the community sport sector
- 25% no sport/physical activity qualifications
- 58% with Higher Education qualifications (including 15% with a higher degree)
- 68% unattached to any sector professional bodies.

2. Facilitation or coordination (25% of the sample):

- 55% female
- 10% from ethnic minorities
- 3% had a disability or impairment
- 85% employed full-time; 8% part-time; 1% self-employed; 3% volunteers
- 44% in first role in the sector
- 80% with Higher Education qualifications (including 20% with a higher degree)
- 57% unattached to any sector professional bodies
- 27% dissatisfied or very dissatisfied with prospects of promotion
- 21% dissatisfied or very dissatisfied with job/role security.

andy pitchford and mike collins

3. Management (26% of the survey):

- 39% female
- 4% from ethnic minorities
- 4% had a disability or impairment
- 94% employed full-time; 1% part-time; 1% self-employed; 3% volunteers
- 23% in first role in sector
- 83% with Higher Education qualifications (including 32% with a higher degree)
- 47% unattached to sector professional associations
- 14% dissatisfied or very dissatisfied with job/role security
- 21% dissatisfied or very dissatisfied with promotion prospects.

In terms of those respondents most likely to be engaged in sport-based social interventions, the following responses were noteworthy:

Of those working with *young people*:

- 32% were in face-to-face roles
- 26% as facilitators
- 23% as managers
- 13% in hybrid roles
- 2% as senior managers
- 37% in their first community sports role
- 74% with Higher Education qualifications.

Of those working in *inner city areas*:

- 28% were in face-to-face roles
- 20% as facilitators
- 28% as managers
- 18% in hybrid roles
- 3% as senior managers
- 39% were in their first community sports role
- 51% were aged under 34 years
- 37% were female
- 72% with Higher Education qualifications
- 26% from Sport Science/Studies degrees
- 8% with a background in community development
- 7% in social work/social policy.

Of those working at *neighbourhood level*:

- 49% were in face-to-face roles
- 18% as facilitators
- 12% as managers
- 16% in hybrid roles
- 3% as senior managers
- 45% in their first community sport role
- 35% were female
- 73% were unaffiliated to sector professional associations
- 35% had no sports-related/NGB qualifications.

Thus moving from group 1 to group 3 the share of female, BEM, disabled, part-time and voluntary, novice, professionally unaffiliated and dissatisfied workers declines; and the proportions with undergraduate or postgraduate qualifications rises. This is in line with the logic and experience of labour markets. But, as in 1995, the 'porosity' of the CSD field is shown by the numbers of new entrants even at management level. And even at that level, the extent of the dissatisfaction with the job role, job security and prospects of promotion is substantial.

In relation to those workers who were least likely to have extensive vocational experience of community sports settings, the following data are notable.

Of those respondents in their *first community sport role* (38% of the sample):

- 27% were in face-to-face roles
- 29% as facilitators
- 16% as managers
- 22% in hybrid roles
- 20% were aged under 24 years
- 37% were between 25 and 34
- 11% were lone workers
- 67% were unaffiliated to a sector professional associations
- 70% had sports-related/NGB qualifications.

Of those respondents *aged under 24 years* (15% of the sample):

- 30% were in face-to-face roles
- 38% as facilitators
- 10% as managers
- 21% in hybrid roles
- 9% were lone workers

- 86% had Higher Education qualifications (including 8% postgraduate)
- 88% had sport-related/NGB qualifications.

It is difficult to find comparable data on job/role satisfaction, but Table 14.4 shows the findings from Pitchford's survey. The two greatest dissatisfactions were security of tenure and prospects of promotion. Regarding the first, as ten years earlier, there are still a sizeable number of time-limited posts in this job market; in 3-year posts, familiarisation/set-up and network formation and wind-down/job-seeking phases can often take up a quarter of the total time, making such funding lower in cost-effectiveness than is often appreciated by politicians and national managers. Regarding the second, there is still no clear career ladder, and people have to move geographically or laterally to gain experience and promotion, since this is often not possible for lone workers or in small teams. The routes into generic middle and top management are only a little clearer that in 1995 (Collins with Kay, 2003).

PERCEIVED TRAINING NEEDS

The existing high level of initial training would suggest that this workforce would be open to more closely targeted, specialised training. In constructing a functional map of educational and training requirements for the community sports development sector, the role of underpinning fields and disciplines needs to be carefully assessed. For example, any assumption that UK under-graduate sports programmes provide an effective understanding of youth and community practice or play work might be misplaced.

In Pitchford's brief survey, it was not possible to gather data on the effectiveness of these SD workers. There is some efficiency to be gained from a clearer picture

Table 14.4 How far are SD workers satisfied with their job/role? (%)

Satisfaction with	Very/Satisfied	Neither satisfied nor dissatisfied	Very/Dissatisfied
Working conditions	80.3	11.2	7.9
Hours of work	74.9	14.2	9.8
Security of job	64.1	18.2	16.2
Prospects of promotion/ development	46.4	31.7	20.5
Training opportunities	66.2	19.8	12.5
Degree of responsibility	74.9	11.4	5.7

of the fields of knowledge which underpinned their work, and any subsequent rationalisation of educational and training products for those fields. Fields of knowledge worth considering might include:

- playwork
- health promotion
- youth work
- criminology/probation work
- social work
- community practice
- physical education
- business management
- marketing.

Some of them, like youth work and community practice, are underpinned by particular values and principles, to the extent that those working in each field are likely to share an ethos, and an interpretation of the worth/status of their work to society in general. In the current climate, in contrast, identifying and articulating a coherent and distinctive set of values that might underpin community sport development work appears to be a more challenging proposition. However, whatever their highest qualification, this sample of probably a fifth of the market were not highly convinced of its usefulness in preparing them for their job: 49% thought it effective or very effective, 31% were neutral, and 14% thought it ineffective or very ineffective.

Pitchford's data suggests that there is a poor match between underpinning knowledge and job functions which is being perpetuated by the fragmented nature of training and education for the sector. Though many in his sample claimed to focus on projects for young people, youthwork and playwork had relatively low profiles in the sector's curricula vitae: of the 41% who identified young people as their key target group, only one in eleven cited youthwork as an underpinning field of study, one in a hundred playwork and only four in a hundred had any connections with either UK Youth or the National Association of Clubs for Young People.

Similarly, in settings where workers operated within a single neighbourhood, only 6% of workers cited community development and community practice as components of underpinning qualifications. Interestingly, one in five of these workers were from Business Management/Business Studies backgrounds.

There is constant complaint from employees that the sports field in general gives low priority and small budgets for training, often limited to senior managers and to short courses, and that many employers offer little financial, time or in-kind support for study, especially if it involves days away from work. For all that, nine out of ten of Pitchford's sample recorded some training in the previous two years by a range of agencies (Table 14.5).

Pitchford's respondents indicated the influence of five factors on their ability to access training, as set out in Table 14.6.

As to the place where training would be most beneficial, 25% cited a campus or other base away from work, 21% their workplace, 12% at home (by distance learning), and 54% some combination of these.

Question 24 allowed respondents to prioritise or identify their own training needs and requirements. More than one in ten of respondents selected topics as a priority training need (Table 14.7).

Table 14.5 Training attended in the previous two years (2004/5)

Provider	%
Local authority	49
National governing body of sport	40
Sport England	38
National Association of Sports Development	21
Youth Sport Trust	20
University or College	19
Institute of Leisure and Amenity Management	16
Institute of Sport and Recreation Management	11
Positive Futures	11
NACRO	6
Other youth sport	5
Other	13

Table 14.6 Factors affecting how much training CSD workers access

Factor	Very/influential (%)	Of limited/ no influence (%)
Cost	71	25
Availability locally	77	19
Timing of training	81	15
Attitudes of managers/team members	49	47
Availability of distance learning	37	57

Source Pitchford, 2005.

Table 14.7   Topics identified as a priority for training

Topics	Listed by %
Funding Manage challenging behaviour Understanding/converging policy agendas Strategy/policy development Sustainability issues	43
Handle local systems/networks Good practice examples Monitor and evaluate Manage finance/budget Deliver sport sessions Awareness of government agency policies Community development practices Managing projects Handling social inclusion issues	25–28
Career development planning Manage volunteers Partnership working	20–24
Child protection Recruit/develop/retain staff Self-management Communication/negotiating skills	15–19
Drug/alcohol awareness	10–14

What is striking is that it would not be unreasonable to expect most of these to have been covered in any initial SD degree course, except perhaps career development planning and drug/alcohol awareness. Particular functional work-groups had their own priorities where understandable items appear, like challenging behaviour by neighbourhood workers (see box).

Neighbourhood workers
- Funding (46%)
- Managing challenging behaviour (40%)
- Sport session delivery (39%)
- Sustainability (28%)

---

andy pitchford and mike collins

Facilitators
- Funding (48%)
- Financial/budget management (29%)
- Managing challenging behaviour (27%)
- Sustainability (26%)

Inner city workers
- Funding (47%)
- Managing challenging behaviour (38%)
- Sustainability (33%)

Coaching and leadership delivery
- Sport session delivery (45%)
- Managing challenging behaviour (43%)
- Funding (37%)

Managers
- Convergence training (42%)
- Strategy, policy development (42%)
- Funding (37%)

Workers under 24 years of age
- Funding (59%)
- Budget/financial management (38%)
- Career development planning (31%)

COURSES ON OFFER

So what do initial and continuing Higher Education courses related to sports development provide? Nationally, the number of students opting for sport-related degree programmes is growing significantly as the following analysis demonstrates. In total, 130 higher and further education colleges offered 1,934 sport-related programmes. The most significant market is undergraduate sport science, which has grown rapidly but is now perceived to be maturing as applications and acceptances to programmes have stabilised. In 2004 there were 8,995 applications to sports science programmes and 7,810 accepted places, compared to 7,959 applicants and 7,024 acceptances in 2002 (Nixon and Settle, 2005).

Undergraduate courses

The provision of honours degrees has mushroomed (www.ucas.co.uk), so that by 2006 there were in Britain forty-three courses, more or less evenly divided between science and arts streams (24:19). These were underpinned by six HND courses, two DipHEs, and most recently seventeen two-year Foundation degrees, with three places offering a third BA top-up year. Fourteen of these honours degrees were just called Sports Development, and only one entitled Community Sport Development (North East Wales Institute of HE). The largest number (sixteen) was explicitly linked to coaching, six to exercise and health, four to educational development, four to PE, and two each to sports studies and sports science. The editor of this volume has some doubts about trying to educate coaches and sports development officers on the same course, because he sees the two conceptually and operationally separate (Collins, 1995; Collins with Kay 2003), but it does provide career options for students.

Is this variety reflected in the composition of the courses? Table 14.8 summarises the broad modular contents of different courses from HEIs recognised as market leaders. Clearly there were a number of common features in topics as well as generic skills, and all demanded a dissertation as a synthetic and critical personal contribution which gives a chance for students to offer something unique in their job interviews. UWIC and Sheffield Hallam clearly showed growth out of conventional sports studies offerings and Northumbria from sports management. Liverpool, NEWI and Gloucestershire offered a wider range of options and links to education, community and youth issues, but the core provision of learning focused on youth is scanty, whatever the slant/emphasis of the course.

One can contrast this with the training arranged by employers (SkillsActive 2006a): health and safety (62%), job-specific (53%), coaching (52 %), induction (46%), management/supervisory (30%), training in new technology (27%), customer service (27%), company administration (17%), marketing (12%), other (8%), languages (2%).

The UK Coaching Certificate has taken off, with 94,000 candidates at the three levels in 2006/7. But the transfer of funds by Learning and Skills Councils, under government instruction from adults to 16–19 year-olds and people with no NVQ Level 2 (29% of workers) started to threaten this growth; now CSPs are entrusted to get candidates coach training. SkillsActive also found large gaps in Level 2 customer-service skills of four out of five frontline staff, and of Level 3 supervisory management skills in seven out of ten managers (SkillsActive, 2006b).

andy pitchford and mike collins

Table 14.8 Module contents of selected undergraduate SD courses

	Liverpool John Moores U	NE Wales Inst of HE	Sheffield Hallam U	Northumbria U	UWIC	U of Gloucestershire
	BA SD + PE	BA Com. SD	SD + coaching	SD + coaching	SD	SD
Year 1 (common foundation)						
	Study/pers skills	Study/pers skills	Study/pers skills	Study/pers skills	Coach science	Study/pers skills
	Opps in sch + commy	Work in CSD	Foundation of SD/leadership	Man/dev sp	Health + spec pops in sp	Sp organisations
	Theory sp/PE	CSD principle	Sp+social incl.	Marketing	Biomechanics	Activity leadership
	Perform sp/PE	Soc hist of sp	Skills for SD	Intro coaching	Functional anatomy	Intro social sp/ex
	Leadership in sp/PE	Instruct sp/exer		Res process	Physiology	Transf SD skills
	Sportslinx weekly placement	*Options*	*Sports options*		Psychology	*3 options from*
		Sp/Ex practice	Games 1,2		Res methods + prof dev	Critic think in SD
		Child protect	Athletics/water		Sports techniques	Fund of anatomy
		Play	Adapted sp			Fund of phil sp/ex
		Work with groups/individs				Intro sp/ex physiol
		Sociol youth + community				Intro to psych of sp/ex/health
Year 2 (2 and 3 core)						
	Pract. Deliv of sp/PE	Res methods	Res methods	Res man	Res meth + prof dev	Res methods
	Facil inclusion	Workplace learning	Sp coaching	Marketing	Practical coaching	Sociol of sp
	Deliv coaching	Comparit. SD	Sp + youth	Strategic plan	Sport man + marketing	Sp + soc inclusion
	Sport context	Sp/cult/society	Learning at work	Res design/ analysis	SD environ't	*3 options from*
	Manage/coord SD	Running sp	SD planning/ processes	Placement	Eval approaches to SD	Psych of ex/health
	Workbased learning	Volunteering				Ex in healthcare
						Adapted PE

Table 14.8 Continued

Liverpool John Moores U	NE Wales Inst of HE	Sheffield Hallam U	Northumbria U	UWIC	U of Gloucestershire
BA SD + PE	BA Com. SD	SD + coaching	SD + coaching	SD	SD
+ 2 options	*Options* ■ Practice of coaching ■ Culture + soc ed ■ Europ perspect. ■ Urban studies	*Options* ■ Multimedia ■ Notation analysis ■ Sp + lifestyle ■ Disab/third age ■ Workbased learn		■ SD practice + bus dev ■ Dissertation	■ Ethical issues in sp ■ Hist of sp organisations ■ Planning for SD ■ Football + community

Year 3 (2 and 3 options)

Liverpool John Moores U	NE Wales Inst of HE	Sheffield Hallam U	Northumbria U	UWIC	U of Gloucestershire
Strand choice ■ Sport manage. ■ Sports dev ■ Health-related fitness ■ Inclusion ■ PE ■ Dissertation	■ Workplace enquiry ■ SD pol + pract ■ Modern sport ■ Dissertation *Options* ■ Adv coach + special pops ■ Clinic practice ■ PA, ex + health ■ Debates in ed ■ Youth cult + arts ■ Support informal learning	■ Coaching children ■ SD in action ■ Dissertation *Options* ■ Internat SD ■ UK sport policy ■ Issues in SD	■ Sp Event Man ■ Facil/op man ■ Sp dev organs ■ Dissertation	■ Coaching science ■ PA, health + spec pops ■ Socio-cult issues in sp ■ Sport injuries ■ Market + man ■ Dev communities ■ Placement ■ Technology in 16 sports + dance	■ Issues in SD ■ Particip + partners ■ Dissertation *Options* ■ Ex + mental health ■ Ex prescription ■ Coaching science ■ Sp ethics theory + practice ■ Performance SD ■ Youth culture + active leisure

Masters level courses

These began to emerge just before the millennium, and are still few in number (www.prospects.ac.uk). Asserting 'sports development has grown as a recognised profession over the last decade', the website for Sheffield Hallam University speaks of a 'recognised need for a specialist masters degree', but no statement is extant from any of the professional bodies to this effect. The decision to split off a sports development stream from a mainstream sports management/sports studies course has been taken by each individual HEI. The entry requirement is a 'good' honours degree, but can also be in relation to 'appropriate' vocational experience, and in Cardiff's case is 'aged over 25' and has held for a minimum of two years a 'position of responsibility of relevance'.

Table 14.9 shows the content of the extant courses in October 2006. They do not show great differences from their predecessor BA/B.Sc. courses, and demonstrate the same lack of material focused on youth.

SD keeps changing; with the evolution of CSPs (see Chapters 3 and 5), Partnership CEOs are insisting that the role is now wider than 'traditional' SD and many are now called Partnership Managers (e.g. with the workforce and training agencies, clubs, etc.). Seeing a skills gap relative to Britain's competitors, HMG had tried to encourage employers to lead in specifying training needs, with a White Paper (DES, 2005), and a series of Sector Skills Councils, that for sport (and children's play and caravanning) being SkillsActive. Each had to analyse its labour market and develop an agreement with employers, giving them a much greater say in the structure and content of training, in return for delivering to government the 'flexible multi-skilled workforce it desires' (Ravenscroft and Gilchrist, 2005: 172).

Ravenscroft and Gilchrist's take on the leisure labour market is that it is a dual one 'consisting of relatively few skilled jobs (generally with relatively low staff turnover) and many relatively unskilled jobs, few of which are filled on a long-term basis' (2005: 173). We would say that this may be true of catering and hospitality, but is overdrawn for sport and the arts. Certainly, however CCT casualised many jobs in contracting companies and to a degree in trusts, and many others run on seasonal or short-term contracts. Certainly these operations, mostly smaller than their predecessor local authority employers, have small training budgets (though GLL provides a training base for the several contracts it runs for London boroughs). But the vocational training–HE divide still exists, and is complicated by the recent formation of National Skills Academies.

Table 14.9 Modules in Masters courses in Sports Development, 2006/7

University of Gloucestershire PgC/PgD/MA Ft/pt	Sheffield Hallam University PgC/PgD/M.Sc. Ft/pt	Northumbria University PgD/M.Sc. Ft/pt	University of Wales Institute Cardiff PgC/PgD/MA Ft/pt
Compulsory ■ Methods of inquiry in PA & SD ■ Sport in society ■ The sport experience ■ Agencies & methods in SD ■ Negotiated independ. study (+ mentoring) Dissertation (3) *Options from* ■ Professional ethics in PA, sport & tourism ■ Strategic management in PA, sport & tourism ■ Prof practice in PA, sport & tourism ■ PA & health referral ■ Cardiac rehabilitation ■ Any modular choice	C1 Advanced skills for SD C2 Researching sport C3 Sport, community regeneration & social inclusion or sport marketing & public relations C4 SD change management project D1 contemporary issues in SD D2 Strategic policy planning in SD D3 developing people in sports organisations D4 managing viability in sports organisations M.Sc. Research project (3)	■ SD in contemporary society ■ SD policy & planning ■ Managing the sport organisation ■ Community SD ■ Sports coaching ■ Sport Event management ■ The Research process Dissertation (3)	*Core:* 1. Research methods & issues 2. Qualitative research methods 3. Principles & practice of SD & coaching Research project (3) *3 options from:* ■ Strategic management & change ■ Issues in SD & coaching ■ Sports marketing ■ Child in PA & sport ■ Coaching process ■ Exercise psychology ■ Independent study

A PROFESSION?

Sports management and development are established occupations, but are they yet a profession? Professions define and control their area of knowledge and expertise, control entry, provide services to their members and provide lobbying and advocacy of a non-political nature. The four very different bodies in this arena were the Chief Leisure Officers Association (CLOA), the Institute of Leisure and Amenity Management (ILAM), the Institute of Sport and Recreation Management (ISRM) and the National Association of Sports Development (NASD). ISRM, based on the Loughborough University campus, had been serving the swimming pool managers – and then recreation managers more broadly – for 105 years, had about 1,800 members, a suite of qualifications accredited on the national framework, close support from the commercial suppliers as national and regional sponsors, and a basic system of CPD. ILAM, formed from a number of earlier interests in 1973, had at one time 5,000 members spread over sport and arts and parks management, children's play and some library and cultural interests. It had more senior officer members than ISRM and its thematic groups had developed some influence with Sport England and DCMS. It had a useful information centre and a range of national courses, but regions of very varying strength. Government, and the Minister for Sport Richard Caborn in particular, wished to deal with a single body, and clearly saw ILAM as its core. NASD was less than a decade old, had some 400 members, mostly young and junior. It had had services from ISRM for two years, but seeing ILAM's star ascending switched partners. CLOA had influence beyond its small numbers because of its members' status, but had little dealings with the other three.

ILAM, ISRM and NASD spent a year in discussion about a possible merged body; but the prospectus produced for members to vote on was vague, and optimistic in projecting a sizeable increase in income without raising subscriptions. In May 2006 ISRM rejected the proposals, because ILAM had a rapidly diminishing membership, large unspecified debts and pension fund commitments. It needed to sell its splendid gentry house HQ south of Reading to cover its commitments, but has not done so, and ISRM's trustees feared that their surplus could soon be swallowed up and its qualifications devalued. This incurred the displeasure of the minister and Sport England.

ILAM sold its offices and took up a smaller staff and base in Reading and reconstituted itself as ISPAL (Institute of Sport, Parks and Leisure) with new trustees and no regional branches, and NASD had disappeared. ISRM's AGM had voted overwhelmingly to keep open the door to a single body, and at the time of writing talks had restarted with a new proposal for a Chartered Institute focused around

281

sport and likely to be based at Loughborough, with the benefits that co-location would bring (see Thorpe and Collins in Chapter 6, pp. 112–16). A case is being prepared for submission to the Privy Council. Houlihan (2008) suggested that after professions had been frozen out by the 'hard managerialism' of the 1980s, both major political parties had more if sometimes ambiguous support, and that sport and recreation had an opportunity to lay claim as a 'civic profession' that,

- builds trust with customers and citizens;
- builds social-political capital in communities;
- develops active citizenship (with its large volunteer force), and provides a key element of civil society.

The facts revealed in this chapter show it still to be a very porous field of work, and the new body would have to sign up more than the constituent partners to pass the Privy Council's threshold of 5,000. And although it has growing numbers of graduates, the majority are not so well qualified yet, and that may be the Achilles heel. Time will tell.

THE UK IN THE EUROPEAN SPORTS LABOUR MARKET

Under the aegis of the European Network of Sports Science Education and Employment, within which eighty-six HEIs and other organisations (eight in England and Wales) are involved in developing European-wide qualification frameworks, four groups have been examining the structure, demand, competencies and curricula for PE, sports coaching, health and fitness and, significantly for this chapter, sports management (Petry et al., 2008).

Camy and Madella (2008a) estimated the sports sector workforce in the twenty-five EU states as 800,000 people, but many more in associated media, sponsorship, manufacturing and gambling. At 0.93% of its population, the UK has twice the level of employment as Denmark, Finland and The Netherlands, and some three times those of Sweden, Germany and France. Based on an EU average annual turnover of 25%, Camy and Madella also estimated the workforce stocks at:

- 120,000 workers at Levels 6 and 7 (Bachelors/Masters) with an annual flow of 30,000.
- 400,000 workers at Levels 4 and 5 (upper secondary/post-secondary) with an annual flow of 100,000.
- 280,000 workers at Level 3 (lower secondary) with an annual flow of 70,000.

Given the figures in sports courses in secondary and Higher Education in Britain, these seem to us to be very conservative. They suggest an oversupply at Levels 6 and 7. Camy and Madella (2008b: 161) comment that 'these highly qualified professionals are not well suited to the job markets' growing demand for diversification, and their high qualification level is not generally appropriate for the jobs on offer ("de-skilling")'. They also suggest a serious undersupply at Levels 4 and 5 with only scattered attempts to provide supervisor/apprenticeship training (tiny also in the UK). Systems of competency assessment and quality assurance are likewise patchy, though here the UK is ahead of most countries. Camy (2008) commented that there is a high level of split and short careers (less than ten years) in sport.

The diversity of European provision is great, wih some 12,000 programmes by 1,800 providers for over 200,000 people a year. The EU will be promoting its 8-level European Qualifications Framework, into which most UK education and training will fit, but given the independence of HEIs and the growing plethora of sub-degree courses, it is unlikely that the UK (and numerous other countries) will move to the amount of harmonisation implied in the 'Aligning a European Higher Education Structure in Sports Science' plan, which others are keen on and which gives them European links and access to European funding they might not otherwise get.

CONCLUSIONS

Pitchford's data from his workshops and survey indicate a clear demand for a national, accredited framework for education and training for the community and sport development sector. Indeed, a highly qualified and receptive work-force is already in place. However, it is also clear that a number of broad issues require immediate consideration if effective systems and strategies are to be put in place to advance the sector, namely: developing standards, underpinning knowledge, how far CSD workers represent the communities they serve, and better communication of learned lessons to prevent the far too frequent reinvention of old and not particularly efficient or appropriate wheels.

Developing standards

While Pitchford's survey generated some indication of the desires of the workforce for training, such perceived needs do not necessarily translate directly into occupational standards. Effective community sport work requires an explicit understanding of the requirements of the welfare field underpinning the interventions, in addition to the application of the skills and competencies implied by the list of (mostly practical/practice-based) workers' preferences presented above.

Constructing meaningful occupational standards requires an acknowledgement of what the form of intervention demands, and what employing agencies require, in addition to articulating the specific functions that characterise particular roles in the sector. In this sense the NVQ Level 4 qualification in SD is too mechanistic, with too little underpinning knowledge, and dependent on local, work-based tutors who are all too busy with their day jobs to customise units.

Underpinning knowledge

At present, it seems clear that a majority of entrants to the sector emanate from sport-focused undergraduate degrees. However, the relationship between those degree programmes and the welfare agendas surrounding community sport development work is less clearly defined. A number of scenarios are perhaps worth considering here. Employing/lead agencies in the sector could, for example:

1. While continuing to recruit from sport-focused degrees, prioritise training mechanisms that familiarise entrants with relevant welfare fields – youth work, community practice, playwork, health promotion, lifelong learning, etc. – according to the setting in question.
2. Recruit those with primary initial education and/or training in relevant welfare fields – youth work, community practice, playwork, health promotion, lifelong learning, etc. – and *then* develop training programmes which familiarise those entrants with sport and sport development.
3. Encourage Higher Education sport course providers to focus more explicitly on the welfare agendas which currently and subsequently shape the sector, and/or
4. Prioritise positive action strategies that empower individuals from marginalised communities to gain employment in the sector, focusing then on CPD pathways which widen access to training, including Further and Higher Education.

Identifying the bodies of knowledge on which community sport development work is founded is clearly a key requirement. Without clarity on this issue, the construction of appropriate occupational standards for both the community

284

sport development sector – and the parallel 'sport development' workforce – will continue to be challenging.

How far do CSD workers represent the communities they serve?

Given that most graduate CSD workers are middle-class by origin or education, there are many people in the system who risk being seen as 'them', outsiders, however well-intentioned, doing good to/for 'us'. The Sport England model is one of aggressive, interventionist managerialism, even when it recognises the importance of being accepted by host communities (e.g. Sport England (2006) on the lessons of successful promotion of participation in two of the twelve Sport Action Zones). The promotion of the community development approach (which often means working more slowly with the aspirations and limitations of what local residents want) is espoused by some local authorities, but has not been offered as an alternative to the managerialist, 'top-down' model. Some authorities like Leicester City have taken the long view in what will be the first British city to have a non-white majority, to identify, train, groom and promote a cadre of middle-level black and ethnic minority and disabled managers, and as the Braunstone SAZ case study (Chapter 10) showed, trained local supervisory staff to give residents confidence in using the new Leisure Centre and outreach programmes. Nottinghamshire CC Arts and Leisure Department did likewise in its Sport Direct scheme to train disabled workers (www.nottinghamshire.gov.uk accessed 25 October 2006). But such schemes are exceptional – both of those just quoted were part of Leicester City's and Nottinghamshire's successful bids for Beacon Council status in 2005/6.

It would be easy, given the strengths implied by our sample, to assume that effective training needs only to build on an established base of graduate skills and competencies, but this would be to oversimplify the sector's requirements. More fundamental answers than the light cross-section presented above are needed in terms of the shape, composition, and above all the dynamics/career routes of the workforce before this can become the accepted position. It is not possible to discern from our data whether any workers are the beneficiaries of positive action programmes or community development strategies. In other words, it is not clear how many respondents have emerged from the communities that they serve, and how many are essentially middle-class graduates 'helicoptered' into that particular setting.

Communicating and disseminating lessons

There is a clear requirement for an effective, coherent communication system for the sector. The cobbling together and cross-posting that Pitchford had to do to get his sample, indicates that SkillsActive does not have a comprehensive database of employers or employees, though it is starting to make efforts to get them. A major problem is that many employers and trainers are tiny, one-person companies who do not keep their contact details up to date and public.

Workers in this sector are likely to be under considerable time pressure, and need to be able to schedule training appropriately. The views of one survey respondent neatly summarise the problems currently perpetuated by a frag-mented, 'cascading' communication system:

> I'm desperate for myself and staff to undertake the Positive Futures training – it was held in the South West (Bristol) this term but at very short notice and not in time for our new community sports coach. Inclusion, youth work, managing challenging behaviour and drug/alcohol awareness would be of great benefit for her role. Can we have another programme please?

Sport England, IDeA and the ISRM are trying to gather Good Practice case studies but the quality of data has to be deeper and more analytic than good journalism (Collins, 2005) to provide rich enough material for reader/viewers to judge how to apply rather than crudely copy methods and lessons.

In 2008 the government launched, via the sector skills council, SkillsActive, a National Skills Academy for Sport and Active Leisure to provide a one-stop shop for employer-led qualifications, especially at Levels 2–4. It aims to sup-port 100,000 new jobs by 2014, and replace the 85,000 people who leave a year with skilled workers. It is planned that employers and others find three-quarters of the cost. After a year 67 training providers had been signed up, and 54 employers were subscribing as members; 500 learners had completed courses and 6,000 were active (www.sportactivensa.co.uk press notice 8 May 2009).

Houlihan and White (2002: 221–3) suggested that the evolution of SD might be leading to four clusters of activity, each supported by a cluster of funding and agencies to form an advocacy coalition, 'each seeking to preserve and expand their share of resources and policy influence even if this is achieved at the expense of other sectors of the sports development network'. The four clusters were:

286

1. excellence – advocated by NGBs, UKSI, BOA, UK Sport, Lottery World Class funding, and selected universities;
2. school & youth – advocated by DfES, Sport England, Youth Sport Trust, and specialist sport colleges;
3. performance sport – sports coach UK, Sport England, voluntary clubs;
4. participation/sport for all – local authorities, Sport England.

They describe the first two as strong and growing, and the others as weaker and less coherent, with local authorities being both drawn and driven from sport for its own sake to sport as development for the external outcomes, meaning that funding is increasingly driven by agencies in other inclusion, cohesion, regeneration and social capital policy areas. Even in the fourth cluster, the case studies and this chapter show the variety of situations involved. It is clear that this is not yet a closed, intimate, strong policy area, and the looseness of fit of the training even at graduate and postgraduate levels shows this relative immaturity, and there is little evidence that it is easy or even possible to hurry up history in such matters.

REFERENCES

Boutall, T. (2003) Competences for sports workers in community cohesion, unpublished report for Positive Futures and Community Cohesion Unit, London: Home Office.

Camy, J. (2008) A new challenge for sport education institutions: 'Education and Training 2010', in K. Petry et al. (eds) Higher Education in Sport in Europe: From Labour Market Demand to Training Supply, Maidenhead: Meyer & Meyer Sport.

Camy, J. and Madella, A. (2008a) Higher Education and employability in sport, in K. Petry et al. (eds) Higher Education in Sport in Europe: From Labour Market Demand to Training Supply, Maidenhead: Meyer & Meyer Sport.

Camy, J. and Madella, A. (2008b) Academic and professional aspects of sport education and training systems and programmes in Higher Edcuation, in K. Petry et al. (eds) Higher Education in Sport in Europe: From Labour Market Demand to Training Supply, Maidenhead: Meyer & Meyer Sport.

Collins, M. (1995) Sports Development Locally and Regionally, Reading: Institute of Leisure and Amenity Management.

Collins, M.F. (2005) Where next with CPA? Recreation 64,12:14.

Collins, M. with Kay, T. (2003) Sport and Social Exclusion, London: Routledge.

Community Development Foundation (2004) *Survey of Community Development Workers in the UK: A Report on Paid and Unpaid Community Workers,* Coventry: CDF.

Department for Education and Skills (2005) *Skills: Getting on in Business, Getting on at Work,* London: DfES.

Houlihan, B. (2008) What being a profession means, paper to ISPAL conference, Warwicks, June.

Houlihan, B. and White, A. (2002) *The Politics of Sports Development,* London: Routledge.

Nixon, I. and Settle, T. (2005) Sport University North East England KSA Partnership, downloaded from www.sportengland.org 9 December 2008.

Petry, K., Froberg, K., Madella, A. and Tokarski, W. (eds) (2008) *Higher Education in Sport in Europe: From Labour Market Demand to Training Supply,* Maidenhead: Meyer & Meyer Sport.

Pitchford, A. (2005) *Community and Sport Development Research Project Report to SkillsActive Community Development Working Group* (mimeo), Gloucester: University of Gloucestershire.

Ravenscroft, N. and Gilchrist, P. (2005) Post-Fordist restructuring and vocational training in sport in the UK, *Managing Leisure,* 10: 168–83.

SkillsActive (n.d.) *Briefing Note: A Summary of the Community Sport Development Research Report,* London: SkillsActive, available from www.skillasctive.com.

SkillsActive (2006a) *Assessment of Current Provision: Sport & Recreation,* London: SkillsActive.

SkillsActive (2006b) *Analysis of Gaps and Weaknesses,* London: SkillsActive.

Sport England (2006) *Understanding the Success in Sport Action Zones,* London: Sport England.

Sport & Recreation Industry Training Organisation (2001) *Social Exclusion and Sport: The Role of Training and Learning,* London: SPRITO.

andy pitchford and mike collins

CHAPTER 15

CONCLUSIONS

Mike Collins

SUMMARY

CIPFA (2009) figures showed the state of sports development in England and in Wales at the point of writing: estimated expenditures in 2008/9 were £172m and £13m respectively, and after income, net were £116m and £10m. These represented only £2.26 and £3.44 per citizen respectively, and subsidies (or depending on one's perspective, public investments) of 69% and 79% respectively. Large urban areas, as one might expect, spent noticeably more than more rural authorities: London boroughs £2.36, metropolitan districts £2.98, unitary authorities £2.09, and non-metropolitan districts £1.78 per head.

These chapters have graphically demonstrated the range of jobs, organisations, settings and network of relationships in which SD is presently employed, a range that would have amazed the early SD officers in the Sports Council's Action Sport projects of the early 1980s or even the National Demonstration Projects later in the decade. Hylton and Totten (2008: 91) called it initially almost 'counter-cultural'. Now it is embedded in the daily work of LAs and NGBs. Whether this work amounts to a range as wide that Houlihan and White mused on in 2002 is something I comment on below. But it does justify a summary of the findings of Chapters 3 to 14 before moving to thematic analysis.

In the case studies focusing mainly on organising or delivering SD, in Chapter 3 Enoch looked at the Active Sports programme introduced after Champion Coaching and which provided a foundation on which larger school club and elite programmes were built. Here the issue of partnership – of what sort and with whom – become much more complex than for its predecessor. She graphically describes how CSPs were introduced to attempt to bridge the sectors of youth, education/schools and local authority leisure and how programmes were rolled out and measured, including data that has not hitherto been on public view (though – a recurring theme – no evaluation was ever done, at least publicly).

The strains of changing policy environments are made clear (and then elaborated by Charlton). Eventually change is not incremental but radical and a new policy architecture emerges. For youth sport at least she believes a strong framework was set. This book eschews evidence and debate on performance sport, but doubts are being raised by external critics about the strength and applicability of Balyi's Long Term Athlete Development tool to all sports, being developed from observation of practice with no theoretical base and no detailed monitoring and evaluation; some NGBs and coaches prefer other approaches, and whether Sport England will continue to single-mindedly support it remains to be seen. Enoch also shows how an opportunity was seized by Sue Campbell and the Youth Sport Trust to provide a training splint across the structural fracture between juvenile and adult and school and club sport and was not only possible but very successful. Yet I believe that it is a patch on a wound and not a fundamental improvement to initial teacher training, which would be much more expensive but long-term and difficult to revoke. If, or rather when, the advocacy coalition that supports the PSSSCL strategy breaks up, will TOPs and the YST work survive if political and financial support goes elsewhere?

Lindeman and Conway look in Chapter 4 at a phase of school provision that preceded CSPs. And in a minority setting where, thanks to a philosophy of community, schools unflinchingly promoted by an education innovator meant that the core of the recreation and culture provision happened at school (found in Cambridgeshire, Cheshire and only a few other places). Municipal provision made up (some of) the gaps in Leicestershire. Now with Building Schools for the Future and extended schools, inexplicably the LEA is withdrawing from that community role.

In Chapter 5 Charlton displays how one of the larger and more complex CSPs organised itself, in Lancashire, and the tension involved in balancing and managing over two dozen relationships, and how partners can wax and wane in interest. Lancashire Sport also demonstrates the turnover of chief officers identified by Enoch, and the limitations of a management tool, *TAES*, developed in another setting.

Thorpe looks in Chapter 6 at sports development in HE, a new area of growth of high-performance sport and community action and volunteering, and a new arena for Sport England. The range of activities at Loughborough is exceptional so although the Lottery has provided a range of physical plant and support services like those found on US campuses funded by sponsors and commercial competitive sport (but an even wider range of activities, which other campuses are selectively developing and specialising in, whether like Lancaster, East Anglia and Hertfordshire for community sport, or Chichester, Bath and Leeds for elite

290

mike collins

sport like Britain/UK in relation to international competition), it will not and cannot go on dominating the student sport championships as it has done in the last two decades. Such spreading of expertise can only be helpful locally.

Scotland has chosen political devolution, and in Chapter 7 Thomson reflects on how far this has affected sport. He finds more continuity than change; what has not changed is that the resources necessary to meet the major challenges of participation have not been made available, and the need is not politically powerful enough to lever up the programmes. So whether managerially culpable or merely the visible object, sportscotland has been the scapegoat for reshaping, though the SNP did not delete it when given the chance (as the Lib Dems have said they would in England (*Guardian* 23 April 09) but are most unlikely to get the chance!). Ironically the champion in Scotland has been a politician, McConnell. But this has not led to a programme that has linked school and club sport, like *PESSCL* in England, nor as in England has it led to enough local authority finance to overcome the obsolescence and shortfall issues, so the challenge of Scotland's mountainous ill-health issues remain.

In Chapter 8 Bell examines another programme that ran for almost a decade but was not evaluated, Champion Coaching. She confirmed the findings in Nottinghamshire that children and parents liked and approved of the programmes and their coaches a lot, that on the whole child-friendly clubs (de Knop *et al.*, 1994) and sections were formed but that it failed to bridge the social gradient between affluent and disadvantaged (except where very specifically targeted, as in Knowsley). When the editor approached a Sports Council senior SD manager to extend this work to two other areas for confirmation, he was told 'that's all in the past . . . we've learned lessons and there will not be the same problems in the new programme' (the National Junior Sports Programme, again transmuted into Active Sports without any public evidence or evaluation). It was only a decade later, that SE chairman, Lord Carter, affirmed the need for all investment to be subjected to proper monitoring and evaluation (2005: 25). Bell systematically pursued participants, parents, teachers and coaches to trace not only the benefits to children's sport, but also the legacy to coaching. The early legacy she found was to strengthen the skills and confidence of some established coaches, but the development of only a few new or inexperienced ones. She also showed that the 'exit route' (a new buzzword at that time) into the Youth Games was effective, and this led on to a pattern of district and county school sport games. In a short time there was action that led into 'a great leap forward' with the development of the National Coaching Certificate, surveys of the number, roles, qualifications and work of coaches and a highly structured and resourced plan for coaching across Britain.

The editor has repeatedly lobbied about the paucity of information about the foundation level of amateur sport in Britain and worldwide – voluntary sports clubs (Collins and Nichols, 2005; Collins, 2008a). In Chapter 9 he and David Sparkes, Chief Executive of the Amateur Swimming Association look at the Association's planning for recreational swimming and its clubs. The context of recreational swimming is of school swimming declining (because of the closure of old on-site pools, the squeeze on curriculum time and the cost of taking children off site to learn and to swim) and adult swimming growing among middle-aged and older people, but replacement of small older pools by larger ones or complexes, not always easily accessible. ASA's programme for modernising its clubs was first to get them to do an audit of their programmes and resources and then to get them to assess what levels of development each wished to adopt – whether to consolidate at their present level or work to moving up. This process was very challenging to the voluntary officers, to specify aims and a development plan, and took a lot longer than anyone originally estimated, and will not be complete by the London Olympics. But the process enables ASA regional Development Officers to know where to direct resources for different purposes.

Recent years have also seen in public swimming programmes like 'free swimming' to attract, first children and then older people to swim. This is backed politically in all three parts of Great Britain to increase participation and gain health benefits. In England 82% of LAs have signed up, but pool managers and development officers have doubts about what proportion of extra swimmers are new swimmers and how many are existing swimmers getting free swims, especially amongst those over 60; they certainly increase management costs; most of these professionals would like to link this effectively with schools and swimming lessons. In her study of the Free Swimming programme across Wales (Chapter 13), Bolton recorded the same concerns that a 'free splash' would not be automatically turned into committed, heath-giving exercise, and the difficulties of attracting ethnic minorities, disabled people and people from deprived areas without other costs, of transport and outreach work; otherwise it can become a recreational 'fire sale'.

In Chapter 10 Walpole examines from an insider's viewpoint really local SD work through the development of Braunstone's Sport Action Zone, the smallest of Sport England's area-based initiatives and at least as great a success as the two singled out in Sport England's reviews (Ipsos/MORI, 2006; Sport England, 2008a–h). Doorstep-level consultation and research, and hiring and training local labour to work in the new leisure centre, provided the programmes requested, with top managers taking the political and financial risks of top-slicing the City's leisure budget to support and commit to the scheme they wanted to succeed in a deprived area. The success turned round the Council's image on the estate and was a major part in the City's award of Beacon status and City of Sport. It is a testament to corporate and professional commitment and patience.

McCormack looks in Chapter 11 at another long-standing local scheme, Streetsport, which has attempted to involve youth in sport in deprived estates in Stoke-on-Trent to divert them from antisocial activities. Its successes come from a similar level of care of and commitment to the young people from the scheme's managers and sports leaders – as Positive Futures (Substance, 2007) and Nichols (2007) found in their field studies. Working with so-called hard-to-reach groups means working with smaller rather than larger groups, over sustained periods. There is no cheap, quick fix, as psychiatrists, social workers, and probation officers will testify in their work. So why do the media and politicians (and consequently many of the public) expect it of sport? What I wrote about this in 2003 (Collins 2003: 218–9) is still true; Positive Futures' five year timescale and large scale was exceptional, but most of its messages about getting trust and slowly encouraging empowerment are not new, as neither were those that Sport England (2008a) listed for Sport Action Zones and ADCF schemes (see pp. 205–7). Such work has a higher unit cost than opening the doors of leisure centres and welcoming people in.

In Chapter 12 Len Almond produces a text of a different texture and style, summarising more than three decades of involvement in promoting Physical Activity related to health, more recently especially of older people. As a Physical Educationalist, he is well aware of the strengths and weaknesses of sport as an attractor to getting people active. Len provides a menu of national and local programmes that involve PA. In many countries there is no divide between sport and PA – they are overseen by the same government ministry. Apart from two years in the early 1990s, it has not been so in Britain. Yet, after ten years when much was made of the health-promoting values of sport, and just three years after the CMO's report, it is ironic that the DCMS' strategy again should separate the health and sports cases. Yet many LAs and PCTs have joint projects and CSPs have been supporting the work of Sport and Physical Activity Alliances (SPAAs). A national Activity Alliance has been launched and the DoH is promoting a campaign called Active4Life among both individual citizens and organisations. As Thomson shows (Chapter 7), in Scotland promoting PA has a high priority and a coherent strategy.

OVERARCHING THEMES

Partnerships

A leitmotif through the eleven case studies – in Active Sports, Champion Coaching, Leicestershire's education projects, Higher Education, Braunston Sport Action Zone, Streetsport, health and free swimming, (Chapters 3, 8, 4, 6, 10, 11, 12 and 13) and of course in CSPs (Chapters 3 and 5) – is of partnerships, which have been embedded in British government since the 1980s. Some say it is necessary to overcome the traditional single-profession, Department-based, 'silo' style of government operations (Clarke et al., 2000), some that 'joined-up' strategy and delivery are essential to cope with the multi-dimensional, cross-cutting, 'wicked issues'. Justifications for partnerships include pooling resources, added value, increased efficiency or effectiveness, and greater legitimacy by gathering a wider range of stakeholders.

Marsh and Rhodes (1992) and Rhodes (1997) saw partnerships as networks: single-issue networks might be short-lived and spatially or thematically narrow (respective examples are the movements against the third runway a Heathrow airport, and the anti-motorsports coalition in the British National Park movement – see Collins, 2008b: 449–53); policy networks are more coherent, long-lasting, negotiated and shared-value communities of individuals or, more usually, organisations. Atkinson and Coleman (1992: 157) saw policy networks as 'dependency relationships that emerge between both organisations and individuals who are in frequent contact with each other in particular policy areas'. This can be true when a central body holds finance or power, but the Marsh and Rhodes conception fits most of SD partnerships better.

In sports policy, partnerships became an explicit element first in the National Demonstration projects which, developing the inner city Action Sport programme aimed at youth, worked not only for particular groups in society, but had an aim to gather resources from organisations with which the Sports Council had never previously worked – health, women, pubs, working men's clubs, probation, and workplace fitness programmes – and thereby set a pattern for the next twenty years (McDonald and Tungatt, 1991). Lindsay (2006) examined ten of the partnerships used to implement the £751m New Opportunities for PE and Sport Programme (NOPES) funded after 2001 by the New Opportunities Lottery Fund (merged into the Big Lottery Fund in 2004). Three were communities of interest from within authorities where he found top-down decision making; two, both Northern Irish Education and Library Boards, were interorganisational networks open to bids from outside and bottom-up, and the remaining five were wide networks with a tight core led by elected members which worked both top-down and bottom-up. Interestingly, nine built on

294

relationships that existed before NOPES (perhaps indicative of the short time-scale for spending the grants and to ensure meeting NOF criteria).

In 2000 the government created School Sport Partnerships, typically of 4 to 8 secondary schools and their feeder primaries, each with a Partnership Development Manager and a (teacher) Coordinator, and by 2007 the scheme covered all English schools. The Institute of Youth Sport's (2006) examination of the operation found some stresses between school within SSPs, because they often competed for primary pupils, and between the SSP and external partners. Some LA SD Units saw them as competitors for youth sport; some had good relations with sports governing bodies and their clubs, especially in affluent areas where they are more plentiful. Partnership does not solve all problems (Houlihan and Lindsay, 2008).

In pursuing their priority areas of sports pathways for youth, and club and workforce development, CSPs are the centre of numerous relationships, some with other networks; indeed, Skelcher (2000: 9) argued that 'partnership bodies are being created to manage the complexities of policy networks', and Goss (2001) spoke of 'new spaces for joint working'. Of four models of governance, McDonald (2005) assigned CSPs to the rational model; the dominant actors being HMG and Sport England, seeking to influence the behaviour of all regional and local players, acting as 'pawns' (policy takers) rather than 'queens' (policy makers), to use Le Grand's (2003) terminology. But relations with partners can wax and wane as Charlton shows (Chapter 5). Power is an issue in all networks, and rarely distributed equally. If a CSP was hosted by an LA, it could be suspected of disproportionate benefit by others (KKP, 2005).

McDonald (2005: 579) suggested that they could be a way of sustaining existing power under the fig-leaf of cooperation. Houlihan and Lindsay (2008) suggested that introducing the PSA 2005–2008 target for youth participation had put pressure on CSPs to focus on participation rather than PESSC links. Henry et al. (2008) found that health and PA agencies were a peripheral domain with relatively few links in their two CSPs, and in the PDMs in one county made few links with LAs, NGBs and the CSP. Changing focuses in national policy affects networks as much as single agencies.

The Audit Commission said (2009: 1) 'Government policy has moved from encouraging partnerships towards mandating them, even though voluntarism is the key to effective joint working'. Partnerships cost time and effort to sustain, often by middle/senior managers; the larger and more complex they become, the greater the organisational cost of keeping them together, keeping everyone involved. The box below shows the numerous major partners that some CSPs in NE England have to satisfy; and the experimental use of social network mapping demonstrated the well over 200 links that two East Midlands CSPs had contacts with more than once a month (Henry et al., 2008). Of course, an irregular, occasional relationship, as over major funding, can be more important than mundane day-to-day contacts. One of Sport England's showcase projects (of which no more was heard) had more than forty partners, what Goss (2001) called an 'unwieldy partnership'. Houlihan and White's (2002: 225) opinion was that 'partnerships are often cumbersome vehicles for policy because each tends to have its own peculiar processes for accessing the particular government funding stream, as well as distinctive requirements for monitoring and reporting, often on an annual basis, resulting in high management costs and frustratingly slow decision-making'.

Partners in NE England sport

Regional Sports Board

- Regional Sports Board
- Sport England NE
- ONE-NE (Reg Dev Agency)
- Government Office North East
- Regional Assembly
- Planning authorities
- Culture North East
- NE Fed for Sport & Recreation
- Regional & county governing bodies of sport
- Chief Leisure Officers
- Sport Development Officers
- Directors of Education
- PE Advisers and Inspectors
- School Sport Partnerships
- School Sport Coordinators
- Universities (5)
- Local sports councils
- Sports Aid
- sports coach UK
- Regional Training Unit

Sport Northumberland

- Alnwick District Council
- BECON
- Berwick-upon-Tweed Borough Council
- Blyth Valley Borough Council
- Castle Morpeth Borough Council
- English Federation of Disability Sport
- National governing bodies of sport
- North East Federation of Sport and Recreation
- Northumberland College
- Northumberland County Council
- Sport England
- sports coach UK
- The Northumberland Care Trust
- The Northumberland Schools Sports Partnerships
- The Youth Sport Trust
- Tynedale District Council
- University of Northumbria
- Wansbeck District Council
- Women's Sports & Fitness Foundation

The IDeA (http;//www.lgpartnerships.com/resources/lead-fivedegrees.asp accessed 4 February 2008) characterised local government partnerships in a very understandable way, thus:

- coexistence – 'You stay on your turf and I'll stay on mine';
- cooperation – 'I'll lend you a hand when my work is done';
- coordination – 'We need to adjust what we do to avoid overlap and confusion';
- collaboration – 'Let's work on this together';
- co-ownership – 'We feel totally responsible.'

Henry et al. (2008) suggested that PDMs in one of their case studies saw the CSP as coexistence, while local authorities usually opted for at least coordination and preferably collaboration; sustaining co-ownership needs close agreement on aims and outcomes and deferring one to another. Despite Sport England's rhetoric in *Shaping Places through Sport* (2008b–f), with clear blue water put between sport and PA and the other cross-cutting issues, the dynamics of CASPs will change. LA SDOs are into other partnerships in pursuit of broader social aims in LAAs and LSAs and may find less need of Sport England than previously.

There is a sizeable literature on partnership evaluation, summarised by Parent and Harvey (2009), which they characterised in five groups, and here I suggest examples from the SD literature:

1. process evaluation (Rigg, 1986 for Action Sport, and McDonald and Tungatt, 1991 for the NDPs);
2. impact evaluation over the short term (Coalter, 2007);
3. outcome evaluation in relation to long-term aims (Bell, Chapter 8);
4. formative evaluation (KKP, 2005 for CSPs);
5. summative evaluation (Ipsos/MORI 2006 and Sport England, 2008a for the SAZs and ACDF projects).

The Audit Commission (2009: 4,7) commented of LSPs that:

- They need active leadership (not domination or control) and purposeful relationship management (where social network analysis and delivery-chain analysis may help).
- They need performance management systems, and common data quality and mechanisms take time to develop.
- Most lack mechanisms for assigning resources from partners' mainstream programmes.

- Government hinders through not having aligned planning and reporting cycles.
- They need a whole-systems model, taking account of the seven 'S's – sustainable community strategies, staff and skills, style of management, synergies, steering mechanisms, systems, and standards.

Most of these comments could equally apply to CSPs.

Leadership

Programmes and projects need leaders, especially those who bring together different professionals from different organisations with different cultures across different spheres of policy. Green (2007: 945) reiterated that in England, as in Australia and Canada, 'what is clear . . . is the absence of a voice of any significant volume for the mass participant'. Previously the Sports Council did that, and local government was a strong ally; but from 1993 to at least 2008 Sport England had not fronted this cause strongly, under pressures to focus on youth and elite performance. Derek Mapp on his appointment as chair of Sport England in 2007 said he felt his 'entrepreneurial background equipped [him] for the task of continually moving community sport to be more centre stage'. James Purnell obviously disagreed! Nor has the Local Government Association spoken up for sport in the last decade. Community SD is no different, as Ipsos/MORI made clear in its overview of lessons from the SAZs and ACDF projects, adding that if possible these leaders should be charismatic, able to charm, encourage, and cajole help from stakeholders, to turn them into contributors. Thomas (2009) says that what is now important in leisure is not the conventional or even the transformational managers but inspirational leaders, with a shift of focus (see box).

Conventional managers are expected to focus on:

- Developing processes
- Hardware and equipment
- Efficiency
- Systems specified by technologists
- Rule-oriented action
- Hierarchical, bureaucratic settings.

---

mike collins

> *Future leaders* need to focus on:
>
> ▪ Organisational development/the 'big picture'
> ▪ People
> ▪ Job satisfaction/output/risk/trust
> ▪ Systems specified by users, individualised
> ▪ Action within boundaries establishing autonomy, creativity, values
>   (while setting minimum safety/quality/finance/performance)
> ▪ Democracy/evolutionary/organic/boundary-free setting.
>
> (after Thomas, 2009)

Charisma cannot be taught, only developed from inner strengths and characteristics. In SD such people are scarce: of politicians, Denis Howell was one, responsible for giving the Sports Council the chance to develop Action Sport and its successors (Chapter 2); of professionals Sue Campbell stands supreme as the policy broker, the champion of coaching (as the first deputy director and second Director of the National Coaching Foundation) and then of teacher improvement and performance/elite development as Director and later Chair of the Youth Sport Trust and then adviser to ministers of sport and education and now Chair of UK Sport and a cross-bench peer. There is a gap on the LA career ladder from Head of SD to chief leisure officer and higher; one of the very few who has made it from the ranks in the 1980s of Action Sport in the West Midlands is Derrick Anderson, then Chief Leisure Officer and Chief Executive of Wolverhampton City Council and now the London Borough of Lambeth, advising ministers of sport, the Arts Council of England, the Home Office and LOCOG 2012 along the way.

SD jobs, training and professionalism

Pitchford and Collins examine in Chapter 14 from Pitchford's 2005 survey how sports development's workforce had developed since Collins' survey a decade earlier. Its average age has risen only a little, and with over a third in only their first job it is still a young 'community of practice'. It is a very well qualified group – 75 per cent graduate – and would make a major contribution if most signed up for a new Chartered Institute, yet two-thirds of those involved in coaching/leadership, three-quarters of those working in neighbourhoods, and half of coordinators/facilitators and managers were not signed up to a professional body, for whatever reasons. It continues to display a huge diversity of job titles and roles, but with fewer DOs focused on specific sports or 'target groups' (other than youth) than in the 1990s. This chimes with wider changes in the SD landscape as does a smaller proportion working for LAs, since a wide range of public commercial and voluntary employer opportunities has emerged.

Pitchford and Collins also show in Chapter 14 the rapid growth of under-graduate and Masters taught courses in the 60 or so HEIs offering sports studies, and more sports development elements are appearing in Foundation degrees. In this field, as in all others, the government has seen no need to bridge the divide with the training sphere; dominated recently by the skill toolkits of NVQs, as bereft of social organisational or human developmental contexts as HEI courses can be of competency skills. But the development of the new national/regional Skills Academy scarcely seems likely to simplify the scene for students or employers.

I close this section with two issues: can one community of practice encompass this growing diversity? Having surveyed the landscape of sports development policy from the 1960s to 2000, Houlihan and White (2002: 219–21) argued that there were clusters of interests – advocacy coalitions – at the different levels of involvement, as reproduced and updated in Table 15.1.

This raises the issue over whether SD is still a single field; I see no theoretical or practical basis for saying that it is not. It is just that the job is done in a wide range of settings, relationships and organisations. Likewise, when Houlihan and White asked whether training for these diverse jobs could be held in single courses, again I do not see why not. The underpinning rationale is in both cases to support and promote access and participation in sport for recreation and competition.

Further, can one foresee a single professional body? Houlihan and White (2002) questioned whether a single profession could serve and encompass the emerging diversity. In practical terms, if it does not do so, a Chartered Institute will lack members and scarcely be credible – the huge Chartered Institute of Management, for example encompasses a great variety of jobs and settings. But the continuing diversity challenges training and education providers, and HEIs may do well to seek specialisations aimed at particular SD roles or settings, if only to have a USP for students applying. Can one see one Institute? If the two bodies now in talks do agree to form a new Institute, the new trustees and leaders will have to do some things neither do at present and do others better, in:

- offering or accrediting a wider range of courses than ISRM;
- reviving the technical/policy groups that ILAM/ISPAL had and combining them with the effective regional presence ISRM has, but for a wider group;

Table 15.1 Clusters of interests in sports development in England

Primary focus	Foundation	Participation	Performance	Excellence
Lead organisations	**PESSCL** **SSPs**	**PESSCL** **SSPs** LAs schools **NGBs** clubs	NGBs clubs **SSColls**	NGBs elite clubs EIS BOA
Supporting organisations	**CSPs**	**CSPs** Sport England	**CSPs** Sport England SCUK	BASES UKSpMedl Sport England UKSp HEIs
Main programmes	TOPs National Curriculum for PE			World Class programme
Primary source of funding	Sport England SE Lottery DCSF LAs	LAs SE Community Sport fund	Clubs' income Sport England, SE Lottery DCSF	Sport England SE Lottery UKSp UKSp Lottery TV income Sponsors
Increasingly marginalised organisations	LAs		LAs	

Source After Houlihan and White, 2002 Table 7.3, with changes in **bold**.

- offering a wider and more coherent standards and ethics base, with a disciplinary arm that would warn, retrain or ban incompetents, as other Institutes do;
- developing the CPD capability;
- attracting more people from the top ranks and the grassroots of the community of practice.

CURRENT CONTEXT AND CHALLENGES

HMG and Sport England have set out some very challenging targets for participation. Are they achievable? What is the current context for these policies?

International comparisons

HMG has compared England with Finland; Finland is the second most equal (after Japan) of twenty-three of the world's richest societies, and England the second most unequal (after the USA); this correlates directly with extremes in general of an index of health and social problems derived by Wilkinson and Prickett (2009). So far as sport in concerned, Finland has much more gender and income equality, better welfare payments, over thirty years of an integrated policy for diet, exercise and health, a stronger belief and practical support for the voluntary sector, including sport (Collins, 2008a). So, even by 2020, this is a gap (passing nineteen other rich countries) that the UK is most unlikely to be able to close, and HMG has set itself up for failure. It would have been difficult but credible to have sought to reach participation and equity levels equal to France, Germany or The Netherlands, in the middle of this distribution. England invests less in sport – in 2002, just £36 per capita compared to the 'peer-group' average for seven advanced economies of £59, with Finland and France providing £84 and £110 per capita (Carter, 2005: 16). Table 15.2 shows how Sport England plans to distribute its resources for community recreation over the next five years.

Table 15.2 Funding sport in English communities, 2009–2013 (2009–2010 indicative funding)

Fund	Exchequer (£m)	Lottery (£m)
Solicited		
NGBs – 20 priority, 13 development, 7 other Olympic and 8 Paralympic sports	66	54
National partners, e.g. Women's S&FF	10	–
CSPs 45 – £200,000 each p.a.	–	10
Children/Youth towards 5 hours of sport a week for 5–19s	18	–
Total solicited	94	64
Open		
Themed rounds – 2 a year, revenue and capital	–	30
Small grants – £300–£10,000	–	7
Innovation – large projects with wide application	–	5
Sportsmatch – £500–£100,000 to lever in other funds	3	–
Total open	3	42
Facilities – large, innovative, sustainable projects	8	2
Total (£213m)	105	108

Source Sport England, 2009.

The domestic context

Inequality

In Britain's very unequal society, how has New Labour been coping with meeting its 1997 vision of reducing social exclusion and inequality? The largest claim was to halve child poverty by 2010 and eradicate it by 2020. Introducing family tax credits and help for pensioners helped initially, but tightening rules on disability benefits did not help, and neither did the failure to tax high earners (until the credit crunch budget of 2009), because that widened the gap and helped to continually raise the level of the 60 per cent median income benchmark for poverty (which implied constantly raising benefits). Hills *et al.* (2009: 349–54) observed thirty-one indicators in *Opportunities for All* (DWP, 2007 and earlier) and the *Households Below Average Income* data series (DWP, 2008 and earlier), and found thirteen improving, eight steadily improving or flat and eight slowing or deteriorating, notably in,

- slowing spending in education and health (mostly pro-poor) and in tax and benefit changes;
- plateauing of child-related spending after 2004;
- reduced momentum in the New Deals for young people and long-term unemployed;
- ending some area-based initiatives.

But health and wealth inequality increased. The publication of the 'households below average income' data (DWP, 2009) was a blow to these hopes; it showed that the Gini coefficient of income inequality (1960 = 100) was, at 138, the highest ever, above the 130 when John Major took over from Margaret Thatcher, and the 131 when Tony Blair succeeded him (*Guardian*, 8 May 2009: 6). In the previous three years, the richest fifth of people had seen an increase in incomes of 3.3%, while the poorest fifth saw a loss of 2.6%. For 2007/8 the HBAI report showed (figures after taking account of housing costs):

- for children, 4 million poor, 9% above 1998/9;
- for working age adults, 7.5 million poor, 12.5% above 1998/9;
- for pensioners, 2 million poor, a fall of 31% on 1998/9;
- a total of 13.5 million poor, a fall of 4%.

Since the Tory opposition had identified tax credits as a source of expenditure savings if they gained power, the situation looks difficult to bleak. Unemployment had also reached 2.2 million – 7.7% (*Guardian*, 14 May 2009) the highest since 1996, and likely to hit the part-time and low-skills parts of the leisure job market harder than others. 2002–2009 saw increasing fiscal challenges in the light of the credit crunch and the limits on public spending necessitated by the government increasing public indebtedness, and Hills et al.'s, last words were (2009: 359): 'The last decade has shown that a more interventionist strategy of "pump up" is hard. The period since 1997 shows that gains are possible, but they require continuous effort to be sustained.'

Public expenditure

Targets for participation and performance linked to a legacy for London 2012 will protect sport from cuts of the size some functions will have to take (DCMS's expenditure was cut by only £168m in the 2009 budget (*Guardian*, 23 May 09)), though Olympics minister Tessa Jowell admitted that HMG would probably not have supported the London bid had it known about the credit crunch! By contrast, rumours were that Germany's sports budget would suffer a cut of 10%. After a decade of slow growth below inflation, local government in England and Wales estimated that there would be a 3.5% cut in 2008/9, more in Greater London (7.0%) and urban unitary authorities (6.7%) (CIPFA, 2009). This is likely to increase in subsequent years.

Time patterns

Shifts in the allocation of time move slowly; women still do the majority of housework, even if they work; leisure time is still dominated by TV, and DCMS/DH and Sport England want people to increase their active physical activity time to undertake an average of 90 minutes per week. The British work longer hours than most European nations, and in 2002 the Henley Centre found 45% of their sample agreeing that 'I am so tired in the evenings that I often don't have the energy to do much' (Rowe et al., 2004: 9). With competition at all ages for increased internet/AV use, any increases in PA are likely to have to come mainly from reducing established patterns of watching TV and making the effort to go out. This would require *very* powerful social marketing.

The continuing challenge of obesity

Obesity continues to increase; for children from 12% to 16.7% in 2000–2005, for adult men from 22.7% to 23.0%, and for women from 23.2% to 24.2% in 2003–2006 (NICE, 2008); this places the UK as the fifth most obese of twenty-one European countries. Fox, member of the Foresight obesity group, reported in 2008:

304

mike collins

- It takes only a 2kg weight gain a year for a decade to move someone from optimal to obese categories.
- Projections to 2035 show an increase of 45% in diabetes and 15% in uterine cancer due to weight gain alone.
- Those doing enough PA to combat obesity decline from 58% and 32% for 16–24 year old men and women to 17% and 12% at age 65–74, respectively.
- There is a worldwide research consensus that PA is needed to obtain and maintain weight loss, and while 30 minutes a day will help, without diet control this could have to reach 60–90 minutes a day.

Zaninotto et al. (2008) reported that if increases continued at the same rate to 2012, prevalence of the obese would be 32.1% and 31.0% for men and women, reaching 43% in manual social classes. A governmental programme *Healthy Weight, Healthy Lives* (COI, 2008: i–xv) recommended five lines of action with a budget of £372m for 2008–2011:

1. starting with promoting healthy lifestyles in children so that there is no 'conveyor belt' problem carrying over into adulthood, aiming to reduce obesity levels in 2020 to those in 2000;
2. promoting diet including less fat, sugar and salt;
3. introducing PA into daily life – walking and cycling to work, school, shops, and hobbies (gardening, allotments, dancing) and exercise and sport;
4. creating incentives to lose weight;
5. personalised help and support.

The future sports market and sports development

Facilities

There is a large backlog of facilities that were built as cheaply as possible in the 1970s, have worked hard over long hours for thirty years and are now obsolescing because of wear and tear, or failure to meet contemporary accessibility, energy or comfort standards. Hence there is a need for increased investment to replace them, let alone meet rising participation. In 2003 Davis Langdon estimated that £550m would be needed just for sports centres. Space for Sport and the Arts finished several years ago, and grants for sports centres are no longer routine from Sport England or the Lottery Fund. My estimate is that adding together PPP/PFI schemes and investment by trusts and contractors, which will dwindle during the credit crunch, new provision is likely to amount only to half what is needed to stand still. Sport England's facilities-planning computer model, set to current participation rates could be recalibrated to the rates aimed for in 2013 and 2020, to give a much clearer indication of the capital planning challenge, and the only reason one can adduce for Sport England not running it is to avoid embarrassing a government whose expenditure and debt has been extremely stretched. But not to do so is again wittingly to court failure. Examining 66 benchmarked centres in deprived areas, Taylor *et al.* (2004: 23) showed that for social groups D and E, disabled and unemployed people and discount leisure card holders and youth aged 11–19 had consistently higher benchmark scores than those in non-deprived areas, attributable to better planning, better intelligence on target group needs, specific targeting and low pricing, backed by LA policy commitment. Surely this is a good social policy investment area?

NGBs and club members

With the development of pay-as-you-play public provision from the 1960s and private sport and fitness centres from the 1980s, the voluntary sector has to a degree been squeezed, but also that model is a mutual self-help one, and assumes an input from most members to fundraising, officiating, administration, and maintaining facilities. Moreover, most clubs have worked on the model of either parents introducing their children, or spotting talent in the school system; they have not sought large numbers of novices who need training from scratch or a basic level, except for swimming and a few other sports. That is, as claimed by Bishop and Hoggett a generation ago (1986), they are mutual help bodies, different from and largely disregarded by the voluntary welfare theorists and powerful coalition of agencies centred round the Home Office and Department for Communities and Local Government which supplies overwhelmingly altruistic services for public good. Sports club membership was assessed by the General Household Survey 2002 at 16.5% (Table 15.5) (including fitness, social and other clubs as well sports clubs at 6.4%). These figures were in line with similar surveys in Scotland and Wales.

Using the same questions, Active People 2006 showed membership of 25.1% (a barely believable 52% increase in four years, and for 2008 24.7% (a minor decrease of 0.4% (Sport England, 2008h)). However, surveys of volunteering had shown sport in Britain and the rest of Europe to be about a quarter of the total, but not all of that had been through clubs. So which figures are nearer the truth and the reliable base – which Active People was intended to be? Sport England's new strategy (2008g) to which the NGB movement has signed up, expects 500,000 new participants via NGBs, with a further 200,000 increasing their

306

frequency and/or intensity of participation (see p. 310 and Table 15.5). By 2000, eight sports promised 1.1 million extra participants (swimming, tennis, association football, rugby union, athletics, cycling, golf and cricket (Sport England *National governing body outcomes 2009–2013*, July 2009). Most involved growth at twice the needed national rate but tennis, cricket and rugby union aimed at eye-watering annual rates of growth of 7.75%, 8.75% and 15.3% respectively – which will severely strain or risk breaking each NGB's voluntary resources.

Is this switch of practice likely at grassroots in thousands of clubs, and are they ready to take part, given the mixed responses found by Garrett (2000) and Harris *et al.* (2009)? (See pp. 8, 307.) In 2002, in an essay commissioned by Sport England, Taylor wrote:

> Faced with a conspiracy of problems caused by societal changes and national institutions' requirements, voluntary sports organizations are hard pressed to deliver their core activities, and many are doing so with diminishing and increasingly hard-pressed volunteer resources. The scope for such organizations taking a lead role in developing participation in sport seems as remote as hoping for significant extra funds for local authority sports development from the Exchequer.
>
> (Taylor, 2002: 105)

Moreover, in the immediate downturn, in 2009 the CCPR surveyed a representative 160 clubs and found that 39% had seen falls in renewing memberships and, as a consequence, two in five had seen falls in subscription incomes and three in five reduced commercial sponsorships. A number thought they would have to close within a year, extrapolated to a national figure of 6,000 local clubs. The CCPR warned Sport England of threats to the 2012 target (see www.ccpr. news/newspages, accessed 7 May 2009).

Ignoring older people

Since the publication of the booklet *50+ and All to Play For: Sport for Older People* in the 1980s (which was reprinted by Sport England several times), the priority, indeed the obsession with sport for young people, has meant that Sport England has ignored the most rapidly growing part of the population, with the greatest personal benefits to gain from improved activity, mobility and fitness and the group that would make the greatest benefit to reducing burdens and costs on the health service (indeed, younger people do the reverse, and make costs through higher rates of injury (Nicoll *et al.*1993)).The COMPASS survey (Sport England, 1999) showed clearly that Sweden and Finland had much higher involvement of people over 60 playing sport at a moderate or intense level twice a week or more often. For Finland the figures were 46% for 60–64s and 46% for the over-65s; for Sweden 19% and 28%, while for England they were only 14% and 10% respectively.

Rowe et al. (2004: 8) of Sport England argued that the ageing of the population is likely to be the biggest influence on numbers participating in sport; using population projections, they suggested that by 2024 the numbers aged 6–15 participating would fall by 250,000 and those over 45 would increase by 1.3 million, but overall participation would fall from 53% to 46%. Sport England does not seem to have picked up on this.

In advising Sport England, the Henley Centre (2003) had spoken of the 'ageless population' where more people were increasingly 'acting young'; but finding time to take up sport and join clubs is a double act of changed behaviour, and it is not clear how the incentives for large numbers of people will be found.

Participation

The General Household Survey had showed a 4% decrease in participation from 1996 to 2002. Stamatakis and Chaudhury (2008) suggested that this might be confounded by changed questionnaire methodology, life expectancy, obesity and leisure patterns, and the growth of ethnic minorities. Stamatakis et al. (2007), using self-report data from the English Health Survey 1991–2004 (developed from Sport England's ADNFS), showed increases in regular sport (playing twice a week or more at moderate or vigorous intensity) among 35–49 year old men, for example, from 26% to 42.6% and for women from 25.1% to 35.4%. This gain included a rise in gym visiting and keep fit, offset by a decline in cycling. For all adults and all PA there was slight increase in meeting the health benefit threshold of 30 minutes a day for five days a week, from 46.8% to 48.5%.

Stamatakis and Chaudhury (2008) extended the analysis of the same data for 1997 to 2006. Even in this short time there were significant (at the 1% level) increases in the average age, mean household income, obesity, non-smokers, car owners, and increased non-occupational and non-sporting PA of five sessions of 30 minutes a week, and decreases in manual workers, those with no educational qualifications, and white ethnic groups (Table 15.3). Increases in regular participation were small for both sexes (under 0.5% for men and 3% for women), and the upward trends were apparent only for non-manual, middle-aged men who were white, in higher income households. As with Rowe et al.'s (2004) analysis of GHS data to 2006, they found no narrowing of the socio-

308

mike collins

Table 15.3 Health Survey for England data on sports participation, 1997–2006

Correlated significantly with participation (<0.001)	Males		Females	
	1997/8	*2006*	*1997/8*	*2006*
Positively				
Average age (years)	46.1	49.2	47.1	49.3
Mean household income (£000)	20.7	30.4	18.8	28.0
Obese (%)	17.2	24.9	20.7	75.2
Non-smokers (%)	72.1	79.6	73.7	79.5
Car available (%)	82.9	85.0	n/a	n/a
Non-sport, non-occupational regular PA (%)	21.7	22.9	23.3	24.8
Negatively				
Manual social class (%)	51.6	43.2	48.5	40.4
No educational qualification (%)	25.2	24.5	34.1	29.0
Ethnic group, white (%)	94.0	91.0	94.4	91.0
Regular sports participation (%)	40.8	41.2	31.2	33.9

Sources Stamatakis *et al.*, 2007; Stamatakis and Chandhury, 2008.

economic and ethnic gaps. They did not mention the effect of population increases.

Taking Part is a DCMS-sponsored survey seeking to measure progress in meeting Public Service Agreement Target 3, and Table 15.4 shows changes over its first three years 2005/6 to 2007/8 on the same basis as the earlier General Household Surveys. It showed statistically significant decreases in participation among women and people with limiting disability and, unlike parallel figures for historic

Table 15.4 Taking Part data for sport 2005/6 to 2007/8 (once a month or more often)

	Active sport		Moderate intensity sport	
	% 2007/8	*Change from 2005/6*	*% 2007/8*	*Change from 2005/6*
Black and minority ethnic	52.6	−0.6	21.0	+1.8
Limiting disability	30.1	−2.2	9.7	+0.2
Lower socio-economic groups	43.8	+0.4	16.5	+1.3
Females	46.1	−1.6	18.6	+0.1

Source DCMS, 2008.

sites, arts events and museums and galleries, failed to meet the PSA sport targets for all four groups.

Sport England's *Active People* Surveys were huge: 363,700 telephone interviews in 2005/6 and 191,000 in 2007/8 (SE, 2008h). Using different measures, they showed a growth of 1% in participation over two years; the growth was slightly larger among men than women, smaller amongst disabled people (Sport England, press notice and summary, 12 December 2008), and did not happen amongst lower socio-economic groups or Black and ethnic minorities. Minister for Sport, Gerry Sutcliffe, said 'this shows the record amount of public money invested in community sport in the last decade is delivering results'. Sport England's CEO was more measured, saying the figures 'highlight some of the challenges we face – such as the gender gap'. This growth is at only half the rate needed to meet the 1 million target by 2012/13, and was helped by the fact that in the intervening two years the English adult population also grew by 1.5%, mostly through immigration. Raising England's levels of moderate or vigorous sport three times a week for an hour and a half, from its 21% to match Finland's 52% just seems incredible.

Table 15.5 attempts too put together these various survey results, targets and projections. Clearly the SE 2012 target relies on a totally different trend to SE's 2004 projections just based on population; *Taking Part* implied a higher once a month rate than *GHS* by 2002, but the baseline 3x30 minute moderate figures from *Taking Part* and *Active People* are of the same order; the increase in the latter were fuelled to an unmeasured degree by an increase in population mainly by immigration; can one expect that to go on helping the 2012 targets? The *GHS* and *Active People* figures for club membership are a long distance apart. GHS suggested that only two fifths of the memberships in any sort of club were in sports clubs (6.4 per cent), half for men but under a quarter for women; if Active People repeats this pattern it raises questions about whether the targets for new members can be raised from the small segment of sports clubs over which NGBs have some influence.

With evidence from thirty-five Australian NGBs over four years, Sotiriadou *et al.* spoke of a sports development process of attracting, retaining and nurturing people; and conclude (2008: 267) for the Australian SD system that it,

> places an emphasis on the development of junior athletes and their transition to elite. Consequently the participation, development, and need of the general population appear to be the least portrayed or receive less attention. This suggests that the sport system in Australia underrepresents recreational and health and fitness membership/ participation pathways.

Table 15.5 Regular participation in sport (regular = once a month or more often) and belonging to clubs (all types), 1987–2026 (%)

Year	87	90	91/2	93	94	96	97	98	99	02	03/4	05/6	06/7	07/8	12	16	26
GHS													*Proj*			*Proj*	*Proj*
All	45	48		47		46				43			47			45	44
M	57	58		57		54				51			56			54	52
F	34	39		39		39				37			39			38	37
Club																	
All						15				17							
M										22							
F										11							
Health Survey England																	
All							n/a				n/a		n/a				
M							41				42		41				
F							31				34		34				
Taking Part																	
All												54	53	54			
Moderate intensity												21	22	23			
Active People															*Tar*		
All												16	17		19		

Table 15.5 Continued

Year	87	90	91/2	93	94	96	97	98	99	02	03/4	05/6	06/7	07/8	12	16	26
Moderate intensity																	
M												19		20			
F												12		13			
Club																	
All												25		25			
M												29		29			
F												21		21			

Sources DCMS, 2008; Sport England, 2004a,b, 2008h; Stamatakis and Chaudhury, 2008; Stamatakis, Ekelund and Wareham, 2007.
Notes Rowe and Moore (2001) projected participation forwards on current (GHS) participation rates for forecast populations in 2006, 2016, 2026 = Pro. Tar = target set by Sport England in its 2008–2011 strategy (an extra million participants). *Active People* 2007/8 participation changes significant at 5% level. mod = those taking part in three 30-minute sessions a week.

This can also be said of England and in particular of older people who still have two or three decades of life ahead of them.

PROSPECTS FOR THE NEAR FUTURE

The editor writes this after thirty-seven years of strategic planning, teaching and training, research and evaluation in British sport. In the short term, I am depressed that a few people in a few months, some with a very short acquaintance with the system, without proper public display of analysis, can radically reverse a decade of a very different policy, from sport for good to sport for sport's sake.

Sport for good loaded sport, as a small policy with modest financial and human resources, with huge expectations in a range of policy areas where, as Fred Coalter has made explicit from the Value of Sport Monitor, there was little evidence of mechanisms and outcomes outside the physical, social and mental health benefit – that is, 'what works where and for whom' (Coalter, 2007). I have argued elsewhere (Collins, 2003, 2008b) that sport should play its part in working for a safer, fairer, greener and more enjoyable society, but it is a modest part relative to other major spheres of employment, welfare, and health.

The target chosen, to make British sport like Finnish sport in twenty years, was hopelessly optimistic, and sets up the sports system and all its leaders for failure and likely to suffer a reduction of resources when not achieved. Finland is a high-wage, high-tax, high-benefit welfare state, where gender equity is very advanced. For over two decades physical activity policy, healthy eating and anti-smoking policy have meshed, and been well resourced, starting from a higher participation base than in Britain. The state (like its three Scandinavian neighbours) believes in supporting active citizenship centrally and locally, to take the lead in civil society and in sport.

By contrast, Britain is a low-wage, low-tax, low-welfare benefit society (even though many citizens, businessmen and politicians will not believe or admit it). Gender equity has a long way to go, even farther in sport than in some other spheres (WSFF, 2008), and Britain faces a larger social-cohesion challenge than Finland. Investment in sport for all facilities and leaders has been modest, and cannot just be driven by the now reasonably resourced youth programmes. Sport ministers have consistently ignored the evidence that facility investment is not keeping pace with obsolescence, let alone the levels needed to meet the 1% per annum compound target.

Green (2007) identified four key themes operating in Australia, Canada and the UK equally since 1960:

313

1. growing central government intervention in the sports sector and policy;
2. policy discourse taking on rational /technocratic styles from business;
3. enduring debates about mass participation versus elite sport;
4. a growing governmental realisation that while mass participation rates remain low, political aspirations to use sport and PA programmes to achieve health benefits remain problematic.

One of the problems is that there is absolutely no evidence that there is a 'trickle-down' effect from elite success in general (Stewart et al., 2004) or the Olympics (Coalter, 2004). Perhaps what is needed is sustained higher level investment across society and coordination of sport and health policies. Did someone mention Finland?

I am naturally optimistic, and not prone to be a Jeremiah. But I fear that DCMS and Sport England are currently heading up a policy cul-de-sac, working against an unhelpful socio-economic context including health, wealth and class inequality, trying to use NGBs to promote participation (for most NGBs traditionally a secondary issue to improving performance), ignoring the older groups offering the greatest health gains and savings, not being upfront about the likely facilities shortfall, and sidelining and downplaying local authorities, the main gateway into sport on an open-access basis. I hope that I am proved wrong by 2012–2015, by those who undertake policy analysis at that time.

My enduring hope is in the passionate, hard-working, committed people who work, paid or voluntary, in grassroots sport in all three sectors about whom I have learned or have met over nearly four decades. They will outlive the flip-flops of bi-partisan policy and the management nostrums, sometimes imported from private industry or from other sectors of government – and even from academia.

REFERENCES

Atkinson, M.M. and Coleman, W.D. (1992) Policy networks, policy communities and the problems of governance, Governance, 5(2): 154–80.

Audit Commission (2009) Working Better Together? Managing Local Strategic Partnerships: Cross-Cutting Summary, London: Audit Commission.

Bishop, J. and Hoggett, P. (1986) Organising Around Enthusiasms: Patterns of Mutual Aid in Leisure, London: Comedia.

Carter, Lord (2005) Review of National Sport Effort and Resources, London: Sport England.

Central Office of Information (2008) Healthy Weight, Healthy Lives: A Cross-Government Strategy, London: COI.

mike collins

Chartered Institute of Public Finance and Accountancy (2009) *Culture, Sport, and Recreation Statistics 2008/9 Estimates* (including charges), London: CIPFA.

Clarke, J., Gewirtz, S. and MacLaughlin, E. (2000) Reinventing the welfare state, in J. Clarke, S. Gewirtz and E. MacLaughlin (eds) *The New Managerialism*, London: Sage.

Coalter, F (2004) in A. Vigor (ed.) *After the Gold Rush?* London: Institute of Public Policy and Research.

Coalter, F. (2007) Sports clubs, social capital and social regeneration: 'ill-defined interventions with hard to follow outcomes'?, *Sport in Society*, 10(4): 537–59.

Collins, M. (2003) *Sport and Social Exclusion*, London: Routledge.

Collins, M.F. (2007) Leisure studies and the social capital discourse, in M. Collins, K. Holmes and A. Slater (eds), *Sport Leisure Culture and Social Capital: Discourse and Practice*, Leisure Studies Association Publication 100, Eastbourne: University of Brighton.

Collins, M.F. (2008a) Public policies on sports development: Can mass and elite sport hold together?, in V. Girginov (ed.) *Management of Sports Development*, Oxford: Butterworth-Heinemann.

Collins, M.F. (2008b) Sport and recreation and the environment, in B. Houlihan (ed.) *Sport and Society* (2nd edn), London: Routledge.

Collins, M.F. and Nichols, G. (2005) Summary – an emerging research agenda, in G. Nichols and M.F. Collins (eds) *Volunteers in Sports Clubs,* Publication 85, Eastbourne: Leisure Studies Association.

Davis Langdon Consultancy (2003) *Condition and Refurbishment of Public Sector Sports Facilities: Update of 1995 Study*, London: Sport England.

Department for Culture Media and Sport (2008) *Taking Part: The National Survey of Culture, Leisure and Sport: Final Assessment of Progress on PSA3: Complete Estimates from Year 3, 2007/8*, statistical release, 11 December 2008, London: DCMS.

Department for Work and Pensions (2007 and earlier) *Opportunities for All: Indicators Update 2007*, London: DWP.

Department for Work and Pensions (2009, 2008 and earlier) *Households Below Average Incomes,* London: DWP.

Fox, K. (2008) Seminar presentation Physical activity and obesity: from research to policy development, Loughborough University, April.

Garrett, R. (2000) Changing their game: the effect of Lottery funding on voluntary sports clubs, in M. MacNamee, C. Jennings and M. Reeves (eds) *Just Leisure: Policy Ethics and Professionalism*, Publication 71, Eastbourne: Leisure Studies Association.

Goss, S. (2001) *Making Local Governance Work: Networks, Relationships and the Management of Change,* Basingstoke: Palgrave.

Green, M. (2007) Olympic glory or grassroots development? Sports policy priorities in Australia, Canada and the United Kingdom, 1960–2006, *International Journal of History of Sport*, 24(7): 921–53.

Harris, S., Mori, K. and Collins, M. (2009) Great expectations: voluntary sports clubs and their role in delivering national policy for English sport, *Voluntas*, 20(4).

Henley Centre (2003) *Strategic Framework for Community Sport in England: Meeting the Challenge of Game Plan: Emerging Insights into the Future of Participation of Sport in England*, London: Sport England.

Henry, I. et al. (2008) *Sports Partnerships Promoting Inclusive Communities: Lincolnshire, Leicester-Shire and Rutland Sports Partnerships*, Loughborough: Institute for Sport and Leisure Policy.

Hills, J., Sefton, T. and Stewart, K. (eds) (2009) *Towards a More Equal Society? Poverty, Inequality and Policy Since 1997*, Bristol: Policy Press.

Houlihan, B. and White, A. (2002) *The Politics of Sports Development*, London: Routledge.

Houlihan, B. and Lindsay, I. (2008) Networks and partnerships in sports development, in V. Girginov (ed.) *Management of Sports Development*, Oxford: Butterworth-Heinemann.

Hylton, K. and Totten, M. (2008) Community sports development, in K. Hylton and P. Bramham (eds) *Sports Development: Policy, Process and Practice*, London: Routledge.

Institute of Youth Sport (2006) *School Sport Partnerships Annual Monitoring and Evaluation Report for 2006*, Loughborough University: IYS.

Ipsos/MORI (2006) *Understanding the Success Factors in Sport Action Zones: Final Report*, London: Sport England.

Knight, Kavanagh and Page (2005) *Active Sport/CSP Impact Study: Year 3 Final Report*, Bury St Edmunds: KKP.

de Knop, P. et al. (1994) *Youth-Friendly Sports Clubs Developing an Effective Youth Policy*, Brussels: Free University Press (VUB).

Le Grand, J. (2003) *Motivation, Agency and Public Policy: Of Knights and Knaves, Pawns and Queens*, Oxford: Oxford University Press.

Lindsay, I. (2006) Local partnerships in the UK for the New Opportunities for PE & Sport Programme: A policy network analysis, *European Sport Management Quarterly*, 6(2): 167–84.

Marsh, D. and Rhodes, R.A.W. (1992) Policy communities and issue networks, in D. Marsh and R.A.W. Rhodes (eds) *Policy Networks in British Government*, Oxford: Oxford University Press.

McDonald, D. and Tungatt, M. (1991) *National Demonstration Projects: Major Lessons and Issues for Sports Development*, London: Sports Council.

McDonald, I. (2005) Theorising partnerships: Governance communicative action and sport policy, *Journal of Social Policy*, 34(4): 579–600.

316

National Institute of Clinical Excellence (2008) *Lifestyle Statistics*, London: NICE.

Nichols, G. (2007) *Sport and Crime Reduction: The Role of Sports in Tackling Youth Crime*, London: Routledge.

Nicoll, J.P., Coleman, P. and Williams, B.T. (1993) *Injury in Sport and Exercise*, London: Sports Council.

Parent, M. and Harvey, J. (2009) Towards a management model for sport and PA community-based partnerships, *European Sport Management Quarterly*, 9(1): 23–45.

Rigg, J. (1986) *Action Sport: Community Sports Leadership in the Inner Cities*, London: Policy Studies Institute for the Sports Council.

Rhodes, R.A.W. (1997) *Understanding Governance: Policy Networks, Reflexivity and Accountability*, Buckingham: Open University Press.

Rowe, N. and Moore, S. (2001) *GHS: Participation in Sport: Past Trends and Future Prospects*, London: Sport England.

Rowe, N., Adams, R. and Beasley, N. (2004) Driving up participation in sport: the social context, the trends, the prospects and the challenges, in *Driving Up Participation: The Challenge for Sport*, academic review papers, London: Sport England.

Skelcher, C. (2000) Changing images of the state: overloaded, hollowed out, congested, *Public Policy and Administration*, 15(3) 3–19.

Sotiriadou, K., Shilbury, D. and Quick, S. (2008) The attraction, retention/ transition and nurturing process of sport development: some Australian evidence, *Journal of Sport Management*, 22: 247–72.

Sport England (1999) *COMPASS: Sports Participation in Europe*, London: Sport England.

Sport England (2004a) *Participation in Sport in England, 2002*, London: Sport England.

Sport England (2004b) *Participation in Sport in GB: Trends 1987–2002*, London: Sport England.

Sport England (2008a) *Impact: Innovation Working in Communities, Increased Participation, Sport Action Zones, ACDF, Magnet Fund, in 3D: Driving Change, Developing Partnerships, Delivering Outcomes*, London: www.sportengland. org, downloaded 10 August 08.

Sport England (2008b) *Shaping Places through Sport: Executive Summary: Developing Strong, Sustainable and Cohesive Communities through Sport*, London: Sport England.

Sport England (2008c) *Shaping Places through Sport: Transforming Lives – Improving Life Chances and Focusing the Energies of Children and Young People through Sport*, London: Sport England.

Sport England (2008d) *Shaping Places through Sport: Increased Prosperity –*

Increasing Skill, Employment and Economic Prosperity through Sport, London: Sport England.

Sport England (2008e) *Shaping Places through Sport: Creating Safer Communities – Reducing Antisocial Behaviour and the Fear of Crime though Sport*, London: Sport England.

Sport England (2008f) *Shaping Places through Sport: Building Communities – Developing Strong, Sustainable Communities though Sport*, London: Sport England.

Sport England (2008g) *Grow, Sustain, Excel: Strategy 2008–2011*, London: Sport England.

Sport England (2008h) *Active People Survey 2007/8 National Summary Sheet; I Million Target; National Demographic Profile Sheets*, available on www. sportengland.org.

Sport England (2009) *Funding Sport in the Community*, London: Sport England.

Stamatakis, E., Ekelund, U. and Wareham, J. (2007) Temporal trends in physical activity in England: the Health Survey for England 1991 to 2004, *Preventive Medicine*, 45: 416–23.

Stamatakis, E. and Chaudhury, M. (2008) Temporal trends in adults' sports participation patterns in England between 1997 and 2006: the Health Survey for England, *British Journal of Sport Medicine*, online, 1–8.

Stewart, B. *et al.* (2004) *Australian Sport: Better by Design? The Evolution of Australian Sport Policy*, London: Routledge.

Substance (2007) *Putting the Pieces Together? 2007 Annual Monitoring and Evaluation Report*, Manchester: Substance Consultants.

Taylor, P. (2002) Driving up participation: Sport and volunteering, in Sport England (ed.) *Driving Up Participation: The Challenge for Sport*, London: SE.

Taylor, P. *et al.* (2004) *Widening Access through Facilities* (mimeo), Sheffield: Leisure Industries Research Centre.

Thomas, P. (2009) Management re-think, Don't panic, just stop managing! and New leaders, managing future, *Recreation*, respectively 68(4): 32–4, 68(5): 32–4 and 68(6): 32–4.

Wilkinson, R. and Prickett, K. (2009) *The Spirit Level: Why More Equal Societies Nearly Always Do Better*, London: Allan Lane/Penguin Press.

Women's Sport and Fitness Foundation (2008) *Women in Sport Audit 2007/8, Backing a Winner: Unlocking the Potential in Women's Sport*, London: WSFF.

Zaninotto, P. *et al.* (2008) Trends in obesity among adults in England from 1993 to 2004 by age and social class and projections of prevalence to 2012, *Journal of Epidemiol Community Health*, online, 1–7.

AUTHOR INDEX

SUBJECT INDEX